VERDI AND PUCCINI
HEROINES

Verdi and Puccini Heroines

*Dramatic Characterization in
Great Soprano Roles*

Geoffrey Edwards and Ryan Edwards

The Scarecrow Press, Inc.
Lanham, Maryland, and London
2001

SCARECROW PRESS, INC.

Published in the United States of America
by Scarecrow Press, Inc.
4720 Boston Way, Lanham, Maryland 20706
www.scarecrowpress.com

4 Pleydell Gardens, Folkestone
Kent CT20 2DN, England

Dustjacket and frontispiece: *Florine*, 1872. John Robert Dicksee. Oil on canvas. Courtesy of the Edwards family collection.

British Library Cataloguing in Publication Information Available

Library of Congress Cataloging-in-Publication Data

Edwards, Geoffrey, 1964–
    Verdi and Puccini heroines : dramatic characterization in great soprano roles / Geoffrey Edwards and Ryan Edwards.
      p. cm.
    Includes bibliographical references and indexes.
    ISBN 0-8108-3935-0 (alk. paper)
    1. Verdi, Giuseppe, 1813–1901. Operas. 2. Puccini, Giacomo, 1858–1924. Operas. 3. Operas—Characters. 4. Operas—Stories, plots, etc. 5. Women in opera. I. Edwards, Ryan, 1941– II. Title.
ML410.V4 E29   2000
782.1—dc21   00-061950

♾™ The paper used in this publication meets the minimum requirements of American National Standard for Information Sciences—Permanence of Paper for Printed Library Materials, ANSI/NISO Z39.48–1992.
Manufactured in the United States of America.

Dedicated with love to

Leila Edwards

CONTENTS

ACKNOWLEDGMENTS

The authors gratefully acknowledge the many friends and colleagues who encouraged the development of this book and who generously shared their scholarly insights and rich performance experiences during the evolution of the manuscript. In particular, thanks to Dr. Richard Alderson, Mme Lucine Amara, Mr. John Ardoin, Mme Martina Arroyo, Maestro Richard Bonynge, Dr. Albert Cirillo, Dr. Douglas Cole, Maestro Anton Coppola, Mr. Frank Corsaro, Mme Mary Costa, Mr. Richard Covello, Mme Gilda Cruz-Romo, Mme Constanza Cuccaro, Mme Phyllis Curtin, Mme Mary Curtis-Verna, Mme Cristina Deutekom, Dr. Walter Ducloux, Mme Eileen Farrell, Mr. Robert Gay, Mme Lorna Haywood, Professor Barbara Hill-Moore, Mr. Désiré Ligeti, Mme Martha Lipton, Mr. Dominic Missimi, Mme Anna Moffo, Mr. David Morelock, Mme Carol Neblett, Maestro Imre Pallo, Maestra Eve Queler, Mme Gail Robinson, Mr. George Shirley, Dame Joan Sutherland, Mme Renata Tebaldi, Mr. Giorgio Tozzi, Mme Marilyn Tyler, Mme Shirley Verrett, Maestra Mara Waldman, and Mme Virginia Zeani.

Special thanks also to Monsieur Jean Dérens, Conservateur en Chef at the Bibliothèque Historique de la Ville de Paris; Professor Franco Rossi, Curator of the Archives of La Fenice; Professor Gianpiero Tintori, Director of the Museo Teatrale alla Scala; and Professor Martin Chusid, Director of the American Institute for Verdi Studies.

INTRODUCTION

New Perspectives

This book comes at a time when opera-lovers, singers, directors, and critics alike are taking a new look at the dramatic soprano heroines created by Giuseppe Verdi and Giacomo Puccini, endeavoring to go beyond inherited scholarly interpretation and come to a richer understanding of these compelling female characters.

Following the creative flood of *Il Trovatore*, which swept away the tradition of *bel canto* romance, the six women included in this book become participants in an unending human quest, a quest for self-knowledge, for comprehension of the individual's place in the cosmic order of existence, for understanding of the values which give meaning and purpose to life. Each of these characters defies critical reductionism; each refuses dismissive stereotyping. They possess a human resonance which time can never dim and custom can never stale.

Unfortunately, much contemporary criticism still seems intent on fitting operatic protagonists into theoretical paradigms[1]—rather than exploring the development of dramatic character through the organic interaction of text, music, and staging.[2] The result for these Verdi and Puccini heroines is an alienation from the source of their dramatic strength: revelation of the human condition.

Spirit of Romanticism

The individuality of these female characters emerges from the rebellious spirit of romanticism. While Napoleon's armies marched across Europe in the early years of the nineteenth century, artists, poets, and musicians exalted the imperial hegemony of France by identifying with the great classical civilizations of Western antiquity. As the resulting dramatically bankrupt, neoclassical tragedies filled the stages of the Comédie Française and the Opéra, however, the general public turned for relief to the lavish spectacle of "Boulevard"[3] melodrama, with its cardboard characterizations, thrilling plots, elaborate settings, special effects, and atmospheric music.

In reaction to both of these artistic extremes, the humanistic counterculture of romanticism was born. While blending the poetry of neoclassical theater with the intricate plots and striking visual effects of the popular melodramas, romanticism gave dramatic primacy to the inner emotional and psychological life of the individual, to exploring the irrational and uncontrollable nature of human existence, to celebrating cosmic mystery and personal faith.[4] Following a Shakespearean model of character development, romantic drama depicted striking individuals who incorporated antithetical elements from the sublime and the grotesque sides of human nature in complex, but unified, portrayals.[5] Thus, the subtle nexus of psychological tensions, ambiguous responses, and conflicting motivations that determined the character's development moment by moment throughout the play was deftly revealed.

Grand et Vrai

Perhaps no single figure was more instrumental in giving voice to the values of romanticism than Victor Hugo. Hugo championed a drama that was "*grand et vrai*" (great and true),[6] a drama that acted as an enlarging mirror, reflecting, but also heightening, real life. In their lavish costumes and gothic surroundings, Hugo's kings and spies, exiled nobles and deformed jesters are far from the reality of ordinary life in either nineteenth-century Paris or modern society. Yet, their complex psychologies and interpersonal relationships provide a powerful image of humanity.

In the scope of its dramatic conflicts, in the magnitude of its emotions, in the expansiveness of its production, and in the elevation of its lyrical expression, opera, too, heightens daily reality. It is hardly surprising, therefore, that nineteenth-century Italian opera should have found the larger-than-life characterizations of the romantic theater particularly suited to the lyric stage. Romantic drama became standard source material for the *bel canto* operas of the 1830s and 1840s, as well as for such Verdian works as *Ernani* (1844), *Rigoletto* (1851), *Il Trovatore* (1853), *La Forza del Destino* (1862, revised 1869), and *Simon Boccanegra* (1857, revised 1881). Further, the ethos of romantic characterization remained an integral part of the best operatic compositions into the twentieth century, even inspiring the transformation of later melodramatic works—David Belasco's *Madame Butterfly* (1900), for example—into true heroic tragedies.

Verdi's Innovations

Not all melodramatic dross was thus alchemized into romantic gold, however. During the *bel canto* period, Italian opera was frequently filled not with the dramatic ideals of romanticism but with the melodramatic clichés of the romance, shunning complex characterization in favor of hackneyed amorous adventure and misfortunes. Similarly, musico-dramatic expression in *bel canto* opera was often reduced to formulaic reliance on such dramatically constraining conventions as artificial set-piece numbers, the ubiquitous *cavatina-cabaletta*, or gratuitous coloratura showpieces for star performers.

Although schooled in the *bel canto* tradition, Verdi pointedly tried to eschew the traps of melodramatic libretti and undramatic musical conventions. Even in early operas—from *Nabucco* (1842) and *Ernani* to *Macbeth* (1847, revised 1865) and *Rigoletto*—Verdi sought out source material rich in powerful, humanistic characterizations, and he continually pressed against the boundaries of established compositional style in his musical illumination of the individual. By the middle of the nineteenth century, however, Verdi clearly felt he had exhausted the potential for artistic growth within the *bel canto* tradition; he was poised to create a new type of *dramma per musica*. Verdi's search for innovative musical forms to express the dramatic essence of his stories and his characters led him inexorably away from the coloratura set-pieces of *bel canto* and toward a continuous, through-composed scoring in which music evolves organically with the action.

Verdi's musico-dramatic exploration of character also led him to develop a new soprano vocal archetype, one in which the lightness, agility, and extended top range demanded in *bel canto* opera were replaced by emotional power and vocal weight in the upper register—a radical change that was often deplored as destructively demanding by nineteenth-century critics.[7] The Verdi soprano that emerged in the composer's later operas, and so profoundly affected the development of

Puccini's *verismo* heroines at the turn of the century, is usually classi-
fied today as a *lirico-spinto* or even a dramatic voice.

Text, Music, and Staging

The characters explored in this book illustrate the musical evolution of
this new type of soprano, while illuminating the dramatic scope and
power of the great Verdi and Puccini heroines. Dramaturgically, each
portrayal draws strength from opera's unique fusion of dramatic arts:
text, music, and staging coalesce to produce a compelling revelation of
character. Attaining full realization of these operas therefore requires
singers, conductors, and directors capable of using the score and libretto
as guides for dramatic performance. The psychological foundations of
the most carefully crafted operatic characterization may be undermined
by performers or directors who are not sensitive to the connection
between language and musical structure. The libretto provides the
framework for musical characterization, but scoring may subvert or
enhance the resonance of a character's words, reveal an emotional
subtext, and highlight a character's inner tensions, psychological ambiguities, or conscious deceptions.

To illuminate the unique dramatic vision embodied in each of the
representative operatic heroines in the present book, the opera's literary
source is used as an interpretive touchstone to explicate significant
points of comparison and contrast; the opera's score is discussed
descriptively to highlight the role of music in the development of character; and authorial correspondence that traces the dramatic evolution of
the operas, as well as reviews and promptbooks from nineteenth-
century European productions, are cited to emphasize the importance of
staging in characterization.[8]

Beyond Realism

In order to appreciate the composer's often radically experimental
dramaturgy, each opera must be understood on its own terms.
Particularly in discussing Verdi's operas, therefore, it is frequently
necessary to leave behind the mind-set of realism. When viewed from a
perspective of conventional operatic realism, *Il Trovatore* is a travesty;
when perceived as an indictment of the inadequate clichés of operatic
romance, however, it is a revelation. As realism, *La Forza del Destino*

is a dismal failure; as an impressionistic vision of the nature of fate and the cause of human suffering, it is a Verdian masterpiece.

Ultimately, the characters discussed in this book have attained artistic immortality because their personal journeys touch upon fundamental issues of human existence which transcend the localization of costume, setting, or plot. *Aida* (1871) is not really a historical evocation of imperialist Egypt, but rather a profound exploration of the personal torment and suffering that can result from humanity's most divine gift—the capacity for love. *Tosca* (1900) is not an indictment of nineteenth-century political corruption, but rather a transcendent affirmation of individual identity. *Turandot* (1926) is not a fanciful Chinese fairy-tale, but rather a triumphant celebration of love's power to redeem a world consumed by hatred and violence.

Verdi and Puccini heroines illuminate the torment, the ecstasy, and the enduring mysteries of existence. Theirs is a universal quest for meaning amidst the transient shadows of human life. In their spiritual and temporal struggles, in their imperishable hopes and dreams, in their suffering and triumphs, in their very lives and deaths, these women are of all humanity, and for all humanity.

VERDI AND PUCCINI
HEROINES

PREVIEW

Although her capacity for love exemplifies the noblest potential of human nature, the character of Leonora in *Il Trovatore* is more symbolic and less individually complex than many of Verdi's earlier heroines. The composer was attracted by the raw emotional power of the situations depicted in García Gutiérrez's source play and hoped to rework those elements into an innovative operatic drama. In the end, however, *Il Trovatore* became both an homage to and indictment of the inherited tradition of *bel canto* operatic romance.

Verdi concentrates the play's high-*frisson* plot, while adding a profusion of melodic inspiration that has made *Il Trovatore* one of the composer's most popular operas. He also manipulates dramatic and musical conventions, using such subversive dramaturgy to illuminate the limitations, failings, and absurdities of the traditional operatic romance.

In the bleak world of *Il Trovatore*, the conventional love of Leonora is pointedly marginalized. Once the fatal love triangle is established in the first act, pitting her beloved troubadour Manrico against Count di Luna, Leonora yields primacy of place to the men. She is quickly reduced to a clichéd helplessness, which continues as Manrico rescues her from di Luna in Act II. Oblivious to the civil war which threatens to engulf them in Act III, Leonora remains completely absorbed in her love for the troubadour. Yet, while the strength of this love leads Leonora to embrace even death itself by the last act, her deflating final moments are notably lacking in transcendent power.

Il Trovatore is the Great Flood of Verdi's operatic Creation. The opera sweeps away an inherited tradition of stage romance, leaving behind the enriched dramatic soil in which Verdi's later humanistic masterpieces will grow.

CHAPTER 1

Il Trovatore

> ### *"Nella vita tutto è morte! Cosa esiste?"*
> ### **"In life, everything is death! What else is there?"**[1]

Giuseppe Verdi's response to criticism about the excessive number of deaths in *Il Trovatore* (1853) strikingly articulates the quest for meaning in human life that weaves throughout the composer's *oeuvre*. In early works from *Nabucco* (1842) to *Rigoletto* (1851), love provides this meaning, offering redemption from the torment of existence in a hostile, often incomprehensible, world. Beginning with *Il Trovatore*, however, such faith in the transcendent power of the heart is tempered by pessimism and a recognition of love's limitations in ameliorating the human condition.

Symbolic Characterization

An almost cosmic, metaphysical dramatic paradigm shapes many of Verdi's later operas, illuminating the eternal question of why misery and suffering seem an inescapable part of life. As a result, the characterization of Verdi's sopranos in these operas often becomes more symbolically weighted and less individually complex than in the composer's early works.

Love, as embodied in the Verdi soprano, remains a central force, but idealism is replaced with uncertainty and doubt: while Amelia in *Simon Boccanegra* (1857, revised 1881) finds love ultimately rewarded with happiness, Amelia in *Un Ballo in Maschera* (1859) and Elisabetta in *Don Carlos* (1867, revised 1884) must suppress love in the name of duty, and Desdemona in *Otello* (1887) discovers that love is powerless in confronting deadly evil.

Leonora in *Il Trovatore* foreshadows this emergent trend of symbolic Verdian characterization; her capacity for love exemplifies the noblest potential of human nature, yet her symbolic function within the opera results in a loss of internal contradictions and psychological ambiguities.

Tradition and Innovation

Verdi had at first hoped that Salvatore Cammarano's libretto for *Il Trovatore*,[2] based on Antonio García Gutiérrez's *El Trovador* (1836), would be the inspiration for a dramaturgically innovative *dramma per musica* in the manner of *Rigoletto*: "*tanto più Cammarano mi presenterà novità, libertà di forme io farò meglio. Faccia pure tutto quello che vuole: tanto più sarà ardito io sarò più contento.*" (The more Cammarano presents me with novelty and freedom of form, the better I will do. Let him then do everything he wishes: the more daring he is, the happier I will be.)[3] To his librettist, Verdi insisted,

> *In quanto alla distribuzione dei pezzi vi dirò che per me quando mi si presenta della poesia da potersi mettere in musica, ogni forma, ogni distribuzione è buona, anzi più queste sono nuove e bizzarre io ne sono più contento. Se nelle opere non vi fossero né Cavatine, né Duetti, né Terzetti, né Cori, né Finali etc. etc., e che l'opera intera non fosse (sarei per dire) un solo pezzo, troverei più ragionevole e gusto. Per questo vi dirò che se si potesse evitare nel principio di quest'opera il Coro (tutte le opere cominciano con un Coro) e la Cavatina di Leonora, e cominciare addirittura col canto del Trovatore e fare un sol atto dei due primi, sarebbe bene, perché questi pezzi così isolati con cambiamento di scena a ciascuno pezzo m'hanno piuttosto l'aria di pezzi da concerto che d'opera.*

(As far as the distribution of numbers, I will tell you that for me, when I am presented with poetry that can be set to music, any form and distribution is good; even more, I am most happy with those that are new and original. If in opera there were neither *cavatinas*, nor duets, nor trios, nor choruses, nor finales, etc. etc., and the entire opera were only (so to speak) a single piece, I would find it more reasonable and proper. Because of this, I will tell you that if one could avoid at the opening of this opera the chorus number (all operas begin with a chorus number) and Leonora's *cavatina*, and begin right with the troubadour's song and make a single act of the first two, it would be good, because these pieces, isolated by a scene shift after every piece, seem to me more like concert pieces than opera.)[4]

Verdi was attracted by the raw emotional power of the situations depicted in García Gutiérrez's play[5] and hoped, perhaps, that Cammarano could rework those elements into a true operatic drama in which the conventional set-piece structure of *bel canto* composition could be jettisoned. But neither the poet—nor, indeed, the composer in his own revision of Cammarano's first sketches—could effect such a transformation. Finally, after Cammarano's untimely death, Verdi reshaped *Il Trovatore*, making it both an homage to and an indictment of the inherited tradition of *bel canto* operatic romance.

Source Play

For all its enduring popularity in Spain, García Gutiérrez's *El Trovador* is merely a well-constructed melodrama. In its twisting story of love and vengeance, characters are only superficially explored. The play is an exciting potboiler, but it is inextricably bound to its era, unable to transcend the period's indulgence in theatrical excess.

Verdi further concentrates the play's high-*frisson* plot, while adding a profusion of melodic inspiration that has made *Il Trovatore* one of the composer's most popular operas:

> This black drama, equalling in horror the wildest imaginations of a Parisian melodramatist, is, nevertheless, strongly interesting, and its striking situations and impassioned scenes afford much scope for musical expression and effect. Of these capabilities the composer has availed himself; and

the opera, when well performed, never fails to make a deep
impression on the audience.[6]

As the composer himself later wrote, "*Quando tu andrai nelle Indie
e nell'interno dell'Africa sentirai il* Trovatore" (When you go into the
Indies and the heart of Africa you will hear *Trovatore*).[7]

Subversive Dramaturgy

Throughout the opera, Verdi continually manipulates dramatic and
musical clichés; the melodramatic excesses of the libretto and the
artificiality of *bel canto* set-piece composition ultimately illuminate the
limitations, failings, and absurdities of the conventional operatic
romance. *Il Trovatore* is not a parody, though it surely invites such par-
odic treatments as the Marx Brothers' *A Night at the Opera*. Rather, it
emerges as a masterful "anti-opera," a creation which so perfectly con-
summates its inherited tradition of *bel canto* romance that it enchants
the audience while simultaneously subverting the foundation of beliefs
upon which such opera was built.

Verdi's depiction of the romantic heroine Leonora lies at the very
heart of this subversive dramaturgy in *Il Trovatore*. With a composer
like Giacomo Puccini, who embraced the ideals of love throughout his
oeuvre, the operatic Leonora might have become a powerfully drawn
tragic figure. But Verdi had clearly lost faith in such idealism.[8]
Anticipating later works from *La Forza del Destino* (1862, revised
1869) to *Otello*, *Il Trovatore* focuses on the dark realities of a human
existence consumed by hatred and revenge.

At the heart of the opera is not the love of Leonora, but the titanic
struggle for vengeance between the gypsy Azucena and the Count di
Luna. Verdi himself, comparing the role of Leonora with that of
Azucena, wrote of the gypsy, "*è prima, primissima, più bella, più dram-
matica, più originale dell'altra. Se io fossi prima donna (il bell'affare!)
farei sempre nel* Trovatore *la parte della Zingara.*" (She is first, the
foremost—more beautiful, more dramatic, more original than the other.
If I were a prima donna (a pretty state of affairs!) I would always rather
sing the part of the Gypsy in *Trovatore*.)[9]

Clichés of the Romance Heroine

In the bleak world of this opera, therefore, the conventional love of the heroine is pointedly marginalized. Significantly, Verdi's instructions for Bardare indicate that the composer decided only after Cammarano's death to upgrade Leonora to the status of a major prima donna role. Leonora is defined simply by her unwavering love for Manrico. As a result, psychological subtext plays virtually no part in her character development. Verdi's Leonora is a distillation of romantic clichés: consumed by a doomed love, she must endure jealousy and denunciations from her lover, make a despairing renunciation of the world, suffer the torment of a reunion already overshadowed by conflict and death, and, ultimately, sacrifice her own life for the man she loves.

Leonora's emotions are painted with broad strokes and given voice in emotionally generalized melodies. While Verdi deftly manipulates the musical formulas of the *bel canto* style to emphasize Leonora's conventionality as a romance protagonist, he pointedly suppresses the elements of the *bel canto* musical tradition that could have lifted Leonora to a new and transcendent dramatic plane.

There is no glorious final apotheosis for Verdi's Leonora in either her words or her music. To the end, she remains a static character, unable to reach a greater understanding of herself or her place in the cosmos, unable to attain true heroic stature. Leonora embodies the inadequacy of romantic idealism in confronting the intractable realities of human existence: the clichés of romance cannot bring her lasting happiness and joy; they cannot save the life of her beloved troubadour; they cannot end the cycle of vengeance that ravages the world of the opera.

Act I

In both musical form and dramatic content, Leonora's Act I *scena*—following a curtain-raising choral exposition—epitomizes the romance conventions of *bel canto* opera.[10] Leonora, a noble attendant of the Princess of Aragon, is in love with a mysterious Black Knight. She had bestowed upon him the victor's laurels at a great tournament, and he has since returned in the guise of a troubadour to sing melancholy songs of love beneath her balcony in the Aliaferia palace. As she lingers in the nocturnal darkness of the garden, waiting for her troubadour to return, Leonora recounts the story of her love to her requisite confidante, Ines.[11]

Tacea la Notte

A few measures of generic orchestral prelude usher in the explana-
tory recitative of this traditional *aria d'entrata*. As Leonora tells Ines
about the tournament and how, with the onset of civil war, the mysterious knight had vanished, the rhapsodic imagery of "*Come d'aurato
sogno fuggente immago*" (Like the fleeting image of a golden dream)[12]
is heightened by the floating vocal phrases and gracious arpeggio
underscoring of a brief *andante*.

Ines demands to know what ensued, and Leonora obliges her with a
lyrically expansive *cantabile*, "*Tacea la notte placida*" (34; The peaceful night was silent). There is little dramatic specificity between words
and music here, but, rather, a generalized evocation of the ecstasy that
surged through Leonora's heart on that silvery night when the
troubadour's song first filled the air. Thus, the vocal line swells *con
espansione* on the somewhat inappropriate phrases, "*dolci s'udiro e
flebili gli accordi d'un liuto, e versi melanconici e versi melanconici un
trovator cantò*" (35-6; sweet and plaintive, the strains of a lute were
heard, and a troubadour sang melancholy verses).

Example 1.1

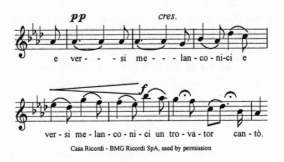

Casa Ricordi - BMG Ricordi SpA, used by permission

Leonora's melody perhaps suggests the instinctive, visceral joy she
felt at the very sound of the troubadour's voice, but it also highlights the
artificiality of the *cantabile*'s strophic form. It is not until the end of the
second verse that Leonora's words finally catch up with the melody:
"*Gioia provai che agl'angeli solo è provar concesso! . . . Al core, al
guardo estatico la terra un ciel sembrò.*" (38-9; I felt a joy that is
granted only the angels to feel. To my heart, to my ecstatic gaze the
earth seemed a heaven.)

Significantly, when scoring Azucena's later narrative describing the horrible death of her mother at the stake, Verdi eschews such artifice, preferring the musico-dramatic specificity of an incisively etched monologue. With Leonora's *cavatina*, however, the purpose is not to depict a complex individual, but simply to establish a "romance heroine." Accordingly, Verdi invokes every hackneyed device that libretto poetry and *bel canto* composition can offer, culminating with what can only be viewed as a tongue-in-cheek cadenza, where the vocal line incongruously plunges over an octave from high C on "*terra*" (earth) to A-flat on "*ciel*" (39; heaven)![13]

Di Tale Amor

Ines voices the usual premonitions of doom, but Leonora will hear none of them, launching into a brilliant *cabaletta*. There is a sense of irrepressible exuberance in the rollicking phrases, gleeful trills, and cascading sixteenth notes of "*Di tale amor che dirsi mal può dalla parola, d'amor, che intendo io sola, il cor . . . il cor . . . il cor s'innebriò*" (42-3; My heart is intoxicated with a love that I alone know, with a love that can hardly be put into words).

The headlong momentum of the *cabaletta* is slowed momentarily as Leonora acknowledges, "*Il mio destino compiersi non può che a lui dappresso*" (43; My destiny can be fulfilled only beside him); but even here, the playful vocal figures on "*compiersi*" and "*dappresso*" evoke an innocent delight barely concealed beneath the weighty image of destiny. Finally, Leonora's repetitions of "*per esso morirò*" (44; for him I will die) hurtle her into the near-comic exaggeration of a cadenza which plunges from high C to low A-flat on "*morirò*" (45). As the artifice of the *cabaletta*'s traditional second-verse repetition highlights, self-sacrifice is not Leonora's tragic fate; it is simply a convention of romance.

Love Triangle

Having given full voice to her feelings, Leonora enters the palace. Count di Luna then appears, preparing to express his own love to the heroine, but he is forestalled by the sound of Manrico's serenade. Hearing her beloved troubadour, Leonora immediately rushes back out into the darkened garden and mistakenly goes to embrace di Luna. The situation is fraught with absurdity, but the rapid pace of events keeps the scene from degenerating into outright comedy: Leonora is deluded for only eight measures before Manrico's righteous indignation reveals her error.

Nearly beside herself, Leonora kneels at Manrico's feet and breathlessly swears, "*A te credei rivolgere l'accento, e non a lui. . . . Io t'amo, il giuro, t'amo d'immenso, eterno amor*" (57-8; I thought I was addressing you, not him. . . . I love you, I swear it, I love you with vast, eternal love). Though she is the catalyst for the actions of Manrico and di Luna, Leonora herself is quickly marginalized. Expressing little more than generic angst, Leonora's vocal line breaks down into isolated interjections, while her suitors confront each other with jealous fury.

As the ensuing trio thunders toward its conclusion, Leonora begs di Luna to turn his rage only on her. Her gesture of self-sacrifice is musically obliterated, however; not only does her vocal line join in unintelligible unison with that of Manrico, but the declamatory bravado of their melody is also clearly more evocative of the troubadour's words than her own.

As one nineteenth-century critic noted, "*Léonor a un peu moins de violence quand elle est seule: on voit que son âme se laisserait aller volontiers à la tendresse, et même à la rêverie. Mais ses farouches amants l'entraînent bientôt dans leur tourbillon, et, malgré qu'elle en ait, elle hurle avec les loups.*" (Leonora has a little less violence when she is alone: one sees that her soul would willingly let itself go to tenderness and even reverie. But her fierce lovers soon sweep her along in their whirlwind, and, in spite of what she would have, she howls with the wolves.)[14]

Having set the wheels of action in motion, the conventional romance heroine must yield primacy of place to the men, and Leonora's clichéd helplessness is symbolized in the final stage directions of the act: "*I due rivali si allontanano con le spade sguainate. Leonora cade, priva di sentimento.*" (The two rivals go off with swords drawn. Leonora falls, senseless.)[15]

Act II

In Act II, Leonora believes Manrico has been killed in the duel, and so she prepares to enter a convent.[16] Arriving at night with her weeping friends, Leonora simply but poignantly explains that without Manrico life no longer holds any joy. Her compressed recitative is enriched by the delicate phrases of a brief *cantabile andante* as Leonora places herself in God's hands: *"Degg'io volgermi a Quei che degli afflitti è solo sostegno, e dopo i penitenti giorni può fra gli eletti al mio perduto bene ricongiungermi un dì"* (176-7; I must turn to Him who is the only support for the wretched, and who, after my days of penitence, may reunite me with my lost love one day among the blessed).

Her vows are forestalled by the Count di Luna, however, who announces his intention of carrying Leonora off and making her his bride. Leonora responds with declamatory indignation, but, before she can proceed any further, Manrico appears. Shock and joy vie for supremacy in her heart as Leonora tries to grasp the troubadour's apparent return from the dead; at last, her breathless *andante mosso* vocal line blossoms into an exquisite melodic statement of transcendent joy: *"Sei tu dal ciel disceso, o in ciel son io con te?"* (180-1; Are you descended from heaven, or am I in heaven with you?)

Example 1.2

Casa Ricordi - BMG Ricordi SpA, used by permission

This rapture of love expressed, however, Leonora shows no further character development in the ensuing ensemble;[17] the confrontation between Manrico, di Luna, and their followers assumes primary importance. Echoing her first wonderment at Manrico's arrival, the tripping sixteenth-note phrases of Leonora's vocal line in the ensemble soar with happiness above the massed voices. While events swirl around her, Leonora remains essentially impervious and, when the others fall silent, she repeats the radiant melody of *"Sei tu dal ciel."*[18] Finally, as the curtain falls, *"Manrico tragge seco Leonora. Il Conte è respinto, le donne rifuggono al cenobio."* (Manrico drags Leonora away with him. The count is driven back, the women take refuge in the convent.)[19]

Act III

By the third act, Leonora is with Manrico in the besieged fortress of Castellor. The civil war rages, and battle with the Count di Luna and his army is imminent; but such events are outside the purview of the conventional romance heroine. Focused exclusively on love, Leonora remarks on the coming war only as a blight on her wedding: "*Di qual tetra luce . . . il nostro imen risplende*" (260; With what gloomy light shines our marriage). In his aria "*Ah, sì, ben mio*" (261; Ah, yes, my love), Manrico vows eternal devotion to Leonora, even if he should fall on the field of battle.

Leonora listens rapturously but seems oblivious to the prospect of her lover's death. Instead, as an organ sounds in the nearby chapel, she joins Manrico for the joyful coda "*L'onda de' suoni mistici pura discende al cor, al cor! Vieni; ci schiude il tempio gioie di casto amor!*" (265; The wave of these pure, mystical sounds descends into the heart! Come; the church opens to us the joys of chaste love!) The innocent lightness of these phrases, like the chiming of wedding bells, blossoms into a tender joining of the lovers' vocal lines that repudiates any thought of the battle to come.

Their romantic reverie is shattered by news that the Count di Luna's men are preparing to burn Azucena at the stake. Revealing to the amazement of his beloved that he is the gypsy's son, Manrico rallies his followers to effect a rescue. Leonora is again reduced to passive onlooking. Her only contribution to the fiery *cabaletta* with which Manrico brings Act III to a close is the clichéd cry, "*Non reggo a colpi tanto funesti. . . . Oh quanto meglio saria morir!*" (272; I cannot bear such dismal blows. . . . Oh, how much better it would be to die!)[20] In Act II by contrast, when Manrico was preparing to leave the gypsy camp and rescue Leonora, Azucena had an entire duet with the troubadour. Verdi's divergent dramatic characterizations of the two women could not be more evident.[21]

Act IV

D'Amor sull'Ali Rosee

By the fourth act of the opera, Manrico has been captured by the Count di Luna and imprisoned, along with Azucena, in the Aliaferia palace. It is night once more, and Leonora arrives outside the prison tower, determined to rescue her beloved even at the price of her own life. Looking up at Manrico's window, Leonora prays that her sighs may float up to comfort the troubadour: "*D'amor sull'ali rosee vanne, sospir . . . dolente, del . . . prigioniero misero conforta l'egra mente*" (285; Go, sorrowful sigh, on rosy wings of love—comfort the troubled mind of the wretched prisoner). Leonora's purity and selflessness of spirit are evocatively captured in the caressing, almost hypnotic phrases of her gracious *adagio*, ornamented with delicate trills and underscored with an elegant orchestration that recalls the *bel canto* use of solo flute to embody innocent love.[22]

Example 1.3

Casa Ricordi - BMG Ricordi SpA, used by permission

Only in the final phrases of her invocation does Leonora add, "*deh! non dirgli . . . improvvido, le pene, le pene, le pene del mio cor*" (286-7; ah, do not rashly tell him the sufferings of my heart). Even here, as Leonora's vocal line mounts to top B-flat, then C, and finally to D-flat before a languid, heavily ornamented denouement, her *dolce* phrases drain the anguish from her words.

Miserere

The strains of a *Miserere* are heard from within the palace, bringing to the fore the reality of death and, perhaps, the damnation awaiting a suicide. For a moment, Leonora is gripped with fear. With effortful, fragmented phrases, she cries, "*Quel suon, quelle preci solenni, funeste empiron quest'aere di cupo terror! Contende l'ambascia, che tutto 'm'investe al labbro il respiro i palpiti al cor.*" (289-90; That sound, those solemn and dismal prayers fill this air with gloomy terror! The anxiety that engulfs me nearly stops my lips' breath, my heart's beating.)

However, the sound of Manrico's voice, bidding an apostrophized farewell to his beloved, recalls Leonora to her sense of purpose. More terrifying than the prospect of her own death is that of her lover. Thus, when Leonora repeats the vocal phrases of "*Quel suon*," her thoughts are focused on Manrico: "*Sull'orrida torre ahi! par che la morte con ali di tenebre librando si va. . . . Ah forse dischiuse gli fian queste porte sol quando cadaver già freddo sarà.*" (293-5; Over the dreadful tower, Death is hovering on wings of darkness. . . . Ah, perhaps this door will be opened only when he will already be a cold corpse.)

Tu Vedrai che Amore

As Manrico implores the spirit of his beloved not to forget him and the monks continue to chant their *Miserere*, Leonora breaks down into a repeated, keening affirmation of eternal devotion: "*Di te . . . di te . . . scordarmi!*" (296; Forget you—you!) In her ensuing *cabaletta*—which is, unfortunately, often cut in performance—fear and grief still color the individual drooping phrases of Leonora's *allegro agitato*; but the strength of her love momentarily transforms suffering and loss into hope and triumph, shaping the short phrases of the vocal line into an arching paean of supreme purpose. The trials of life are swept away by an irresistible wave of love and faith: "*Tu vedrai che amore in terra mai del mio non fu più forte*" (302; You will see that there was never a love on earth stronger than mine).

The traditional second verse of the *cabaletta* reinforces Leonora's sense of immutable purpose, and the romantic ideal of love triumphant even in death is given consummate musical expression in the ascending phrases of the concluding coda: the vocal line sweeps to a blazing high C before the final resolution of the *cabaletta* as Leonora cries, "*con te . . . nella . . . tomba scenderò*" (310; I will descend with you into the tomb).

Bargain with di Luna

The Count di Luna appears outside the palace, and Leonora launches into her chosen path of action. She begs for Manrico's life, offering her own to appease di Luna's fury: "*calpesta il mio cadavere, ma salva il Trovator!*" (318-9; Trample on my corpse, but save the troubadour!) Significantly, however, her thrusting vocal line conveys nothing of pitiful debasement. Instead, Leonora's declamatory phrases in this whirlwind duet are propelled by a single-minded urgency of purpose which equals the intensity of di Luna's hatred and desire for vengeance.

When all pleas are in vain, Leonora offers herself to the count, though privately affirming, as she swallows the poison hidden in her ring, "*M'avrai, ma fredda esanime spoglia*" (327-8; You will have me, but a cold, lifeless corpse). When di Luna accepts her proposal, Leonora voices her joy to God in the duet's *allegro brillante cabaletta*: "*Vivrà! Contende il giubilo i detti a me, Signore . . . ma coi . . . frequenti palpiti . . . mercè . . . ti . . . rende il core!*" (328-9; He will live! Joy denies me words, Lord, but with its rapid beating my heart gives thanks to You!) There is certainly joy in the cascading runs of her headlong vocal line, but there is also a sense of finality in the downward-thrusting phrases which recalls the imminence of death.

Final Moments with Manrico

Leonora is already dying by the time she enters Manrico's cell; she begs her intractable lover to flee, only to find herself unjustly cursed. Such a climactic scene virtually demands the type of virtuoso finale which traditionally concluded *bel canto* tragedies. But no such transcendent vocalism ennobles Leonora's final moments. Instead, Verdi allows her to be overwhelmed by the harsh realities of existence, thus mercilessly exposing the ultimate inadequacy of the ideals by which Leonora has lived her life.

As she pleads in vain with Manrico to save himself, there is none of the majesty of spirit which inspires, for instance, Donizetti's Lucrezia Borgia in her rending final aria, "*M'odi, ah m'odi*" (Hear me, ah, hear me).[23] Instead, Verdi provides Leonora with only a supporting role in a trio dominated by the melodic sweep of Manrico's denunciations and Azucena's dreams of her mountain home. Denied melodic scope, Leonora's frantic repetitions convey only the hollow futility of her idealistic self-sacrifice: "*oh come l'ira ti rende, ti rende cieco! oh quanto ingiusto, crudel, crudel sei meco! T'arrendi, fuggi, o sei perduto, nemmeno il cielo salvar ti può.*" (358-65; Oh, how rage makes you blind! How unjust and cruel you are to me! Yield, flee or you are lost, not even Heaven can save you.)

With blind fury, Manrico curses Leonora for giving herself to di Luna. Fainting from the effects of the poison, Leonora abandons all hope of saving the troubadour and turns her final words to effecting a reconciliation. She hurriedly explains that the poison is already working, then launches an exquisitely lyrical affirmation of her unwavering love: "*Prima che d'altri vivere . . . io volli tua morir*" (370-1; Rather than live as another's . . . I wanted to die yours).

Example 1.4

Casa Ricordi - BMG Ricordi SpA, used by permission

The promise of transcendent love is tantalizingly evoked in the ascendant phrase which carries this vocal line from G to top A-flat; but a precipitous octave drop for "*io volli*" drags Leonora's melody back to earth, back to the reality of the grave. The heroic joy she felt at the prospect of being united with Manrico forever in death seems to drain away in Leonora's gasping final phrases and ritualized farewell. She experiences no musical apotheosis. Her love and faith are true, but they ultimately have none of the transfiguring power that infuses, for example, the dying moments of Verdi's Gilda with divine serenity and heavenly hope in the last scene of *Rigoletto*: "*Lassù in cielo, vicino alla madre*" (Up there in heaven, near to my mother).[24]

Great Flood

With Leonora's death, the ideal of redemptive love—so often clichéd in operatic romances—is obliterated in a maelstrom of vengeance. The infuriated Count di Luna sends Manrico to the executioner's block, only to discover, too late, that he has killed his own brother. As Azucena voices her terrible dying cry of pyrrhic victory, "*Sei vendicata, o madre!*" (378; O Mother, you are avenged!), the count is left with a crushing recognition of the hell into which his annihilatory hatred has led him. Such are the grim life paths in *Il Trovatore*: one road leads to meaningless death, the other to existential devastation.

Il Trovatore is the Great Flood of Verdi's operatic Creation. The opera sweeps away an inherited tradition of stage romance which the composer had come to view as irredeemable. Yet, even in this wave of disillusionment, Verdi's artistic quest for meaning in life is not ended. His essential question of human purpose continues to reverberate,

"*Nella vita tutto è morte! Cosa esiste?*" (In life, everything is death! What else is there?) Their destructive fury spent, the obliterating waters of *Il Trovatore* will quickly recede, leaving behind them the enriched dramatic soil in which Verdi's later humanistic masterpieces will grow.

PREVIEW

In *La Forza del Destino*, Verdi creates an operatic equivalent to Shakespeare's "Problem Plays," focusing on the ambivalent realities of a world in which goodness is not always rewarded and flashes of heroic anagnorisis or understanding are few and far between.

Freely adapting Saavedra's source play, Verdi probes the ambiguous power of destiny in guiding human life. Time and again, Verdi shows human hatred, pride, and arrogance to be far more instrumental in causing suffering than the malign influence of abstract destiny. But he then goes beyond this premise to explore an even more corrosive question: what if the fault which plunges humanity into misery and degradation were a virtue such as love? Thus, the heroine Leonora is doomed not by evil, but by an ability to love which is the very essence of her self.

Through his impressionistic dramatic adaptation, Verdi depicts a world of cruelty, horror, and disillusionment in which the recurring metaphor for life is war; a world of isolation and alienation; a world of existential despair in which virtue and vice, goodness and evil, love and hatred are equally damning.

Tortured from the beginning of Act I by her irreconcilable filial and romantic loves, Leonora is then consumed by guilt and remorse after her father's death. Pursued in Act II by her vengeful brother, she hopes in vain for peace in the isolation of a hermit's cave. Only in her death at the end of Act IV, however, does Leonora at last find release from the wheel of her suffering and, like the tragic heroines of classical drama, affirm a divine order in the universe which gives meaning to human life.

CHAPTER 2

La Forza del Destino

Problem Opera

In exploring the infinite complexity of human existence, Giuseppe Verdi often emulated the dramatic eclecticism of his theatrical idol, William Shakespeare. Each of Verdi's operas views the world through a slightly different lens, and the result is a compositional *oeuvre* offering an unparalleled richness of perspective and insight. In *La Forza del Destino* (1862; revised 1869),[1] Verdi creates an operatic equivalent to such challenging Shakespearean "Problem Plays" as *Measure for Measure* or *Troilus and Cressida*, focusing on the ambivalent realities of a world in which goodness is not always rewarded and flashes of heroic anagnorisis or understanding are few and far between. *Forza* is one of Verdi's great "Problem Operas" not, as many critics have suggested, because of its ostensibly flawed dramatic structure, but because of its haunting chiaroscuro vision of humanity.

Providence and Individual Will

The power of destiny in guiding human life—in theological terms, the balance of divine Providence and individual Will—is an age-old topic

of debate, and Verdi probes the ambiguities of this issue with theatrical
élan as he unfolds the inexorable destruction of the House of Calatrava.
The force of destiny can be felt throughout the story, most notably in
the innumerable coincidences which continually bring the characters
into situations of potential crisis. Yet, once these situations have been
contrived, the human natures of the individuals involved determine
the results.

Thus, destiny may bring the Marquis di Calatrava onto the scene at
the precise moment that Leonora and her lover, Alvaro, are preparing to
elope, but it is the nobility of Alvaro's nature which prompts him to
throw down his pistol in surrender to the marquis, accidentally killing
him. Destiny may cause Alvaro and Carlo, Leonora's vengeful brother,
to meet at the monastery of Hornachuelos, but it is Carlo's blood-thirsty
arrogance and Alvaro's pride which precipitate their duel. Destiny may
lead the two duelers within sight of the inaccessible grotto where
Leonora has secretly taken refuge, but it is Carlo's implacable hatred
which drives the dying man to stab his sister when she rushes to his aid.

Time and again, Verdi shows human hatred, pride, and arrogance to
be far more instrumental in causing the suffering of the characters than
the malign influence of abstract destiny. This concept, though a radical
departure from many of the conventional operatic scenarios of the time,
was of course well established in theater. Significantly, the idea that
humanity brings about its own degradation through weakness and sin
only to attribute its failings to the "will of the gods" is admirably
expressed in one of Verdi's favorite Shakespearean plays, *King Lear*:

> This is the excellent foppery of the world, that when we are
> sick in fortune—often the surfeits of our own behavior—we
> make guilty of our disasters the sun, the moon, and stars, as
> if we were villains on necessity, fools by heavenly
> compulsion, knaves, thieves, and treachers by spherical pre-
> dominance; drunkards, liars, and adulterers by an enforc'd
> obedience of planetary influence; and all that we are evil in,
> by a divine thrusting on.[2]

As Cassius reminds Brutus in *Julius Caesar*, "The fault, dear Brutus,
is not in our stars,/ But in ourselves."[3]

Fault of Love

In *Forza*, Verdi suggests that the misery of human existence stems as much from who we are as from the malevolent power of destiny. But he then goes beyond this premise to explore an even more corrosive question: what if the fault which plunges humanity into misery and degradation were not an evil such as pride, hatred, or debauchery, but a virtue such as love?

Leonora di Vargas is doomed to a life of suffering because of a fault, but that fault is not, as she believes, her negligible role in her father's accidental death or her tainted love for a supposedly unworthy suitor; Leonora is miserable well before the fatal accident which triggers her desperate flight and tormented search for peace. Her fault is her capacity for love. Like Aida, Leonora is tortured by the irreconcilable claims of filial and romantic love. The events brought on by destiny exacerbate her torment, but they do not cause it: she would have been just as wretched eloping with Alvaro and betraying her father, or remaining at home and betraying Alvaro. Her guilt and suffering come from an irrevocably divided soul. She is doomed not by evil, but by an ability to love which is the very essence of her self. For Leonora, only death can bring release from such suffering.

Source Play

La Forza del Destino is a radical reconception of the Spanish source play, *Don Alvaro, o la Fuerza del Sino* (1835), by Angel de Saavedra, Duke of Rivas. Inspired by the works of Victor Hugo, this sprawling drama is often hailed as a Spanish *Hernani* because of its importance in the history of romantic theater.[4] It is very much a concept drama, tracing the destiny which guides the Incan prince Don Alvaro in his hapless destruction of his beloved Doña Leonor and the entire House of Calatrava. The numerous locales and free-wheeling action of the play provide opportunities for abundant pageantry and local color. Although Verdi retains many of these theatrical trappings, he abandons much of the meticulous plotting which gives the original play a certain patina of realistic plausibility.

Dramatic Impressionism

The libretto for *Forza*, written by Verdi's frequent collaborator Franceso Maria Piave with detailed guidance from the composer himself, is a revolutionary work of theatrical experimentation. The tenets of realism by which it is usually judged—and found wanting—are simply inadequate to capture the achievement of Verdi's instinctive artistry. While he was certainly not one for theory and philosophy, Verdi pressed continuously against the boundaries of established musical and dramaturgical conventions in his operas. A true romantic dramatist, Verdi was always searching for new forms capable of providing ever more compelling insights into the human condition. In *Simon Boccanegra* (1857; revised 1881) he explores the dream state of proto-expressionism by tracing one man's search for meaning in his life; in *Otello* (1887) he harnesses the power of Shakespearean metatheatricality[5] to ensnare the audience as an unwitting accomplice in Jago's destruction of Otello and Desdemona. In *Forza*, he jettisons conventional realism in favor of a richly metaphoric impressionism.

This dramatic structure has troubled generations of critics: "Confusion and coincidence run riot through the somber pages of *La Forza del Destino*. No one, in a hundred years, has ever been satisfied with the plot lines, and rare is the director who does not make some kind of alteration or rearrangement in the sequence of events."[6] There is no doubt that by any standards of realism, the story of *Forza* borders on the ludicrous. Yet, the orderly unfolding of plot was never one of Verdi's primary concerns. Throughout his career, character truth and psychological reality remain his unshakable goals; plot action serves to illuminate the characters rather than assuming independent importance. Judged as a nineteenth-century *pièce bien faite* in the manner of the well-made melodramas of Scribe or Sardou, *Forza* is seriously flawed. And so, too, are a catalogue of theatrical masterpieces from Shakespeare to Beckett and Ionesco.

Verdi wrote of *Don Alvaro, o la Fuerza del Sino*, "*Il Dramma è potente, singolare e vastissimo: a me piace assai e non so se il pubblico lo troverà come io lo trovo, ma è certo che è cosa fuori del comune*" (The drama is powerful, remarkable, and vast: it appeals to me very much; I don't know if the public will find it as I do, but it is certainly something out of the ordinary).[7] It seems clear that what attracted Verdi to the play was not the realism of its plot, but the magnitude of its vision. As Verdi noted in another context, "*Copiare il vero può essere una buona cosa, ma* inventare il vero *è meglio, molto meglio*" (To copy the truth may be a good thing, but *to invent the truth* is better, much better).[8]

Rather than concerning himself exclusively with the trials of one person or one family, Verdi creates a universalized image of human existence through an impressionistic series of scenes. In doing so, he tellingly shifts the thematic focus of the opera from illustrating the *force* of destiny to illuminating the *nature* of destiny.

War as a Metaphor for Life

Through both his adaptation of scenes from the original play and his interpolation of new material, Verdi depicts a world of cruelty, horror, and disillusionment in which the recurring metaphor for life is war. Although meretriciously hailed as a rollicking and beautiful undertaking by the gypsy Preziosilla in the second act tavern scene, war in *Forza* is far from the gloriously naive, patriotic celebration found in many earlier *Risorgimento*-period operas. Such clichés as "*È bella la guerra*" (War is beautiful)[9] are ultimately subverted by Verdi's interpolation of a later scene inspired by Friedrich Schiller's *Wallensteins Lager*.

Given the vastness of the original Spanish play, it might seem odd that Verdi felt the need to add material to his libretto, but the thematic content of the new scene elucidates his vision: the sordid realities of war become apparent in an actual military camp outside Velletri in Italy (Act III.ii). In place of sentimentalized platitudes about the beauty of war, Verdi shows war's haggling profiteers and looters, lamenting conscripts, and anthems of nihilistic abandon: "*viva la pazzia*" (269; hurray for madness).[10]

The coincidental arrival of the comic Fra Melitone from Spain, just in time to denounce the degradation of the camp, provides a culminating caption for the scene. As he rails against the sinning humanity which has turned the world upside down, there is an undeniable truth in his words. At the same time, however, Melitone is no austere classical seer speaking with the voice of divine authority. As revealed later by his exasperation while feeding beggars at the monastery of Hornachuelos (Act IV.i), Melitone is just as prone to weakness and vice as those he condemns in the military camp. Thus, he not only serves to denounce the fallen state of humanity, but ultimately to illuminate the gap between human ideals and actions: while Melitone espouses the ideal of devotion to the teachings of God, he often falls short in the living of his own life.

Alienation

In the bleak, warring world of *Forza*, individuals find themselves isolated and alienated—by prejudice and hatred, pride and arrogance, guilt and fear. In contrast to the conclusion of *Simon Boccanegra*, for example, even love provides no redemption in *Forza*. Leonora and Alvaro are neither consoled nor strengthened by the spiritual power of their love. Mysteriously driven apart after the first scene of the opera, they pursue separate paths until the final bloody conclusion of Act IV. Theirs is a relationship of miscommunication and misunderstanding.

As with the conflicting recollections in the classic tale of *Rashomon*, there is no way in *La Forza del Destino* to reconcile the lovers' contradictory memories of the fatal night they were parted. While Leonora is convinced that Alvaro abandoned her, "*l'ho seguito e il perdei*" (118-9; I followed him and lost him), Alvaro insists that he fell wounded that night and, after recovering, searched a year for his beloved only to find that she had died. Their love plunges them into a shifting quicksand of disillusionment and misery which neither can escape.

Significantly, the spiritual, psychological, and even physical alienation epitomized by Leonora and Alvaro is also manifest in the other principal characters of *Forza*. Although Leonora's brother, Carlo, evidences none of the inner torment and self-doubt of the lovers, he is equally alienated from the rest of the world by his implacable vengeance and hatred. Always concealing his true identity as he searches the land for his sister and Alvaro, Carlo is obsessively fixated on avenging his family's honor through the lovers' deaths. He dedicates his entire life to a soulless existence of negation.

Ironically, even the holy Padre Guardiano finds himself alienated from the rest of the world—not by hatred, but by faith. Living apart in his monastery, Guardiano has achieved a serenity unmatched by those who must cope with the outside world. The lives of Alvaro, Leonora, and Carlo cross his own without any lasting unsettling effect. But only by consigning himself utterly to the will of God, by completely renouncing any identity other than that of God's instrument on earth, can Guardiano achieve the peace which comes from supreme emotional detachment.

Thus, Verdi weaves the seemingly disconnected dramatic threads of *La Forza del Destino* into the meshes of an artistic net. And in that net he captures the despairing, existential essence of life, the plight of a hapless humanity for which virtue and vice, goodness and evil, love and hatred are equally damning, for which the only escape lies in total self-abnegation or death.

Act I

Forza opens with the famous overture which Vincent Godefroy strikingly describes as "a Dantesque picture of a lost soul desperately searching for rest eternal, perpetually haunted and hunted. Such is the destiny of Leonora di Vargas, whose plight ennobles her and lifts her musically to the highest altitudes of soprano heroism."[11]

As the curtain rises, the Marquis di Calatrava is discovered bidding a fond goodnight to his daughter, Leonora, in their home in Seville. Using underscoring strings to infuse the scene with a graceful warmth and old-world nostalgia, Verdi emphasizes the marquis' gentle paternal affection. Tormented by her own thoughts, however, Leonora takes no solace from her father's love, only murmuring to herself, *"Oh angoscia!"* (13; Oh, anguish!)[12]

Recognizing his daughter's unhappiness, the marquis tries to convince her, over increasingly uneasy orchestration, that their recent sojourn to the country has brought peace to her heart through renunciation of an unworthy love. But for all her father's wishful thinking, Leonora's heart is not peaceful. Knowing that she has vowed to elope with Alvaro that very night, Leonora tries to tell her father the truth, but she cannot.

As words fail her, Leonora finally throws herself into her father's arms, clinging with poignant futility to a filial bond which she has already vowed to forsake. The marquis, recognizing that Leonora's love for Alvaro is far from forgotten, is not eager to pursue the discussion and escapes the awkward situation with a final blessing and farewell.

Awaiting Alvaro

Left alone with her maid Curra, Leonora is hopelessly adrift during the intermittently punctuated recitative which follows the marquis' departure. Torn between her love for her father and her love for Alvaro,

Leonora is nearly paralyzed by the emotional strain: "*decidermi non so*" (16; I cannot make up my mind).

When confronted by Curra, Leonora does finally avow her matchless love for Alvaro, offering as proof of her feelings her renunciation of everything else she loves in the world: "*Patria, famiglia, padre per lui non abbandono?*" (18; Am I not abandoning homeland, family, and father for him?) Yet, while Leonora's overwhelming grief is incisively revealed, there is no hint of joy or happiness to come, no promise that her love for Alvaro will fill the void created by her losses. The deep sadness in the sighing, fragmented phrases of her vocal line for "*Patria, famiglia*" thus finds no relief, but culminates in the intense, expansive lament "*Ahi troppo! . . . troppo sventurata sono!*" (18; Ah, I am too, too unfortunate!)

Me Pellegrina ed Orfana

To emphasize Leonora's unassuaged despair, Verdi adds a new monologue to the scene in Saavedra's play. This interpolation was lifted from Antonio Somma's libretto for *Re Lear*, which Verdi planned to set but never completed.[13] Originally expressing Cordelia's grief at being disinherited and banished from her father's court, these adapted verses add a new weight of tragic suffering to Leonora's plight. Introduced by ethereal woodwinds which seem to exude an ephemeral remembrance of things past, Leonora's flattened, *mezza voce* phrases and the mournful underscoring of cello arpeggios provide a compelling musical image of isolation and loss: "*Me pellegrina ed orfana, lungi dal patrio nido*" (19; Wanderer and orphan, far from my native home).

As Leonora thinks of the inexorable fate which drives her into exile, her fading vocal line seems to wander like a winding path into the uncharted regions of the imagination. Her love for Alvaro has brought only misery, and Leonora's agony finds expression in a vocal line which drags itself, *crescendo ed accelerando*, to a *forte* top G on the key word "*misera*" before a plunging descent: "*Colmo di tristi immagini, da' suoi rimorsi affranto è il cor di questa misera, dannato a eterno pianto*" (19-20; Full of sad images, crushed with remorse is the heart of this wretched one, condemned to unending tears).

With terrible self-knowledge, Leonora repeats these words, her tormented, lunging line reaching high B-flat then collapsing nearly two octaves on her final "*dannato a eterno pianto.*" The fact that Leonora uses the present tense in this lament is critical, for it reveals that she is doomed to a life of misery long before the fatal accident which introduces the force of destiny.[14]

In a foreshadowing of Aida's "*Oh patria mia,*" Leonora bids an almost ritualistic farewell *col massimo dolore* to the homeland she is sacrificing for her love. Once again, however, it is significant that this love for Alvaro offers no comfort in replacing what Leonora is abandoning: "*Per me, per me non avrà termin sì gran dolor*" (21; For me, so great a sorrow will have no end).

Finally, when her feelings can be contained no longer within the formalized phrases of the lament, Leonora repeats her cries with an outpouring of emotion that crescendos through a dramatic octave leap to high A on "*dolor*" before a resigned denouement (22). Although leaping intervals in the vocal line at the conclusion of this *romanza* suggest the unabated torment in Leonora's heart, the traditional sense of structural closure, as mournful minor tonalities yield to major in the concluding cadence, emphasizes psychological resolution. Leonora has made up her mind to elope with Alvaro, no matter how painful that decision may be.

Alvaro's Arrival

Seeing that it is after midnight and Alvaro has not arrived, however, Leonora thinks that perhaps the agonizing execution of her decision can be postponed. She eagerly seizes on the hope that Alvaro "*non verrà*" (23; will not come), but despite the notation *con gioia*, her flattened unaccompanied recitative conveys only anxiety. A moment later, Alvaro arrives and throws himself rapturously into Leonora's arms. He passionately declares that God has transformed their apprehensions into happiness, but Leonora's fragmented interjections highlight the psychological gap between the lovers. Alvaro's soul is undivided, and he can look forward to the future with unconstrained enthusiasm. Leonora cannot.

Hence, although the two lovers' vocal lines join in unison for a sequence of accented F-C oscillations, Alvaro's "*Seguimi, lascia omai la tua prigion*" (Follow me, leave your prison at last) contrasts with Leonora's "*no, risolvermi non so*" (27; no, I cannot resolve myself). They share a feeling of emotional *frisson*, but Alvaro's excitement comes from romantic eagerness, while Leonora's anxiety stems from a supreme effort to steel her resolution and act upon her decision to elope.

Seeing Leonora's agitation, Alvaro tries to calm her with an expansive, lyrical vision of their future life together as husband and wife. His efforts are in vain, however, for Leonora is on the verge of complete emotional collapse. In a torrential flood of consciousness not found in Saavedra's play, Leonora begs Alvaro to delay their departure one more day, long enough for her to see her father once again.

As she tries to convince herself that Alvaro is content with such a delay—"*tu contento, gli è ver, ne sei?*" (31; it is true, you are happy about it?)—Leonora's patent self-delusion pathetically reveals her need for release from the inner tensions which are destroying her. Even while she now insists that her heart is full of joy, there is only sobbing anguish in the suffocated, drooping phrases of Leonora's "*io t'amo*" (33; I love you).[15]

Ah! Seguirti Fino agli'Ultimi

Alvaro interprets Leonora's ambivalence as a sign that her love does not equal his own and offers to release her from her vows. But Leonora does love Alvaro, and his palpable hurt spurs her to action. Interrupting him, she launches into a whirlwind *cabaletta*: "*Ah! Seguirti fino agl'ultimi confini della terra*" (35-6; Ah, to follow you to the ends of the earth).

Example 2.1

Ah! Se - guir - ti fi - no a- gl'ul-ti-mi con-fi - ni del - la ter - - ra

Casa Ricordi - BMG Ricordi SpA, used by permission

With its brittle, martial melody and pounding meter, this *allegro brillante con slancio* explosion is an exercise in willful self-deception. In her virtual call to arms, Leonora compels herself to force all troubles from her mind. Her vision of life with Alvaro as a war against destiny, however, drains the ostensible joy from her words, "*con te sfidar impavida di rio destin la guerra, mi fia perenne gaudio d'eterea voluttà*" (36; let facing fearlessly with you the war of evil destiny be an everlasting joy of ethereal delight).

The lovers' ensuing duet sounds far more like a traditional fraternal battle cry, in the manner of *I Puritani's* "*Suoni la tromba*" (Let the trumpet sound), than any expression of transcendent, romantic devotion. Even when Alvaro picks up Leonora's melodic line, the two lovers remain fundamentally divided, expressing different thoughts with alternating musical phrases until the final lines of the duet. As the sound of the approaching marquis and his men is heard outside the chamber, the lovers' final repetition of "*dividerci il fato, no, no, non potrà*" (40; fate will not be able to part us) already seems hollow and ironic.

Confrontation with the Marquis

At this critical moment, Leonora abandons herself to destiny. Evidencing her still-divided soul, Leonora first shows her concern for Alvaro, urging him to hide, and then shows equal concern for her father when she sees Alvaro draw his pistol. Yet, when the marquis enters, heralded by the ominous "Destiny" motif in the orchestration, Leonora simply removes herself to the sidelines of the scene. As if subconsciously understanding that no action on her part can reconcile her conflicting emotions, Leonora choses to resign herself to watching the drama unfold to its destined conclusion.

Although insulted and demeaned by the outraged marquis, Alvaro surrenders to his beloved's father. But as he throws down his pistol, the weapon accidentally discharges, mortally wounding the old man, who curses his daughter with his dying breath. Destiny thus galvanizes Leonora's lifelong quest for peace, a quest born from the essence of her divided soul. And so, as Alvaro drags her from the room, Leonora gives voice to a final climactic cry of "*Cielo, pietade*" (47-8; Pity, Heaven), her top G-sharp extended over some eight measures.[16]

Act II.i

Inn of Hornechuelos

Some months pass between the first and second acts of the opera, months in which Leonora is mysteriously separated from Alvaro, months in which she assumes male attire and continues her flight alone. By the beginning of Act II, Leonora has arrived at the village inn of

Hornechuelos and discovers she has been pursued there by her vengeful brother Carlo.[17]

There is an inescapably mythic aura about this discovery scene: disguises blur personal identity and gender to create a sense of universality, and the stage tableau recalls the Aeschylean doom of a hapless victim pursued by the Furies of retribution.

Clinging timidly to a doorway at the back of the inn, Leonora recognizes Carlo in his student disguise and is immobilized with fear, "*Fuggir potessi!*" (75; If only I could flee!) Ironically, this recognition occurs at the very moment Carlo and the other revellers in the tavern kneel and add their voices to the prayer of a group of passing pilgrims who implore God's mercy.

Leonora is physically and emotionally removed from the crowd; her utter alienation from the world around her is clear in the desperate, plunging phrases of the prayer she counterpoises with the words of the ensemble: "*Ah, dal fratello salvami*" (77; Ah, save me from my brother). Alone and relentlessly pursued by Carlo, isolated by her own suffering even when surrounded by other people, Leonora falls back on a traditional appeal for divine intervention to save her.

Only after she repeats variations on "*Signor, pietà*" (86-9; Lord, have mercy) some five times, does Leonora at last join with the massed voices of the crowd. The superficial effect of this ensemble moment is a fleeting sense of solidarity through faith; but the more profound and lingering impression is one of futility, as Carlo and Leonora both pray for a peace which their very natures make impossible.

Act II.ii

Madonna degli Angeli

Leonora retreats to her chamber, while Carlo relates to the tavern patrons his version of the events surrounding the killing of his father and his own quest for vengeance. Although Leonora is not on stage for this narrative, she overhears it and flees in the next scene to the mountainous sanctuary offered by the church of the Madonna degli Angeli.

Swept along on the orchestral tide of the thunderous "Destiny" motif, Leonora arrives outside the church on the verge of total psychological collapse: "*Son giunta! . . . grazie, o Dio!*" (116-7; I have arrived! Thanks, O God!) Her erratic recitative, with its wild swings of range and dynamics, reveals the mental toll of the emotional strain Leonora has been enduring.

Recalling her own memory of her father's death, she launches a cry of unbearable grief at the thought of Alvaro's supposed flight to America: "*Ed or mi lascia, mi lascia, mi fugge!*" (119; And now he leaves me, he leaves me, he flies from me!) With no personal knowledge of Alvaro's fate, Leonora readily believes Carlo's story, a story which is patently untrue. This complete confusion over the actual events which transpired after Leonora and Alvaro escaped at the end of Act I, the inconsistencies even between the lovers' own stories, suggests that the perspectives which individuals bring to an event are perhaps more significant in the unfolding of human life than the reality of the event itself.

Guilt-stricken by what she perceives to be her role in the marquis' death—"*io del sangue di mio padre intrisa*" (118; I, drenched with my father's blood)—Leonora now takes upon herself the added sin of loving a supposedly faithless man. Falling to her knees and praying for peace in the aria of lamentation "*Madre, pietosa Vergine*" (120; Holy Mother, merciful Virgin), Leonora pleads, "*m'aita quell'ingrato dal core a cancellar*" (120-1; help me strike that ingrate from my heart).

Underscored by agitated orchestration, the broken descending phrases of her aria, with their propulsive double-dotted rhythms and absence of melodic scope, suggest Leonora's desperate state of mind. Ironically, however, while her torment is quite genuine, it is sadly unfounded. Leonora is no more responsible for her father's accidental death than she is guilty of loving an unworthy man. As the next act will reveal, Alvaro has not abandoned her, and his love remains undiminished by time or travails. Leonora's suffering is a tunic of Nessus which she wears as much through choice as compulsion.

Continuing the pattern of supplication begun at the end of Act I and continued in the tavern scene of Act II, Leonora cries, "*deh! non m'abbandonar, pietà, pietà di me, Signore*" (121-2; ah, do not abandon me . . . have mercy on me, Lord). With the fragile support of tremolo strings, Leonora tries to lift her voice and spirit to heaven, her vocal line dragging *con passione* first to top G-sharp and then to A-sharp as her entreaty is repeated. The need for spiritual solace captured in these twin phrases is almost palpable, but it also remains unrealized as the exhausted vocal melody returns inexorably to earth once more.

Example 2.2

deh!   non m'ab-ban-do - nar, pie-tà,   pie-tà,   di   me, Si- gno - re.

Leonora hears the strains of "*Venite, adoremus*" (122; Come, let us adore Him) emanating from within the church monastery, and the ascendant harmonies of the monks' prayer seem an answer to her plea for peace: "*inspirano a quest'alma fede, conforto e calma*" (123-4; they inspire this soul with faith, comfort, and tranquility). But is she truly inspired or only self-deluded?

The fragmented nature of Leonora's interjected comments during the monks' prayer does not suggest any fundamental change in her spiritual state. She remains alienated—physically, emotionally, and musically—from the serenity within the monastery. Indeed, Leonora's return to her original yearning supplication of "*pietà, Signor*" (125) at the end of the aria suggests that the wheel of her suffering continues to turn.[18]

Plea to Padre Guardiano

Leonora rings the monastery bell, and a rather grumpy Fra Melitone finally agrees to summon Padre Guardiano, the Father Superior. When left alone with the pious old man, Leonora entreats him with nearly hysterical agitation, "*Infelice, delusa rejetta, dalla terra e dal ciel maledetta che nel pianto prostratavi al piede, di sottrarla all'inferno vi chiede*" (132-3; Unhappy, deluded, rejected by earth and cursed by Heaven, prostrate in tears at your feet, she implores you to save her from hell).

Though surprised to learn that this wretched woman is Leonora di Vargas, Guardiano invites her to share in the inspiration of religious faith. Kneeling before the rough stone cross which stands in front of the church, Leonora kisses it and declares that she is now calmer, that her father's bleeding ghost no longer pursues her on this holy ground.

Yet, for all her protestations, Leonora's music is hardly peaceful. Rather than picking up Guardiano's tranquil melody, her vocal line writhes over unsettled orchestration. The serpentine contours of

Leonora's phrases and exaggerated use of mechanical, even rhythms—as if in denial of the volcanic emotions which still explode on the word "*maledir*"—suggest an effort at virtual self-hypnosis: "*Più non sorge sanguinante di mio padre l'ombra innante; nè terribile l'ascolto la sua figlia maledir*" (135; The bloody shade of my father no longer rises before me; nor, terrible, do I hear him curse his daughter).

Guardiano, the undisputed man of God, assures Leonora that the phantoms which plague her are no more than the Devil's snares and are powerless on holy ground: "*Sempre indarno qui rivolto fu di Satana l'ardir*" (136; Satan's boldness was always directed here in vain). But Leonora is not calmed by the holy man's absolution; her torment is internally generated rather than externally imposed, and it is therefore not so easily assuaged. As Leonora insists that she wishes to retreat to a hermit's cave and devote her life to God, the hypnotic undulations of the vocal line continue.

Leonora's willful effort seems to succeed. Interwoven with Guardiano's solemn warning against precipitate action she might later regret, Leonora's vocal phrases take on new melodic shape as peace and order descend on her spirit: "*Ah, tranquilla l'alma sento dacchè premo questa terra*" (138; Ah, my soul feels tranquil since I touched this ground). Imbued with this new sense of calm, Leonora is able to answer Guardiano's questions about the death of her father in a factual monotone, without the hysteria of her earlier outpourings. But the fragility of this new-found serenity is exposed when Guardiano suggests that she retire to a cloister rather than to a hermit's cave. With breathless desperation, Leonora vows to abandon herself to the mercies of the wilderness if Guardiano denies her the solitary life she has determined to embrace.

Leonora's Calling

In Saavedra's play, Doña Leonor's refusal to enter a convent stems from her fear of being identified and shamed, but Verdi's heroine offers no such logical rationale. Instead, her invocation of the voice of Heaven, which she now claims to have heard, clearly demonstrates the way in which human beings attribute their own desires to "a divine thrusting on."

Although there has been no suggestion of heavenly revelation in the course of her duet with Guardiano, Leonora now believes she has heard the voice which Guardiano promised her as she knelt before the cross:

"*Ah, sì, del cielo qui udii la voce*: Sálvati all'ombra di questa croce" (142-3; Yes, I heard the voice of Heaven: "Take refuge in the shadow of this cross "). Moreover, she is equally convinced, although there is no such indication in the words she repeats, that Heaven supports her own desire to flee humanity and retreat to a hermit's cave.

Accepting whatever is to come as the will of God, Guardiano agrees to Leonora's plan and calls upon Melitone to prepare the monks for a formal rite of benediction. As the duet draws to its conclusion, Leonora responds to Guardiano's assent with a blissful effusion of lyrical rapture: "*Tua grazia, o Dio, sorride alla rejetta*" (149-50; Your grace, O God, smiles on the outcast).

Freed from the angst which has permeated most of her earlier music, Leonora's vocal line dances with innocent joy, her poised four-measure phrases underscored with the heavenly lightness of harp arpeggios. Guardiano's earlier assurances of absolution could not relieve her spirit, but Leonora now believes that since "*il Signor, mi perdonò*" (151; God has pardoned me) she has truly found redemption from her suffering.

Act II.iii

The scene changes to the interior of the church of the Madonna degli Angeli, and Leonora, flanked by a double file of candle-bearing monks, kneels before Guardiano for her formal benediction. Supported by the full majesty of the Church, blessed by the monks' prayers and protected by their holy malediction of any intruder who might disturb her, Leonora is suffused by a peace she will never know again.[19] Repeating the monks' invocation, she lifts her voice with translucent purity, her ethereal phrases underscored with the delicate strains of woodwinds and harp: "*La Vergine degli Angeli mi copra del suo manto*" (169; Virgin of the Angels, cover me with your mantle).

Yet, even in this scene of faith triumphant, there are visual portents of the alienation Leonora herself has chosen and will never escape: the final stage directions state that Leonora, having kissed Guardiano's hand, rises and departs from the church alone; Guardiano extends his arms after her in blessing. Although sheltered by the Church and dressed as a male penitent, Leonora remains an outsider to the monks' brotherhood, and the solitary life upon which she is embarking will cast her once again into the maelstrom of her own mind and heart.[20]

Act IV

By the last scene of the opera, several years have passed, and it is immediately apparent that the peace of "*La Vergine degli Angeli*" was at best only fleeting and at worst sheer delusion. The stage setting for this scene is richly symbolic: a cave is seen surrounded by rocky crags, and over the entrance is a bell; the sun is setting, and soon the moon shines forth in all its splendor (346). The dusk of Leonora's life has come upon her here in this desolate retreat, but even as the darkness of death prepares to envelop her, a radiant light of hope will appear.

Pace, Pace, Mio Dio

Introduced by the relentless thundering of the "Destiny" motif in the orchestra, the first word of Leonora's great *melodia* "*Pace, pace, mio Dio*" (Peace, peace, my Lord) is a cry of despair that echoes from within the cave (346). Although performance tradition has often turned the first word of the aria into an exercise in *pianissimo* singing, such technical display subverts the dramatic intensity of Leonora's agony.

Forte and unaccompanied, her first "*Pace*" is literally the sound of a voice crying in the wilderness, offering a haunted recognition of Leonora's inability to find spiritual peace in an earthly vale of tears. As Leonora emerges from the cave, her wilting repetitions of the word "*pace*" are colored by plaintive woodwinds and the ironic sweetness of a harp embodying the peace which is always just beyond her reach.

With a keening self-knowledge that lays bare the innermost reaches of her heart, Leonora laments *con dolore*, "*Cruda sventura m'astringe, ahimè, a languir; come il dì primo da tant'anni dura profondo il mio soffrir*" (347; Cruel misfortune compels me, alas, to languish; my suffering has lasted so many years, just as profound as on the first day).

How many times over those years has she prayed in vain for peace, for release from her suffering? Now, almost ritualistically, Leonora once again repeats the word "*Pace*" (347), first with *forte* and then with *pianissimo* dynamics that reflect her inner tension between enduring need and hopeless despair. Confessing that she loved Alvaro, and, indeed, loves him still, Leonora seems to teeter on the brink of madness.

Her strained upper-middle vocal line, with its flattened phrases and unsettling dotted rhythms, suggests a mind caught in an endless vortex of guilt and recrimination: "*L'amai, gli è ver! . . . ma di beltà e valore*

cotanto Iddio l'ornò, che l'amo ancor" (348; I loved him, it is true! But
God had adorned him with such beauty and worth that I still love him).

Example 2.3

Her confession is capped with the explosive outburst of *"Fatalità!"*
(348; Fatal destiny!), the word coming as a near scream on a series of
repeated top Gs, then twice repeated with utter desolation an octave
lower. Significantly, however, this fatal destiny is now associated in
Leonora's mind with her separation from the man she loves, not with her
father's death. Thus, the familiar sound of the "Destiny" motif is heard
only at the end of Leonora's next line, after her thoughts have turned
from the original *"delitto"* to a lyrically melancholy recognition of her
doomed love: *"Un delitto disgiunti n'ha quaggiù! . . . Alvaro, io t'amo,
e su nel cielo è scritto: non ti vedrò mai più!"* (348-9; A crime has torn
us apart in this world! . . . Alvaro, I love you, and it is written in heaven:
I will never see you again!)

Her *agitatissimo* vocal line tortured with irregular rhythms and
heavy accenting as it sweeps along on a tide of building orchestration,
Leonora longs for death as the only release from the universal suffering
of human existence: *"Oh, Dio, Dio, fa ch'io muoia; chè la calma può
darmi morte sol. Invan la pace qui sperò quest'alma in preda a tanto, a
tanto duol, in mezzo a tanto, a tanto duol."* (349-50; Oh, God, let me die,
for death alone can give me tranquility. In vain this soul hoped for peace
here below, at the mercy of so much sorrow, in the midst of so much sorrow.) At last, Leonora's agitation yields to a sense of transcendent longing in an ethereal repetition of *"Invan la pace"* (350), which floats toward
the heavens on a *pianissimo* high B-flat before a caressing denouement.

Leonora's *melodia* is not a formal prayer; it has no ritual conclusion
in either text or music. Instead, it is a single moment in a seemingly

eternal cycle of suffering, recrimination, and hope for release. With an abrupt shift, the orchestration returns to the mundane realities of daily life. As Leonora reluctantly collects the bread that Padre Guardiano has left to sustain her, she hears the sound of someone approaching. Before concealing herself once more in the cave, however, Leonora curses those who would profane this holy ground, launching a shattering four-fold repetition of *"maledizione!"* (351; a curse!), which climaxes on a high B-flat over apocalyptic orchestration.

It is frequently concluded that Leonora's curse stems from abject terror, perhaps from fear of violence at the hands of robbers or other intruders.[21] But Verdi's music suggests otherwise. Instead of a fragmented, wandering, disoriented vocal line analogous to those used in earlier moments of fear, Leonora voices her curse in tightly controlled phrases that convey a terrible weight of authority, the authority of the Church which has proscribed any violation of her solitude. In her years of retreat from the world, Leonora has come to the understanding that she will achieve peace only in death, and it is precisely this release that she awaits. Her curse is thus a violent rejection of any intrusion which threatens to draw her back into a world she has renounced or to divert her from the path to salvation.

Alvaro's Arrival

No sooner has Leonora returned to her cave than Alvaro enters. Having mortally wounded Carlo in their duel, he comes in search of the unknown hermit to give his nemesis the Last Rites. Leonora sounds the bell to summon Padre Guardiano, then steps from her sanctuary and forcefully commands the rash intruder to flee the wrath of Heaven. In an instant, the long-parted lovers recognize each other, but their reunion brings not even the most fleeting celebration of joy.[22] In a whirlwind recitative, Alvaro tells the horrified Leonora that he has Carlo's blood on his hands; his beloved rushes from the scene with a terrible cry to aid her dying brother, and the unforgiving Carlo stabs her.

Terzetto Finale

In the original St. Petersburg version of the opera, the death of Leonora precipitated Alvaro's own unhinged suicide, paralleling Saavedra's play, in which Alvaro leaps from the cliffs with the mad cry,

"*Infierno, abre tu boca y trágame; esparce por el mundo tus horrores;
húndase el cielo; perezca la raza humana. . . . Exterminio, destrucción,
exterminio.*" (194; Hell, open your mouth and engulf me; reveal your
horrors for the world; deluge the heavens; destroy the human race. . . .
Extermination, destruction, extermination.) After much soul-searching
in the process of revising *Forza*, however, Verdi and his new collaborator, Antonio Ghislanzoni, settled upon a denouement which focuses not
on the enduring misery of earthly life, but on the glorious promise
of heaven.[23]

In a magnificent *terzetto finale*, Guardiano counsels Alvaro to hum-
ble himself before the holy and just God who "*adduce a eterni gaudii
per una via di pianto*" (360-1; brings us to eternal joys by a path of
tears). Leonora, too, implores her lover to weep and to pray so that he
may obtain God's forgiveness. Her vocal line here is largely fragmentary
and monochromatic; just as she has resigned herself to the will of God,
so musically she only supports Guardiano, the true voice of the Church,
rather than taking any real melodic initiative.

Alvaro yields, and now, in her final moments, Leonora is flooded
with a joy she has never experienced in the rest of her tortured existence.
Her ascendant, *cantabile dolcissimo* vocal melody foreshadowing the
lyrical effusion in the final scene of *Aida*, Leonora envisions a heaven of
eternal, guiltless love: "*Lieta poss'io precederti alla promessa terra . . .
là cesserà la guerra, santo l'amor, santo l'amor sarà.*" (364-5; Happy, I
can now precede you to the promised land . . . there, war will cease, and
love will be holy.)

Example 2.4

Cantabile dolcissimo

Lieta poss'io pre-ce-derti   alla   promes - sa ter - ra...

là cesserà la guer - ra,   santo   l'amor,   santo l'amor   sa - rà.

Casa Ricordi - BMG Ricordi SpA, used by permission

Her moment of salvation is at hand, and the trio builds to Leonora's final soaring promise to Alvaro, "*in ciel t'attendo, addio*" (366; farewell, I await you in heaven).

In her death, Leonora finds release from the wheel of her suffering and, like the tragic heroines of classical drama, affirms a divine order in the universe which gives meaning even to the inescapable misery of human life. Her final death "*grido*" (367; cry) is a haunting reminder of the earthly struggle Leonora is now leaving behind.[24] But while the travails of life remain, Leonora has found the peace which comes only when the troubled human spirit becomes one again with its Creator. Guardiano intones, "*Salita a Dio*" (367; Ascended to God); and the shimmering strings and harp which bring down the final curtain with a transcendent reprise of her "*in ciel t'attendo*" melody confirm that Leonora's struggle has ended at last with the radiant peace of heaven.

PREVIEW

In adapting Mariette's original scenario for *Aida*, Verdi incisively focuses on the psychological effects of the heroine's inability to privilege romantic, filial, or patriotic love.

Aida's divided soul makes suffering an intrinsic part of her being, an inevitable consequence of her human heart; this vulnerability, in turn, becomes the defining essence of Aida's humanity. Particularizing realism is, thus, pointedly undercut throughout the opera; images of race, gender, and social status drift into the distance like sand carried on the desert wind. Aida's capacity for love is virtually all the audience knows of her, and all it needs to know.

From the early scenes of Act I, Aida evidences an apparent diffidence, which is actually the result of profound emotional enervation. Loving her father and her country but divided in her loyalties, loving Radamès but unable to see her love brought to fulfillment, Aida finds meaningful action impossible and, therefore, retreats from any action at all.

Aida is tormented by her rival, Amneris, in Act II and bullied by her father into betraying Radamès in Act III. Only in the final moments of Act IV does she finds peace: unable to bear life without Radamès, she joins him in a transcendent *Liebestod*.

Aida's beatific release from earthly torment only highlights the unending agony of Amneris, who remains prostrate on the stone sealing the lovers' tomb. As the curtain falls, Amneris' lingering, broken plea for peace seems transformed from a prayer for the dying to one for the living, for those who remain behind to endure the suffering which is an inescapable part of human existence.

CHAPTER 3

Aida

Love and Suffering

The capacity for love shines as humanity's crowning glory; and the search for fulfillment through love, even when doomed to failure, is a timeless quest in opera, a quest symbolizing the eternal longing for temporal redemption from the suffering of life. Operatic plots traditionally trace the path of a single romantic relationship through various vicissitudes to its final outcome. In *Aida* (1871),[1] however, Giuseppe Verdi focuses on the conflicts among competing loves within a single individual: he incisively reveals the psychological effects of Aida's inability to privilege romantic, filial, or patriotic love.

Suffering becomes an intrinsic part of Aida's being, an inevitable consequence of her human heart. The operatic cliché that were it not for "the yoke of inauspicious stars"[2] love would triumph and all would be well is laid bare as a cruel illusion. In a profoundly haunting vision of existential despair, Aida's capacity for intense love leads not to temporal salvation, but to a life of Promethean suffering.

Particularizing Realism

This vulnerability to suffering becomes the defining essence of Aida's humanity; images of race, gender, and social status in the opera thus drift into the distance like sand carried on the desert wind.[3] For all its grandiose display, its ballets and processions, its scenic vistas and exotic local color, *Aida* is a searing, intimate exploration of the human soul.[4]

Hence, particularizing realism is pointedly undercut throughout the opera: the plot of *Aida* is "old-fashioned and generic,"[5] its depiction of ancient Egypt overflowing with inaccuracies and anachronisms,[6] its characters lacking in personal antecedents or quotidian context. Aida's capacity for love is virtually all the audience knows of her, and all it needs to know. The rest of her life is impenetrable and incomprehensible, an existential void illumined only by the blazing lightning-flashes of love which, terribly, both give meaning to her existence and drive her inexorably toward death.

Act I

Heralded by the mournful, longing clarinet motif which is identified with her throughout the opera,[7] Aida first appears in Act I as the quintessential melancholy, passive operatic maiden; "love, submission, sweetness are her principal qualities."[8] Aida takes no active initiative in the dramatic proceedings. Even her asides, which should provide a glimpse into her thoughts and feelings, are obscured in the opening scenes by a lack of *parole sceniche*, the captioning words or phrases which Verdi routinely employs elsewhere.

Questioned by Amneris

Aida unwittingly intrudes on the Princess Amneris' romantic overtures to Radamès just at the moment when her Egyptian rival's jealous suspicions are most fully aroused.[9] With disingenuous concern and protestations of sisterhood, Amneris probes the secret of Aida's sorrow, but Aida is not so easily deceived, replying, "*Per l'infelice patria, per me . . . per voi pavento*" (19; I fear for my unhappy country, for myself, for you). The building, monotone phrases of her vocal line, propelled by driving dotted rhythms and heightened by string doubling, emphasize Aida's palpable agitation.

Yet, there is a sense of truncation in this brief outburst, and Aida's careful understatement of *"per voi,"* down a sixth from the preceding *"per me,"* is particularly conspicuous. By attempting to diminish the personal importance she attaches to the fate of the Egyptians, Aida tries to mask the romantic implications of her first passionate glance at Radamès. The secret love she shares with the young Egyptian captain has already been revealed to the audience, however, in Radamès' *"Celeste Aida"* (7, Celestial Aida), and Aida's protestations of patriotic concern are thus clearly only a partial truth.

Trio

Amneris herself is hardly convinced. She resumes her questioning, demanding to know whether there is not some other, deeper concern which weighs on Aida. But, before Aida can reply, Amneris incongruously turns away to voice her inner feelings of jealousy and wrath. Amneris' aside leads in turn to a full trio, as all three principals reveal their private thoughts. Through his manipulation of this patently artificial stage convention of simultaneous asides, Verdi focuses the opera immediately on the characters' inner lives, rather than on external realities. Given this psychological context, therefore, it is particularly significant that Aida's thoughts remain obfuscated, her words obscured.

Aida might have been expected to initiate the trio by responding to Amneris' demand, *"nè s'agita più grave cura in te?"* (19; does no graver care trouble you?) Instead, she is reduced to silence. Only after the Egyptian princess has fully expounded her dire enmity and Radamès has followed with his own apprehension over Amneris' suspicious countenance does Aida speak. Shaped into an obbligato jeremiad supported by woodwinds, the long, dying phrases of her vocal line keen against the dominant melodies of Amneris and Radamès. Denied the prominence of even a single *parola scenica*, Aida's confession that her sorrow stems not only from patriotism but also from an ill-fated love is virtually unintelligible.

For the moment, the audience must experience Aida's suffering viscerally, without fully understanding it intellectually; the result is a powerful sense of dramatic suspense. Even at the end of the trio, there is no release of the accumulated dramatic tension, for no sooner has the pounding stretta carried Aida to a *fortissimo* high B on *"sventurato amor"* (28; unfortunate love) than a flourish of brass announces the arrival of the Egyptian king and his court. Amneris' questioning of Aida remains unresolved.

Aida's Retreat

Aida's initial image of meekness and submission is already beginning to dissolve, however. The intensity, weight, and scope of her vocal line is simply not consonant with a characterization of subservience and passivity. Instead, Aida's apparent diffidence is the result of profound emotional enervation. Loving her country but divided in her loyalties, loving Radamès but unable to see her love brought to fulfillment, Aida finds meaningful action impossible and, therefore, retreats from any action at all. She seems de-individualized, a dramatic cipher at the opening of the act, not because that is her fundamental nature, but because she has withdrawn from the outer world into the recesses of her own mind and heart.

This retreat within herself is again conspicuous in the ensemble scene following the arrival of the king and court. The *Disposizione Scenica* from the original La Scala production indicates that Aida was positioned near center-stage just to the right of the king.[10] This placement, although realistically inappropriate, keeps Aida at the focal point of the stage picture and thus highlights her conspicuous silence throughout both the messenger's report of the Ethiopian invasion and the ensemble's call for war.

Aida's only audible participation at the beginning of this scene comes in two *parole sceniche*: first, she reacts to news of the Ethiopian warrior-king Amonasro with the aside, "*Mio padre!*" (32; My father!); and, second, she murmurs to herself, "*Io tremo*" (35; I tremble) when Radamès is named commander of the Egyptian forces.

Su! del Nilo al Sacro Lido

After the king and Ramfis, High Priest of Egypt, launch the battle hymn "*Su! del Nilo al sacro lido*" (36; On! to the Nile's sacred shore), however, Aida can no longer internalize her torment: "*Per chi piango? per chi piango? per chi prego?*" (39; For whom do I weep? For whom do I weep? For whom do I pray?) Though on opposite sides of the stage, Aida and Radamès step away from the rest of the ensemble for a moment.[11] Their voices join in a presumptive duet, but the effect is one of bitter irony. They are not singing together, only simultaneously, and their vocal lines remain dissimilar. In a musical caption of the gulf that divides their thoughts at this critical moment, Aida's anguished *pianissimo* obbligato, doubled by woodwinds, is juxtaposed with the martial grandiosity of Radamès' call for Egyptian victory.

Amneris hands Radamès the banner of Egypt with a vigorous reprise of the "*Su! del Nilo*" melody, which in turn is taken up by the assembled masses. But even as the melodic current sweeps inexorably toward a fateful call for Radamès' victory, Aida voices her torment in a desperate counter-melody of plunging phrases and anguished top notes. Although silent during the Egyptians' call for war against her homeland, Aida cannot bear the thought of harm coming to her lover, and so she joins her voice to the thunderous choral imperative, "*Ritorna vincitor!*" (50-1; Return victorious!)

At this moment, with unrealized prescience, she places her love for Radamès over country, over family, over everything else in her existence. Yet, as soon as the words are spoken, Aida recoils in horror at the implications of her cry. As the Egyptian cohort sweeps from the stage, Aida's testament to her love for Radamès propels her into the great *scena* which will reveal at last the depth of her own profoundly divided soul.[12]

Ritorna Vincitor!

As fluid as the torrent of her stream of consciousness, Aida's volatile five-part monologue "*Ritorna vincitor!*" is a psychological *tour de force*.[13] Having joined in the call for Radamès' victory, Aida now repeats the words "*Ritorna vincitor!*" (52), an *allegro agitato* tempo and explosion of desperate eighth-notes highlighting her recognition that triumph for her lover must inevitably mean death or enslavement for her father and brothers.

Like the bloody vision of Macbeth's imagined dagger, haunting woodwind and string figures seem to draw Aida, transfixed with terror, ever further into a nightmare of her own making.[14] She sees Radamès, stained with her brothers' blood, paraded before the Egyptian throngs, and behind his chariot "*un Re . . . mio padre . . . di catene avvinto*" (53; a king . . . my father . . . bound in chains). With a scream on "*avvinto*," her top G punctuated by *fortissimo* strings, Aida starts from her trance.

Accelerating to a *più mosso* tempo, she tries to obliterate this unbearable vision from her mind, imploring the gods to restore her familial bonds and crush the Egyptian oppressors of Ethiopia: "*al seno d'un padre la figlia rendete; struggete, struggete, struggete le squadre dei nostri oppressor!*" (54; Return the daughter to a father's breast; destroy, destroy, destroy the legions of our oppressor!)

There is a sense of willful self-delusion in the incantatory undulations of her prayer, with its unsettling string syncopation and violent octave leaps on "*struggete.*" In vain, Aida tries not to think of the fate which her new entreaty will bring down on Radamès. An inarticulate cry of anguish overwhelms her, however, bursting forth on a *fortissimo* high B-flat before plunging in despair: "*Ah! . . . sventurata! che dissi?*" (54-5; Ah! unfortunate woman! What have I said?)

Emotional Enervation

Once more, the tempo shifts, now to an *andante poco più lento della prima volta*, as Aida sinks again into the paralysis of emotional enervation. She cannot deny her love for her father, for her country, or for Radamès. As she thinks of her lover, the melodic motif first heard in the opera's prelude and associated with Aida since her initial entrance moves, for the first time, into her vocal line: "*e l'amor mio? . . . Dunque scordar poss'io questo fervido amore che, oppressa e schiava, come raggio di sol . . . qui mi beava?*" (55; And my love? Can I then forget this fervent love which, like a ray of sunlight, made me happy here, though a slave and oppressed?)

Example 3.1

Casa Ricordi - BMG Ricordi SpA, used by permission

When she exclaims, *"Imprecherò la morte a Radamès . . . a lui ch'amo pur tanto"* (55; Shall I imprecate death for Radamès, for him whom I love so much), the motif breaks down; Aida's very being is inextricably bound to her love for Radamès. The loss of him, the loss of that love, would mean the loss of herself. By the end of the opera, Aida will reach this conscious understanding, choosing death with Radamès rather than life without him. For the moment, however, she still cannot bring herself to place the claim of romantic love above her love of family and country. She remains trapped and exhausted by her unresolved emotional struggle.

Self-Knowledge

As Aida moves into a *triste e dolce allegro giusto poco agitato* tempo, both emotional strain and sorrow are evident in her headlong vocal line with its narrow range of pitch, dying phrases, and restless string underscoring: *"I sacri nomi di padre . . . d'amante nè profferir poss'io, nè ricordar"* (56; The sacred names of father, of lover, I can neither bear to utter nor recall).

Looking into her own heart, Aida recognizes the oppositions of love which are the cause of her suffering: *"Per l'un . . . per l'altro . . . confusa . . . tremante . . . io piangere vorrei . . . vorrei pregar. Ma la mia prece in bestemmia si muta . . . delitto è il pianto a me . . . colpa il sospir . . . in notte cupa la mente è perduta . . . e nell'ansia crudel vorrei morir."* (56-7; For the one . . . for the other . . . confused and trembling, I wish to weep . . . I wish to pray. But my prayer is changed into blasphemy . . . weeping is a sin for me . . . sighing is guilt. My mind is lost in gloomy night . . . and in cruel anxiety; I wish to die.)

Significantly, this moment of self-knowledge was an addition to the original Verdi-Du Locle outline of the *scena* which moved directly from Aida's thoughts of Radamès to her final prayer for release in death: "Rhadamès (sic) whom I hold dearer than my life . . . defeated . . . wounded . . . dead perhaps . . . ending his miserable existence in the depths of a dark dungeon. Gods, take my life! Through death deliver the miserable Aida from her torments and her grief!"[15]

Prayer for Peace

Finally, Aida offers to heaven a shimmering prayer for peace, her translucent *cantabile* underscored by ethereal strings: *"Numi, pietà del mio soffrir! Speme non v'ha pel mio dolor. . . . Amor fatal, tremendo amor spezzami il cor . . . fammi morir!"* (58; Gods, take pity on my suffering! There is no hope for my sorrow. . . . Fatal love, tremendous love,

break my heart . . . make me die!) It is a supplication for release from
the essence of herself, from the vulnerability to suffering which comes
from her very humanity. Her vocal line swells *poco stringendo* to a
despairing high A-flat before a broken three-fold repetition of *"Numi,
pietà del mio soffrir,"* a desolate *fil di voce* dissolving at last into
exhausted silence as Aida "staggers, anguished and afflicted" offstage.[16]

Act II

By the time Aida enters Amneris' apartments in the second act, she has
internalized her suffering once more. She responds to the Egyptian
princess' insinuating protestation of sympathy for the Ethiopians' defeat
in battle only with a guarded *"Felice esser poss'io lungi dal suol natio,
qui dove ignota m'è la sorte del padre e dei fratelli?"* (91-2; Can I be
happy far from my native soil, here where the fate of my father and
brothers is unknown to me?) Aida's insistence on patriotism and family
parallels her deflection of Amneris' questioning in Act I; and here,
again, the strain in her *più mosso* vocal line suggests the more profound
emotional tension she is concealing. Now, however, Amneris is not to
be diverted. She continues relentlessly, probing the secret of Aida's
heart, holding out hope that the god of love may yet bring happiness.

Aida's brittle facade of self-control begins to crack. Unable to
restrain her surging emotions, she reveals in an animated *allegro* aside
the paradox of her love for Radamès: *"Amore, amore! gaudio . . . tormento . . . soave ebbrezza, ansia crudel . . . ne' tuoi dolori la vita io
sento"* (93-4; Love, love! joy . . . torment . . . exquisite elation, cruel
anxiety . . . I feel life in your sorrows). As the "Aida" motif in *"Ritorna
vincitor!"* revealed her love for Radamès to be the essence of her being,
here her words are symbolically set to a reprise of that same motif.

Amneris' Trap

Observing her rival's mounting turmoil, Amneris presses her advan-
tage, laying a trap for Aida by announcing that Radamès has died in
battle. The last remnants of Aida's emotional control immediately dis-
integrate with the shattering cry, *"Che mai dicesti! misera! . . . Misera!
. . . Per sempre io piangerò!"* (96-7; What did you say! Wretched and
unhappy, I will weep forever!) Amneris then delivers her *coup de grâce*,
declaring that Radamès is actually still alive. Aida falls to her knees, her

uncontrollable outpouring of joy exploding on a high A over *tutta forza* orchestration: *"Vive! ah grazie, o Numi!"* (99; He lives! Ah, thank you, O gods!)

Aida's joy quickly turns to ash in the flames of Amneris' jealous fury. Significantly, Aida initially responds to Amneris' hectoring with the fiery defiance of one who is a princess in her own right. There is no sign of meekness or submission as Aida rises, "turning with pride to Amneris."[17] On the verge of revealing the secret of her own royal birth, Aida confronts her rival with an electrifying *"Mia rivale! . . . ebben sia pure . . . Anch'io . . . son tal."* (100; My rival! well then, so be it. I, too, am such.) Suddenly realizing that a personal challenge cannot serve her love for Radamès, however, Aida determines to subordinate her pride to her love. She abases herself before Amneris, accepting the role of "slave," burying in silence her own royal birth as she begs for pity.

In a plaintive *adagio*, her vocal line doubled by flute and supported with woodwinds, Aida implores, *"Tu sei felice . . . tu sei possente . . . io vivo solo per questo amor!"* (101; You are happy . . . you are powerful . . . I live only for this love!) She is saying whatever she thinks may assuage Amneris. Her tone is consciously obsequious, and the affectation is emphasized by the stylized ornamentation of *"solo per questo."*

Example 3.2

Tu sei fe - li - ce... tu sei pos - sen - te... io vi - vo

so - lo   per que - sto a -mor!

Casa Ricordi - BMG Ricordi SpA, used by permission

Amneris, unappeased, warns of her terrible vengeance; and Aida can only repeat her plea, the artificiality of the reprise highlighting her own scripted performance.

When her supplications are all in vain, Aida finally abandons herself to a nearly hysterical repeat of the death-wish expressed in *"Ritorna vincitor!"* Her hurtling vocal line, with its jarring rhythmic stresses and headlong underscoring, is a tempestuous flood of inchoate despair sweeping Aida toward her doom. A scream of primal anguish carries her to a *fortissimo* high C, before a two-octave plunge that brings her down to the brink of oblivion: "*quest'amor . . . nella tomba io spegnerò*" (107-8; I will extinguish this love in the grave).

Commanding her slave to follow, Amneris departs in scornful triumph to greet the returning armies of Egypt and their victorious commander, Radamès. Cries of "*guerra e morte allo stranier*" (109; war and death to the foreigner) are heard from the offstage populace, and Aida realizes the terrible paradox of her situation: even if Amneris could be won over, Aida's inner conflict among love for her family, love for her country, and love for Radamès remains as intractable as ever. Her mind thus returns to the prayer for peace that ended "*Ritorna vincitor!*" Once again, the wheel of her suffering turns; once again, the haunting melody sounds; once again, the audience hears her desolate *fil di voce* dissolve into silence as Aida haltingly staggers from the stage.

Triumphal Scene

In sharp contrast to this psychological enervation, the Triumphal Scene which closes the second act offers a striking insight into the personal strength Aida possesses when not paralyzed by her own divided heart. In her initial shock at seeing Amonasro a captive of the Egyptian army, Aida blurts out, "*Mio padre!*" (150; My father!) She quickly recovers her composure, however, heeding her father's warning of caution and launching a powerful, eloquent plea for clemency for the vanquished. At first, Aida follows Amonasro's lead, appropriating his established vocal line for "*Ma tu Re, tu signore possente*" (154; But you, king, you powerful lord). She quickly moves beyond simply echoing her father, however, and puts his words to her own arresting, individual vocal melody.

Supported initially by the massed voices of the populace, Aida's line soon soars above the throng with a majestic dignity that transfigures her words of supplication into a paean of familial and patriotic love, culminating in the emotional effusion of a melting cadenza. Aida returns for an instant to Amonasro's original melody but then launches into a heroic descant in the final stretta, her vocal line ascending at last to a blazing high C that seems to embody the regality of her soul and the strength of her love.

Amonasro is spared; but just at this moment of triumph, Aida is stricken by the announcement of Amneris' betrothal to Radamès. While the assembled multitudes proclaim the glory of Egypt, Aida and Radamès voice their shock and despair. The spiritual bond of love which connects them is captured in the desperate unison of their vocal melodies, as Radamès cries that the throne of Egypt is not worth the loss of Aida and she laments, *"Qual speme omai più restami? A lui . . . la gloria, il trono . . . a me . . . l'oblio . . . le lacrime d'un . . . disperato amor."* (184-8; What further hope is left to me now? For him, glory, the throne . . . for me, oblivion, the tears of a desperate love.)

Musically, their threnody echoes Edgardo's suicidal aria *"Fra poco a me ricovero"* (Soon, shelter to me)[18] from the final act of Donizetti's *Lucia di Lammermoor*. Their outcry is a tortured recognition of the futility of existence; the leaping intervals in the vocal lines reveal the torment of two souls; the explosive top B-flats become agonized outcries of hopelessness and loss.

Example 3.3

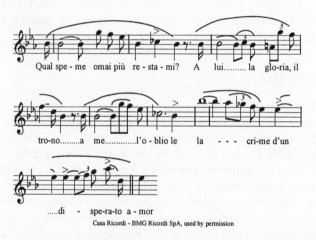

Casa Ricordi - BMG Ricordi SpA, used by permission

Even Amonasro's exultation at the prospect of revenge for the fatherland goes unheard by Aida as she continues to voice her blind despair. In the melee of the final stretta, Aida and her lover are symbolically swept apart by the current of unfolding events until, at last, Aida finds her melodic line joined in unison, not with Radamès, but with Amneris. Their voices mounting repeatedly to the extremes of B-flat and C-flat *in alt*, the two women provide a stunning testament to the absolute power of love: the agony of Aida's abject misery over love lost is counterpoised musically with the ecstasy of Amneris' supreme joy at love fulfilled.

Act III

By Act III, when Aida arrives at the Temple of Isis beside the Nile to
await Radamès, a miasma of futility and despair already overshadows
the last glimmer of hope in her murmured "*Qui Radamès verrà!... Che
vorrà dirmi?*" (209; Radamès will come here! What will he want to tell
me?) Aida's apprehensive "*Io tremo*" (209; I tremble), colored by pal-
pitating tremolo strings, leads immediately into the outpouring of "*Ah!
se tu vieni a recarmi, o crudel, l'ultimo addio, del Nilo i cupi vortici mi
daran... tomba... e pace forse... e pace forse e oblio*" (209-10; Ah!
if you are coming, cruel one, to bring me a final farewell, the dark
whirlpools of the Nile will give me a grave . . . and, perhaps, peace . . .
and, perhaps, peace and oblivion).

Aida's tempestuous, surging vocal line, underscored by eddying
strings which spectrally embody the turbulent currents of the Nile itself,
gives way to a *morendo* calm at the thought of peace. But Aida quickly
recognizes that such release from the pain of her ill-fated love for
Radamès inevitably entails the loss of everything else that she loves
as well.

Oh Patria Mia

In her *romanza* "*Oh patria mia*," Aida's love for her homeland is
foregrounded for the first time in the opera, completing the nexus of her
patriotic, familial, and romantic emotional bonds. By adding this
romanza to his original draft of the score, Verdi creates a far more
complex dramatic exploration of Aida's internal conflicts than is found
in the French scenario by Mariette, which speaks only of her romantic
devotion: "*Les arbres, le fleuve sacré qui baigne ses pieds, ces collines
lointaines où dorment depuis des siècles les ancêtres de celui qu'elle
aime, elle prend tout à témoin de sa constance et de sa fidélité*" (The
trees, the sacred river which bathes her feet, those distant hills where
through the centuries the ancestors of the man she loves sleep, she calls
all to witness her constancy and fidelity).[19]

Like a mysterious, longing call from the distance, an oboe's plaintive undulations turn Aida's thoughts to the homeland she will never see
again. There is a feeling of numbing loss in her obsessive repetition of
"*Oh patria mia, mai più, mai più ti rivedrò*" (210-1; Oh my homeland,
never more, never more will I see you). At last, transported on a stream
of evocative orchestral melody, Aida loses herself in a vision of her

native land. The *cantabile* "*O cieli azzurrî*" (211; O blue skies) weaves a hypnotic spell with its dreamy phrases, graceful ornamentation, delicately shaded *dolce* dynamics, and translucent orchestration.

Yet, at the same time, there is an inescapable undercurrent of tension in the propulsive momentum of eighth- and sixteenth-note rhythms and notable lack of *bel canto* melismatic elongation of syllables in Aida's vocal line. "*O cieli azzurrî*" is not simply a resigned farewell, but a subtle revelation of Aida's intense, passionate patriotic love, a love that only exacerbates her inability to find inner peace.

With a manic-depressive polarity which subtly recalls Aida's earlier oscillations between hope and despair in her love for Radamès, the vocal line leaps an octave from the bleak monotone of "*mai più*" to the first tender phrases of the *cantabile*. This same pattern is repeated for the second verse, "*O fresche vallî*" (213-4; O cool valleys), with a structural, melodic parallelism that highlights Aida's relentless cycle of suffering. The futures of *patria* and *amore* are intimately bound together. Her country was to have been the lovers' refuge; now, if Radamès is lost, Aida will seek peace in death, never seeing her homeland again.

With the dream of reconciling her conflicting loves disintegrating, Aida still clings to an inextinguishable hope. Though she repeats "*mai più*" (215), her vocal line makes a celestial ascent to a *dolce* high C as if striving for transcendence of her suffering. Even in the final phrases of the *romanza*, Aida reaches out for the unattainable, her voice rising toward heaven with a *smorzando* high A that dissolves at last into orchestral reverie.

Confrontation with Amonasro

A man appears, but it is not Radamès. "Aida, turning in surprise and terror at seeing Amonasro, exclaims *Ciel! mio padre*."[20] Aida's instinctive response reflects her unspoken realization that her divided loyalties are about to be placed in active and irreconcilable conflict. She still desperately wants to believe that a happy resolution to her plight is possible, and she is easily seduced by Amonasro's promise that country, throne, and love can all be hers. Blindly, she repeats his beguiling words of home, losing herself in the proffered bliss of reconciliation, in the dream of a return to Ethiopia with Radamès beside her: "*Un giorno solo di sì dolce incanto*" (219; One single day of such sweet enchantment).

Amonasro deftly manipulates Aida's rapture by reminding her of Ethiopia's lurid fate at the hands of the invading Egyptians. Aida remembers all too well. As she prays for peace, her stricken vocal line blossoms with an emotionality born of her own inner pain: "*per noi ritorni l'alba invocata de' sereni dì*" (221; return to us the invoked dawn of peaceful days). For Amonasro, however, peace can come only through victory. He needs the details of Egyptian troop movements, which Aida alone can coax from Radamès. In a flash of terrible revelation, Aida realizes that her father's promise of reconciliation is only a cruel illusion. To regain her family and homeland, she must betray Radamès.

Departure from Mariette's Scenario

In Mariette's scenario, Aida evinces no hesitation in her decision: "*Vaincue par les supplications de son père, par les souvenirs de son enfance, par la joie de posséder celui qu'elle aime loin d'une terre où elle n'a que trop longtemps subi les tortures de l'esclavage, Aïda promet*" (Overcome by her father's entreaties, by the memories of her childhood, by the joy of possessing the man she loves far from a land where, for too long, she has suffered only the tortures of slavery, Aida promises).[21]

Verdi's Aida, however, recoils in horror at the implications of her father's demand, her declamatory "*No! no! giammai!*" (223; No! no! never!) punctuated by violent *tutti* orchestration. Yet, her emphatic rejection is subtly subverted by the truncation of Aida's ascending vocal line at top G. Aida does not want to betray Radamès, but how can she deny the claims of love for her own father and homeland? In rising only to a G, Aida's vocal line suggests the fundamental emotional ambivalence which leaves her defenseless before Amonasro's full-scale psychological assault.

With savage fury, Amonasro denounces his daughter, painting a sanguinary vision of the slaughter her treachery will unleash: "*per te la patria muor!*" (226; Because of you the homeland dies!) Aida's cries for pity fall on deaf ears as Amonasro couples his patriotic rage with a cutting evocation of broken familial bonds, conjuring a spectral image of Aida's mother cursing her faithless daughter.

The *Disposizione Scenica* indicates that at these words "Aida, absolutely terrified, frees herself from her father, takes two steps to the right, then turns to him pleadingly; Amonasro withdraws from Aida, but she follows him and throws herself at his knees, which she attempts to embrace."[22] He is implacable. Declaiming that she is no longer his daughter but a slave of the Pharaohs, "Amonasro, at the height of his fury, once more seizes Aida's left arm; she emits a piercing cry, *Ah!* while her father pushes her back so forcefully that she falls to the ground, almost lifeless."[23]

Completely crushed, Aida capitulates. Dragging herself to Amonasro's knees, she renounces her hope for love with Radamès and piteously pleads to be returned to the bosom of her family and her country.[24] Her decision is met with Amonasro's warm reassurance that only through her action can their martyred people rise again. In bleak despair, Aida resigns herself to the inevitable loss of Radamès, her vocal line swelling to a sustained high A-flat before a plunging, *morendo* denouement: "*Oh patria! oh patria . . . quanto mi costi! o patria! . . . quanto mi costi!*" (231-2; O my homeland, my homeland, how much you cost me! O my homeland, how much you cost me!)

Radamès Deceived

In Mariette's scenario, Aida still believes she has a future with Radamès, and so, when her lover finally arrives on the scene, she makes no effort to obscure her intentions:

> Aïda tour à tour menace et prie. Elle fascine son amant, elle l'entraîne, elle le subjugue. Éperdu d'amour, Rhadamès se jette à ses pieds. Ni la patrie, ni le monde, ni les serments sacrés qui le lient, ne valent un regard, un sourire d'elle. En vain l'honneur le réclame. Il trahira son roi, il trahira la foi jurée, et en échange ne demande aux dieux que l'amour de celle pour laquelle il voudrait mourir.

> (Aida by turns threatens and pleads. She fascinates her lover, she sweeps him away, she captivates him. Mad with love, Radamès throws himself at her feet. Not homeland, not the world, not the sacred oaths which bind him are worth a look, a smile from her. In vain honor recalls him. He will betray his king, he will betray his sworn faith, and in exchange ask nothing of the gods but the love of the woman for whom he would die.)[25]

In the opera, by contrast, Aida goes through the carefully scripted motions of a love scene with Radamès solely to prepare for her disingenuous question, "*Ma, dimmi: per qual via eviterem le schiere degli armati?*" (249; But tell me: by what road shall we avoid the armed

ranks?) Aida's guile transforms this presumptive love duet into a
cynical charade, for her duplicitous manipulation of Radamès is executed with calculated efficiency. First, she challenges the sincerity of his
love. Radamès' exuberant vocal line is met only by Aida's scornful, flattened, declamatory response: he does not love her; he is Amneris'
husband now and does not have the courage to escape his fate.

Spurning Radamès' plans for an appeal to the king, Aida then insists
that he can prove his love only by fleeing the country with her. Radamès
is aghast, but Aida spins out a seductive vision of the utopia awaiting
them beyond the borders of Egypt. As in "*Oh patria mia*," an oboe's
exotic call sounds in the distance when Aida urges, "*Fuggiam gli ardori
inospiti di queste lande ignude*" (239-40; Let us flee the inhospitable
heat of these barren lands). Significantly, however, the oboe melody is
not the same as in the earlier aria; it is not the true call of Ethiopia, but
a Siren's ruse.

While Aida dutifully pictures a land of cool, virgin forests where
love can, at last, be completely attained, her vocal line never takes real
melodic flight. Though superficially pleasing, her vision remains a
mirage. Her lover, however, is easily seduced. When he hesitates
momentarily, Aida's renewed scorn swiftly settles the issue. With
passionate resolve, Radamès cries, "*Ah no! fuggiamo!*" (246; Ah no! let
us flee!), initiating a driving, *allegro assai vivo* as he abandons himself
to delusion. At this point, Aida is content to follow his melodic lead for
a second verse and an ironic reprise of Radamès' exuberant entrance
music for the concluding coda. His initial ardor now seems to be reciprocated, but the lovers' paean is no more than a mockery.

Pausing mid-flight, Aida queries which road will be free of Egyptian
troops. No sooner has Radamès disclosed that his army will pass
through the gorge of Napata than Amonasro leaps from his hiding place
with a cry of triumph. Radamès is overcome with horror and self-
loathing at his own unintended treachery, but it is Amonasro, rather than
Aida, who tries to comfort him. Aida voices only perfunctory interjections to calm Radamès, while her father tries to persuade the Egyptian
captain that a future of love still awaits him. Aida herself, however,
knows better. Aida's silence, as Amonasro drags her off and Radamès
surrenders to Amneris and the priests at the end of the act, underscores
her resignation to a loss which became inevitable as soon as she
privileged the claims of family and country over her romantic love.

Act IV

Aida does not reappear until the end of Act IV. Her intervening escape from the Temple of Isis, as well as Amonasro's death, are only vaguely reported by Amneris before Radamès is condemned for treason and buried alive in a tomb beneath the floor of the Temple of Vulcan.

Foreseeing Radamès' doom, however, Aida has secretly returned, hiding herself in the crypt in order to die with him. Yet, even now, the claims of her heart remain irreconcilable. Embracing eternity with Radamès means turning her back on family and country. Thus, when she steps from the shadows to greet her beloved, the dirge of Aida's vocal line is infused with vitality only at the thought of their final union. Marked *con passione*, her phrases swell to a *dolce* climax before a *morendo* denouement: *"qui lontana da ogni umano sguardo nelle tue braccia desiai morire"* (298; here, far from all human sight, I desired to die in your arms).

After all her suffering, Aida finds peace, but the price she pays is her sanity, for the renunciation of family and country is an act impossible for her conscious mind to accept. So she drifts into delirium, and, in her madness, everything but Radamès melts away. She makes no mention of her betrayal at the Temple of Isis and its deadly aftermath. Instead, with a musical abandon recalling the great mad scenes of *bel canto* opera, Aida imagines the angel of death who will lead the lovers to eternal bliss: *"Già veggo il ciel dischiudersi . . . ivi ogni affanno cessa . . . ivi comincia l'estasi d'un immortale amor"* (300-1; Already I see heaven open . . . there every anguish ceases . . . there begins the ecstacy of an immortal love). And now, for the first time, Aida's voice soars with innocence and delight. Pain and torment fade away, leaving only the euphoric transcendence of her freed spirit.

Liebestod

While Amneris and the priests chant their requiem for the dead in the temple above, Aida and Radamès bid farewell to their earthly vale of tears in *"O terra addio"* (303-4; O earth, farewell). Turning their eyes toward the eternal light of heaven, they at last join their voices in loving unison during the final moments of the opera and, together, find peace. As one nineteenth-century critic wrote of this final duet, *"l'adieu suprême, l'extase amoureuse dans la mort: O terra addio, addio valle di pianto! Une mélodie céleste, je ne sais quoi d'ailé, de pur, le sillon lumineux d'une âme s'envolant vers l'infini, car cette partition tonnante et fulgurante, cette oeuvre grosse de toutes les tempêtes de l'instrumentation moderne, finit par un soupir d'amour."* (the final farewell, the loving ecstasy in death: "O earth, farewell, farewell, vale of tears!" A celestial melody, something winged, pure, the luminous trail of a soul flying toward the infinite, for this score of thunder and lightning, this work full of all the tempests of modern instrumentation, finishes with a sigh of love.)[26]

Peace illumines the darkness of the lovers' tomb, suffusing their very beings, exalting the radiant phrases of their final ethereal hymn to life everlasting: *"si schiude il ciel e l'alme erranti . . . volano al raggio dell'eterno dì"* (304; heaven opens, and our wandering souls fly to the light of eternal day). Pressed in each other's arms, the lovers welcome their *Liebestod*.

Example 3.4

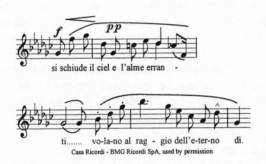

si schiude il ciel e l'alme erran -

ti...... vo-la-no al rag - gio dell'e-ter-no   dì.

Her soul ascending with the soaring bliss of a final, transcendent B-flat, Aida enters the gates of heaven first to await her lover, her beatific release from earthly torment only highlighting the unending agony of Amneris, who remains prostrate on the stone sealing the lovers' tomb.[27] For Amneris, there is no deliverance. As the curtain falls, the Egyptian princess' lingering, broken plea for *"pace"* (310; peace) seems transformed from a prayer for the dying to one for the living, for those who remain behind to endure the suffering which is an inescapable part of human existence.

PREVIEW

In Puccini's operas, men and women alike endure life's inevitable physical and psychological tribulations; but only the heroines of these operas are able to transform the torment of existence into the majesty of tragic understanding, of true anagnorisis.

In adapting Murger's source novel, Puccini and his librettists dramatically alter the character of Mimì, creating a heroine capable of revealing to opera audiences in all times and places the ideals of their own humanity.

Mimì comes from the ranks of the underclass, but while her feet are in the gutter of existence, her eyes are lifted to the stars. A dream of love burns within Mimì, and the flame of this dream suffuses her with the radiance of supreme humanity. The perfection of Mimì's dream sets her apart from the masses that never fully recognize or embrace the ideal of love.

From the moment the floodgates of her heart are opened in the first act, Mimì's love is absolute and immutable, untainted by the sordidness of her world, unshaken by the jealousy and rages of her beloved Rodolfo, undiminished in the face of death itself.

Even as Mimì reaches the tragic understanding that human life must always fall short of human dreams, she still embraces as much of the dream of love as life will allow. Thus, the peace Mimì feels, even as death claims her, is the spiritual serenity of a heroine who, throughout her mortal span, embodied and exalted the glorious potential of the human spirit.

CHAPTER 4

La Bohème

Puccini's Tragic Heroines

The great heroes of tragic drama find themselves engulfed in worlds of torment and affliction—created at times by their own actions, at times by the whims of the gods. Suffering, tragedy asserts, is an inescapable part of human life. Yet, the presence of a tragic hero, of one who can transform this pain into a new and transcendent understanding of life and of humanity's place in the order of the universe, stands as a radiant testament to the infinite potential of the human spirit.

In the operas of Giacomo Puccini, men and women alike endure life's inevitable physical and psychological tribulations; but only the heroines of these operas are able to transform the torment of existence into the majesty of tragic understanding, of true anagnorisis. Puccini thus creates an unprecedented operatic *oeuvre* dominated by tragic heroines, rather than the traditional tragic heroes. Mimì in *La Bohème* (1896) is a case in point: her physical illness is counterpoised with the emotional torment of her lover Rodolfo; but only Mimì comes to a greater understanding of human mortality and the source of meaning in a transient existence.

Source Novel

While drawing upon various episodes in Henry Murger's *Scènes de la Vie de Bohème* (1848), Puccini and his librettists Giuseppe Giacosa and Luigi Illica freely adapt the original story and interpolate new material to create a truly unique stage work.[1] In the nineteenth century, Murger's serialized vignettes of bohemian artistic life in 1830s Paris titillated readers with colorful chronicling of outrageous antics, fights, penury, and promiscuity.[2] Today, however, the novel has the diminished feeling of a formulaic adolescent "coming of age" movie: after a period of youthful indiscretion, sexual indulgence, and defiance of establishment authority, the characters enter into the ranks of middle-class respectability.[3]

In transforming Murger's novel, Puccini and his librettists evidence a complete disinterest in both adolescent titillation and reassuring bourgeois complacency. The vision they offer is one of tragic amplitude. The original character of Mimì is conflated with Murger's minor figure Francine, a gentle, consumptive young woman who devotes the final months of her brief life to a blissful interlude with her beloved Jacques.[4] The wantonness of Murger's Mimì is suppressed,[5] and a compelling new heroine is created, *"un solo personaggio cui si potrebbe benissimo in luogo dei nomi di Mimì e Francine dare quello di: Ideale"* (a single character whom one might well give, in place of the names of Mimì and Francine, that of Ideal).[6] Puccini's Mimì becomes a heroine capable of revealing to opera audiences in all times and places the ideals of their own humanity.

Mimì's Dream of Love

Mimì comes from the ranks of the underclass. A poor seamstress, she lives alone in a freezing garret and embroiders artificial flowers. But while her feet are in the gutter of existence, her eyes are lifted to the stars. A dream of love burns within Mimì, and the flame of this dream suffuses her with the radiance of supreme humanity. The perfection of Mimì's dream sets her apart from the masses that never fully recognize or embrace the ideal of love, which is the glory of the human spirit.

In *La Bohème*, Mimì alone epitomizes the dream of love. The painter Marcello and the flighty Musetta share a light and easy love which is delightful and even genuinely touching at times; their boisterous tantrums and desultory liaisons are hardly the stuff of romantic idealism, however.[7] And while the poet Rodolfo's ardor at first suggests that he is Mimì's true soul mate, it soon becomes clear that his words are not matched by his spirit. Rodolfo's love for Mimì is tainted from the beginning by superficiality and betrayed in the end by guilt and misjudgment.

The vision of *La Bohème* is profoundly humanistic. There is no comforting promise of an afterlife where *"comincia l'estasi d'un immortale amor"* (begins the ecstacy of an immortal love).[8] Instead, the opera exalts the tragic triumph of the individual who, in the face of her own mortality, unwaveringly sustains the fragile dream which affirms her essential humanity and brings meaning to her ephemeral existence.

Act I

When Mimì first appears at the door of Rodolfo's garret in the first act of the opera, the quiet simplicity of Puccini's scoring sets her apart from the other boisterous bohemians. A sudden draft has extinguished her candle as she was ascending to her apartment; too weak to return to the concierge and have it relit, she has reluctantly knocked at her neighbor's door for assistance.[9] An ethereal orchestral foreshadowing of Mimì's aria *"Mi chiamano Mimì"* (They call me Mimì) immediately evokes a sense of unspoken longing, suggesting the private hopes and dreams sheltered behind the young woman's proper public persona. Her words are fragmentary and monochromatic, signalling Mimì's sense of embarrassment at the impropriety of her intrusion: *"Scusi. Di grazia. mi s'è spento il lume."* (54-5; Excuse me. Please. My candle has gone out.)

As dissonant shadows in the orchestration ominously hint at the insidious disease which has pervaded her body, Mimì is overwhelmed by the unmistakable cough of the doomed consumptive. She faints, dropping her key and candlestick, and Rodolfo, alarmed, lifts her into a chair. When Mimì revives, Rodolfo offers some wine to help restore her, murmuring to himself, *"Che bella bambina!"* (58; What a beautiful child!) Mimì clearly overhears his remark, for, although she makes no direct reply, she immediately rises to collect her candlestick and depart with all the haste demanded by virtuous propriety: *"Ora permetta che accenda il lume. È tutto passato."* (58; Now permit me to light my candle. It is all passed.)[10]

It is soon evident, however, that this seemingly unremarkable exchange has had a profound effect on Mimì. In the moment they share

together, Mimì realizes she loves Rodolfo. Love for Mimì is not a grad-
ual evolutionary process of deepening affection; love is an ocean of
feeling contained within her heart and awaiting release. For Mimì there
is no falling in or out of love. Her love is absolute and immutable; it has
never before been offered to another.

Confused and obviously flustered by her surging emotions, uncertain how to respond to the unaccustomed intimacy in which she finds
herself with Rodolfo, Mimì conceals her feelings with a polite though
precipitate departure. A moment later she returns, however, realizing
she has forgotten her key. For the first time, Mimì's vocal line blossoms
with a lyrically expansive phrase, blending lingering reticence with
passionate effusion: "*Oh! sventata, sventata! La chiave della stanza
dove l'ho lasciata?*" (58-9; Oh, careless, careless! Where have I left the
key to my room?) The key she has left behind is not just the key to her
room, but, metaphorically, the key to her happiness.

Example 4.1

© Casa Ricordi - BMG Ricordi SpA, used by permission

Both of their candles blow out in quick succession, leaving Mimì
and Rodolfo alone in the twilight to search for her lost key. Although he
quickly finds it, Rodolfo hides the key in his pocket in order to prolong
Mimì's visit. For her part, Mimì willingly joins in the charade, and the
two continue their search until at last their hands touch.[11] Rodolfo seizes
upon the moment to tell Mimì of his life as a poet and of his romantic
dreams. His effusive aria "*Che gelida manina*" (64; What an icy little
hand) in turn encourages Mimì to open her own heart to this man who
seems to share her dream of love.

Mi Chiamano Mimì

After a brief hesitation, she begins, "*Mi chiamano Mimì ma il mio nome è Lucia*" (69-70; They call me Mimì, but my name is Lucia). The spontaneous free association in Mimì's description of herself contrasts sharply with the polished swagger of Rodolfo's apparently well-rehearsed narrative. With conversational understatement, Mimì speaks of her simple life: "*La storia mia è breve. . . . A tela o a seta ricamo in casa e fuori*" (70; My story is brief. I embroider on canvas or silk, at home and outside).

But when Mimì's thoughts turn to her dream of love, a dream which she associates with the warmth of spring and the magic of poetry, the delicate *dolce* phrases of her *andante calmo* vocal line are enriched by a new fullness of orchestral texture. Puccini's scoring here paints an evocative picture of Mimì's inner life, capturing the syncopated beating of her fluttering heart and her happy memories of the bird songs which are the voices of spring: "*Mi piaccion quelle cose che han sì dolce malìa, che parlano d'amor, di primavere . . . che parlano di sogni e di chimere . . . quelle cose che han nome poesia*" (70-1; I like those things that have such sweet enchantment, that speak of love, of spring-times . . . that speak of dreams and illusions . . . those things that have the name poetry).

When Rodolfo assures her that he understands, Mimì resumes her story with a new lightness of expression, which bespeaks her sense of rapport with the poet. Repeating that she is called Mimì, she emphasizes her solitary and virtuous life; a *rallentando* accents "*prego assai il Signor*" (I pray much to the Lord), while an unaccompanied, *a piacere* phrase highlights the innocence of "*Vivo sola, soletta*" (72; I live quite alone).

Finally, casting aside her natural reserve, Mimì opens her heart to Rodolfo with expansive emotion. An introductory quarter-note rest, extended with a fermata and followed by a double bar and *andante molto sostenuto* marking, signals the dramatic shift in Mimì's narrative (72). Though still simple and without flamboyant affectation, Mimì's vocal line is now infused *con molto anima* and *grande espansione*, weighted with an emotional intensity that is reinforced by orchestral doubling: "*ma quando vien lo sgelo il primo sole è mio . . . il primo bacio dell'aprile è mio!*" (73; but when the thaw comes, the first sun is mine . . . the first kiss of April is mine!)[12]

Example 4.2

Mimì speaks of springtime, but for her the "*bacio dell'aprile*" symbolizes a far more profound, and as yet unrealized, love. Recognizing the gap between her dreams and the realities of her life until this moment, Mimì's shyly returns to the safety of ordinary conversation: "*sono la sua vicina che la vien fuori d'ora a importunare*" (74; I am your neighbor, who comes at the wrong time to trouble you). But there is no turning back, for Mimì feels that with Rodolfo the dream of love can become a reality.[13]

Spiritual Union

In the love duet that brings Act I to a close, Mimì rapturously abandons herself to the realization of her dream, crying "*Ah! tu sol comandi, amor*" (78-9; Ah, Love, you alone command); the lovers' voices join together in ecstatic abandon, intertwining and caressing in a musical embodiment of consummate spiritual union. Parrying Rodolfo's more physical advances,[14] however, Mimì suggests accompanying the poet to the Christmas Eve festivities at the Cafè Momus, and the two raise their voices together in a rapturous repetition of "*Amor*" (82), celebrating Love Universal and Triumphant. Although Rodolfo traditionally joins Mimì for her final ethereal high C, the score calls for him to remain on a more symbolically appropriate harmonic E: the lovers may be in spiritual harmony at this moment, but Rodolfo has not truly reached the heights of Mimì's ideal love.

Act II

Mimì's largely peripheral role in the merriment of Act II serves primarily to emphasize the discontinuity between her dream of love and the realities of the world around her. Rodolfo seems to identify with Mimì's dream when he introduces her to the other bohemians: "*son io il poeta; essa la poesia*" (103-4; I am the poet; she, poetry). But, unconsciously, Rodolfo also acknowledges the divide separating him from Mimì: while he is a poet, he is not poetry; while he is a lover, he is not love.

Mimì is guided by a pure and untainted ideal of love, but Rodolfo's affections are more earthbound. Even in these first honeymoon moments of bliss, unfounded suspicions that Mimì is interested in other men plague Rodolfo: "*All'uom felice sta il sospetto accanto*" (100; Suspicion is always close to the happy man).

The two lovers' different perspectives are starkly emphasized when the painter Marcello is tormented by his sometime mistress Musetta. As Musetta arrives on the arm of a wealthy older man and then uses every trick in her not inconsiderable repertoire to arouse Marcello's jealousy, Rodolfo informs Mimì that, unlike Marcello, he would never forgive; she responds with surprise, "*Io t'amo tanto, e sono tutta tua! . . . Chè mi parli di perdono?*" (128-9; I love you so, and I am completely yours! Why do you speak to me of forgiveness?)

The spectacle of Marcello and Musetta with their tempests, tantrums, and torments leads Mimì to sympathy and compassion as she murmurs, "*l'amor ingeneroso è tristo amor*" (138; ungenerous love is sad love); but Rodolfo responds to the scene with hostility, declaring, "*È fiacco amor quel che le offese vendicar non sa!*" (137; It is weak love which does not know how to avenge offenses!) The disparity between Mimì's dream of ideal love and the reality she has found with Rodolfo is already ominously evident.

Act III

In the third act of the opera, some weeks have passed. It is February, and Mimì has travelled to an inn on the outskirts of Paris in search of Marcello.[15] On the verge of physical and emotional collapse, she asks a maidservant to call Marcello, her effortful, fainting vocal line underscored with haunting strings. When Marcello emerges, Mimì listens quietly as he talks, with typical ebullience, of how he has passed the last month painting the facade of the inn while Musetta gives singing lessons to the visitors. The deathly sound of Mimì's cough forestalls any further chatting, however, and Marcello invites her into the warmth of the inn.

An aching evocation of her inner suffering sounds in the orchestra as Mimì refuses; Rodolfo is inside, and she cannot face him. In a desperate outburst of need and tormented confusion, Mimì cries, "*O buon Marcello, aiuto!*" (182; Help, good Marcello!) Her vocal line as turbulent as the emotional maelstrom which is engulfing her, Mimì reveals her hidden personal torment, her almost inexpressible grief as the love of which she dreamed seems to be slipping away: "*Rodolfo, Rodolfo m'ama, Rodolfo m'ama e mi fugge, il mio Rodolfo . . . si strugge per gelosia*" (182-3; Rodolfo, Rodolfo loves me . . . Rodolfo loves me and flees from me . . . my Rodolfo is consumed by jealousy).

As she recounts Rodolfo's jealous rages in broken, disoriented phrases, it is clear that Mimì, unwavering in her own feelings, cannot comprehend the cause of these scenes. She knows only that she loves Rodolfo and that he is renouncing her. Mimì's vocal line builds with electrifying intensity as she laments, "*Mi grida ad ogni istante: non fai per me, ti prendi un altro amante, non fai per me! Ahimè! ahimè!*" (184-5; Every moment he shouts at me: "You are not for me, take yourself another lover, you are not for me!" Alas! alas!)

Finally, emotionally exhausted, Mimì sinks into a paralyzed monotone as she asks Marcello for guidance. His advice that the lovers should stop living together elicits a strikingly ambivalent response.[16] Although in her mind Mimì can agree with Marcello, her heart can never accept the end of her dream. Thus, her vocal line surges to a top A with *forte* orchestral underscoring in an outpouring of emotion that subverts the ostensible finality in her words: "*Dite ben, dite bene*" (186; You are right, you are right).

Mimì begs Marcello to help her part from Rodolfo, but throughout this exchange the uncontrollable eruptions of feeling in her vocal line clearly indicate a subtextual desire for reconciliation, not separation. Had Mimì truly wished to leave Rodolfo, there would have been no need for her to come in search of Marcello at all; Rodolfo had already stormed out during the night shouting, "*È finita*" (190; It is finished).

Mimì's torment reveals the terrible tension between a dream of love which will not be abandoned, and an actual relationship which is at the point of disintegration. Guided by the ideal of love as an eternal and omnipotent bond, Mimì is adrift as she tries to cope with the frailty of human relationships; hence, the ambiguity in her plea to Marcello, "*Fate voi per il meglio*" (188; Act for the best).

Mimì Overhears

Marcello promises to help and then, hearing Rodolfo inside the inn, tells Mimì to go home. Hoping that somehow all will be well, Mimì instead conceals herself behind a plane tree and lingers to overhear the friends' conversation.[17] Marcello chides Rodolfo, and the poet at last confesses that his jealous tantrums were only to conceal his feeling of helplessness in the face of Mimì's impending death.

At first, Mimì does not fully grasp the significance of what she has overheard, murmuring, "*Che vuol dire?*" (199; What does he mean?) In her youth and innocence, she has never recognized the severity of her illness or confronted her own mortality. Now, as the reality of death faces her, Mimì is nearly paralyzed, her weeping, broken interjections culminating in the anguish of "*Ahimè, ahimè! È finita! . . . O mia vita!*" (202; Alas, alas! It is finished! O my life!)

At last, words fail her completely. Shaken by uncontrollable sobs and coughing, she is discovered by Rodolfo and Marcello, who rush to her aid. Hearing Musetta's flirtatious laugh, Marcello quickly returns to the inn, and Mimì is left alone with Rodolfo. Significantly, after the initial shock in the poet's "*M'ai sentito?*" (203; Did you hear me?), no further allusion is made either to Mimì's death or to Rodolfo's earlier misguided cruelty. The poet simply tries to continue as if nothing had occurred, but his denial of reality offers little comfort.

Donde Lieta

No longer sure of Rodolfo's love, Mimì withdraws back into herself. Struggling to cope with the inevitable—the disillusionment, loss, and death which are intrinsic to human life—Mimì bids farewell to Rodolfo in tightly controlled, narrow-ranging phrases, underscored by a poignant orchestral echo of the "*Mi chiamano Mimì*" motif from Act I: "*Donde lieta uscì al tuo grido d'amore, torna sola Mimì*" (206; Mimì returns alone to the place she happily left at your call of love). The torment she feels at this return is clear, however, in the heightened vocal *tessitura* and the plunging orchestral figures[18] underscoring Mimì's "*al solitario nido. Ritorna un'altra volta a intesser finti fior!*" (206-7; to the lonely nest. She returns once more to intertwine artificial flowers!)

But for all the pain Mimì is enduring, she has not abandoned herself to the abyss of despair. Recalling the happiness of Act II, the sprightly woodwind melody which dances at the conclusion of her phrase glimmers like a gentle smile, a smile of remembrance for the past and of reassurance for a future in which the dream of love will endure, if only within her own heart, to give her courage in the face of death.

Parting "*senza rancor*" (207; without bitterness), Mimì pauses to say she will send the concierge to collect her few small possessions from Rodolfo: a prayer book and ring. Symbolically, these items represent the holy bonds of a union which may not have been blessed by the Church, but which was to Mimì a spiritual marriage. Any sense of bathos is avoided, however, in the careful understatement of Puccini's scoring. As a result, the very casualness of her conversational phrases takes on a particular poignancy.

With a sighing "*Bada*" (208; Mind you), over *pppp* accompaniment, she turns her thoughts to the pink bonnet Rodolfo bought her as a token of their love during the Christmas Eve festivities. Trying to maintain her composure, she begins "*Se vuoi*" (209; If you want) three times before she can put her feelings into words. At last, she offers the bonnet to Rodolfo as a remembrance of their love, her vocal line soaring to a climactic high B-flat for "*se vuoi serbarla a . . . ricordo d'amor*" (209; if you want, keep it in remembrance of love). The word "*amor*" remains suspended on a top A-flat like a musical embodiment of Mimì's transcendent dream.

Temporary Reconciliation

Mimì murmurs "*Addio*" and, after an emotion-laden pause, repeats, "*addio senza rancor*" (209; farewell without bitterness). Her vocal phrase echoes Mimì's farewell earlier in the aria, but it is now raised a third and colored by dissonant orchestral underscoring in evidence of her heightened emotion. Ironically, no sooner has Mimì finished speaking than Rodolfo tries to recast their earlier troubled relationship as a nostalgic idyll: "*Addio sogni d'amor*" (209-10; Farewell, dream of love). The words of idealistic love continue to flow easily for Rodolfo, and Mimì can only remind him with a gentle smile of his jealousies, rebukes, and suspicions. Mimì now fully recognizes the imperfection of their bond of love, the gap between her dream and their life together.

Yet, Mimì also senses from Rodolfo's reaction that in his own way he does still love her, and always has. For all its imperfection, a bond remains between them, and thus there is a spontaneous connection of thoughts in their bittersweet "*Soli d'inverno . . . è cosa da morire! . . . Mentre a primavera c'è compagno il sol!*" (212; To be alone in winter is something to die of! While in springtime there is the sun as companion!)

Mimì has already reached the tragic understanding that human life must always fall short of human dreams. But now she also recognizes that the dream of love is a dream of sharing, the yearning for the ultimate communion with another soul. Even if the perfect realization of that dream remains an illusion, she now determines to embrace as much of the dream as life will allow: Rodolfo and Mimì agree to stay together, at least until the spring.

When the perennially feuding Marcello and Musetta emerge from the inn, their shouts and insults contrast sharply with the ironic imagery of springtime joys intoned by Mimì and Rodolfo. While Marcello and Musetta flare with passionate fire, Rodolfo and Mimì flicker with the dying embers of a fading relationship. The aching lyricism of their music is tinged with loss and regret. The spiritual and emotional distance between Rodolfo and Mimì is clear when her statement of eternal love "*Sempre tua per la vita*" (220-1; Always yours, for life) is met only with his "*Ci lascieremo*" (221; We will leave each other).

Her vocal line suspended with infinite longing, Mimì wishes that she could hold back the inevitable parting that will come in springtime: "*Vorrei che eterno durasse il verno!*" (221-2; I would wish the winter would last forever!) But, ultimately, the scene concludes with Rodolfo and Mimì mechanically repeating their effortful "*Ci lascierem alla stagion dei fior*" (222; We will leave each other at the season of flowers).

Example 4.3

Ci la - scie - rem al-la stagión dei fior!

Act IV

Love and death, the two great realities of existence, come together in Mimì's final appearance during Act IV. Months have passed since she parted from Rodolfo, and now she returns to spend her last moments with the only man she has ever loved. The intervening events are barely sketched through vague rumors and fragmentary reports.

It is clear that as the bonds of love which gave meaning to her life dissolved, Mimì, like Violetta in Verdi's *La Traviata*, gave herself up to a self-destructive existence and early death. Alluding to Mimì's liaison with a wealthy viscount, Marcello reports seeing her dressed like a queen and riding in a carriage; Musetta later relates how she discovered the dying Mimì, who had left her protector and was wandering the streets alone, barely able to drag herself along the street.[19] Yet, Mimì's dream has not been destroyed, and she returns to affirm with her dying breath the ideal love which will pass only with the passing of life itself.[20]

Mimì's Return

For Mimì, there is a joyful feeling of renewal at being once more in the room where, however fleetingly, her dream of love became reality. Her voice soars as she tells Rodolfo, "*si rinasce. Ancor . . . sento la vita qui. . . . No . . . tu non mi lasci più!*" (252-3; one is reborn. Again I feel life here. No, you will not leave me anymore!)

She greets her friends weakly and then pretends to sleep until she is left alone with Rodolfo. While the others are out in search of a doctor and medicine, Mimì finds the strength to sit up in her bed, gently place her arms around Rodolfo's neck, and offer her final testament, an *andante calmo* affirmation of her dream: "*Sei il mio amor . . . e tutta la mia vita!*" (262; You are my love . . . and all my life!) In the simple faith of this phrase, Mimì finds peace.

Example 4.4

Sei il mio a-mor....... e tut - ta la mia vi - ta!

© Casa Ricordi - BMG Ricordi SpA, used by permission

She accepted her human destiny months ago, and while Rodolfo typically declares that she is "*Bella come un'aurora*" (263; Beautiful as a sunrise), Mimì gently responds, "*bella come un tramonto*" (264; beautiful as a sunset). For a moment they recall the joys of the past—the bonnet he bought for her, the search for her lost key, the first touch of their hands—until a new coughing spell jars them back to the present reality of her impending death.

As Mimì falls back exhausted, the other bohemians return with medicine and a muff, paid for with Musetta's jewelry and Colline's over-coat. Slipping the muff onto Mimì's freezing hands, Musetta assures her that this generous and selfless gift is from Rodolfo. And so Mimì passes serenely from life, her last words radiant with the dream of love she has never forsaken: "*Quì amor . . . sempre con te! . . . Le mani . . . alcaldo . . . e . . . dormire.*" (273; Here, love . . . always with you! My hands . . . in the warmth . . . and . . . to sleep.)[21]

The peace Mimì feels even as death claims her, the spiritual serenity of a heroine who throughout her mortal span embodied and exalted the glorious potential of the human spirit in face of disillusionment and suf-fering, is juxtaposed with the torment which engulfs Rodolfo at Mimì's passing. As the orchestra screams *fff tutta forza* the melody of Mimì's final testament like the guilt-amplified echo within his mind, Rodolfo seems to recognize for the first time the priceless treasure he has lost. He cries out Mimì's name *colla massima disperazione* before sinking into the silence of unutterable despair, perhaps finally understanding what the audience has long recognized—the gulf between his own affections and Mimì's transcendent dream of love.

PREVIEW

One of the most daring explorations of feminist characterization in the operatic repertory, Puccini's *Tosca* transforms the source melodrama by Sardou into a tragedy for the modern age.

In the first act, Tosca is conspicuously objectified, marginalized from the male power struggles that dictate the unfolding of events in her world. Tosca consciously plays the expected part of nineteenth-century "Woman;" but, by subordinating her true self to a scripted role, by accepting a patriarchally imposed dehumanization, Tosca becomes engulfed in a vortex of degradation and individual annihilation.

By Act II, however, Tosca recognizes that salvation will come only by accepting and affirming her true self, by casting aside the roles the men in her life have forced upon her, by empowering herself as an individual and shattering the icon of passive victimization. Out of suffering comes redemption. Tosca is freed, and her personal emancipation reverberates through the last act of the opera in the emergence of a vital new conception of human love, in the birth of hope for a better society, in the triumph of faith in a divine order of creation which transfigures even death itself.

When Tosca rushes to the parapet of the Castel Sant'Angelo to embrace her destiny, she ascends into the pantheon of tragic heroines, celebrating her individual identity and embracing the righteousness of Heaven. So she rises *in excelsis*, suffering and despair musically transfigured in a triumphant moment of tragic joy as Tosca launches herself into eternity.

CHAPTER 5

Tosca

Revolutionary Feminism

Giacomo Puccini's *Tosca* (1900) is one of the most daring explorations of feminist characterization in the operatic repertory, a watershed for the lyric stage as revolutionary as Ibsen's *A Doll's House* (1879) was for the spoken theater. Though the elegance of its classically tragic design has been defaced almost beyond recognition by decades of critical graffiti,[1] the work remains monumental. And when the grime of accumulated clichés, preconceptions, and banalities is stripped away, *Tosca* emerges as an artistic masterpiece which compels a revisionist reinterpretation.

Puccini and his librettists Giuseppe Giacosa and Luigi Illica transform Victorien Sardou's 1887 melodrama into a tragedy for the modern age. Sardou's *La Tosca* is an intricately wrought *pièce bien faite* in which plot machinations are paramount and flamboyant splashes of historical color and spectacle camouflage an essential reliance on static character types.[2] Sardou's heroine herself is little more than a construct of the "Diva." As the title of the play proclaims, she is not "Tosca" the woman, but "La Tosca" the star. From her first entrance in Act I, La Tosca's character is delimited: loving and jealous, quick-tempered and defiant, a helpless pawn in the political intrigues that surround her. She manifests not the slightest hint of either personal growth or developing understanding during the remaining four acts of the play.

Self-Recognition

Puccini's *Tosca*, in contrast, undergoes a stunning metamorphosis. At first, Tosca is conspicuously objectified, marginalized from the male power struggles that dictate the unfolding of events in her world.[3] Tosca consciously plays her expected part, conforming to a stereotypic image of nineteenth-century femininity. But by embracing this role in the first act out of love for Cavaradossi, Tosca accepts a patriarchally imposed dehumanization which leads inexorably to her sexual assault by Scarpia in the second act.[4] Subordinating her true self to a scripted role of "Woman," Tosca is engulfed in a vortex of degradation and individual annihilation.[5]

Yet, in the depths of her most abject suffering at the hands of Scarpia, Tosca experiences a moment of profound recognition, of classical anagnorisis. Out of suffering comes redemption, new understanding of her own identity and her place in the world: "Sing sorrow, sorrow: but good win out in the end."[6] The only escape from oppression lies in self-affirmation; and so, in slaying Scarpia, Tosca symbolically destroys the patriarchal order and takes control of her identity, of her destiny. In a single breathtaking gesture, she irretrievably shatters the icon of nineteenth-century femininity. Tosca is freed, and her personal emancipation reverberates through the opera in the ascendancy of a vital new conception of human love, in the birth of hope for a better society, in the triumph of faith in a divine order of creation which transfigures even death itself.[7]

Gender Marginalization

In the first act of Sardou's play, Mario quickly insists that La Tosca be kept ignorant of his intrigues with Angelotti: "*je ne suis pas pour associer les femmes à ces sortes d'aventures*" (I am not for associating women with these kinds of adventures).[8] When Angelotti questions, "*Même celle-là qui vous est si dévouée?*" (Even that one who is so devoted to you?), Mario expounds emphatically:

Même celle-là! —Son concours nous est inutile, n'est ce pas?. . . . Biffons l'inutile. Si petit que soit le risque à lui parler, il est moindre encore à ne lui rien dire, et nous sup-primons du coup les questions, les inquiétudes, la fièvre, les nerfs, etc. . . . Pensez surtout qu'elle est dévote, que la confessionnal est un terrible confident, et que la seule femme vraiment discrète est celle qui ne sait rien.

(24-5; Even that one! Her cooperation is useless to us, is it not? Let us do away with the useless. However small the risk of telling her, it is still less to say nothing, and we head off the questions, the anxieties, the feverishness, the nerves, etc. . . . Think, above all, that she is devout, that the confes-sional is a terrible confidant, and that the only woman who is truly discreet is the one who knows nothing.)

Mario's ostensible qualms, however, are no more than a tissue of prejudice and half-truths, of clichés and female stereotypes. He dismisses La Tosca as so devout that no secret would be safe from her confessor, but in reality she clearly follows the dictates of her own mind. La Tosca recounts how Father Caraffa ordered her to destroy a copy of *La Nouvelle Héloïse* which Mario had given her: "'*Mon enfant, brûlez vite ce livre infâme, ou c'est lui qui vous brûlera*'" (33; My child, burn that infamous book quickly, or it will burn you). Yet, far from burning the proscribed novel, La Tosca chuckles, "*je l'ai lu! . . . Et il ne me brûle pas de tout ce livre.*" (33; I read it! And that book didn't burn me at all.)

The good padre also ordered her to convert her revolutionary lover: "'*Et d'abord obtenez de lui qu'il sacrifie cet insigne révolutionnaire qu'il étale effrontément par les rues avec des airs de défi*'" (35; First of all, get him to give up that revolutionary insignia which he shamelessly displays with looks of defiance in all the streets). Although La Tosca promised to persuade her lover to shave his offending moustache, she never actually said a word because, after all, "*Elles te vont si bien*" (35; It looks so good on you). Clearly, La Tosca is marginalized not because of her religious devotion, but simply because of her gender.

Act I

So too, in the opera, Cavaradossi treats Tosca as an intrusive outsider, despite the passionate devotion expressed in "*Recondita armonia*" (Profound harmony).[9] His political business is beyond "Woman's" purview, so, upon hearing Tosca's voice outside the church doors, Cavaradossi reassures Angelotti, "*È una donna . . . gelosa. Un breve istante e la rimando.*" (33; It is a jealous woman. One brief moment and I'll send her off.) Puccini, however, uses this patent objectification to launch a startling exploration of the role of "Woman" that Tosca is enacting.

Idealized Tosca

With Angelotti safely secreted away, Cavaradossi responds to the increasingly irritated summons from his lover. He unlocks the doors, and the orchestra begins an expansive *andantino sostenuto, dolcissimo e con tutta l'espressione* as Tosca "*entra con una specie di violenza, guardando intorno sospettosa*" (36; enters with a sort of violence, looking about suspiciously).

The romantic contours of this *andantino* are traditionally interpreted as an embodiment of Tosca herself: "To this broad melody (in the solo cello doubled by the flute and accompanied by string arpeggios) Tosca sweeps into the church. This melody describes her physical poise, her absolutely female presence."[10] Yet, as Mosco Carner notes, "Puccini appears so anxious to seize on this great opportunity for lyrical music that dramatically he starts with it too soon, overlooking the discrepancy between the state of irritation and suspicion in which Tosca enters and the languid 'Tosca' melody of the orchestra."[11]

Far from a miscalculation, however, Puccini's use of the orchestral motif is a dramatic master stroke, embodying the inescapable male gaze. The melody of the *andantino* does not really embody Tosca, but rather the image of an "Idealized Tosca" which Cavaradossi projects onto her. In contrast to the intense dialogue between the painter and Angelotti, this motif sounds cloyingly sentimental, providing a trenchant evocation of the artificial romantic roles Cavaradossi and his "Idealized Tosca" play with each other. Thus, the motif commences precisely as Cavaradossi assumes his "tender lover mask," opening the doors for Tosca with calculated nonchalance, preparing to act out a requisite mawkish love scene unconnected to the reality of Tosca's initial agitation and jealousy or his own desire to return as quickly as possible to the business of Angelotti.

Genuine Feeling and Scripted Performance

Cavaradossi begins to go through his paces, trying to embrace Tosca, but she will have none of it. She rejects him brusquely and demands in a fragmented monotone, *"Perchè chiuso?"* (37; Why locked?) Tosca refuses to join in the orchestral motif that Cavaradossi assumes *con simulata indifferenza* for *"Lo vuole il Sagrestano"* (37; The Sacristan wanted it). Insisting that she heard a woman with Cavaradossi, she cries, *"Lo neghi?"* (38; You deny it?), the flash of a top A-flat offering a compelling insight into the real depth of Tosca's feelings, into her need for love.

Tosca desperately wants Cavaradossi to allay her doubts and, hence, eagerly accepts his protestation, *"Lo nego e t'amo"* (38-9; I deny it, and I love you). With her genuine anxiety relieved, Tosca now begins to play her part in the scripted love scene, accepting the role of "Idealized Tosca." As Cavaradossi tries to kiss her, she coyly demurs, *"Oh! innanzi la Madonna"* (Oh! in front of the Madonna), kittenishly adding *"No, Mario mio, lascia pria che la preghi, che l'infiori"* (39; No, my Mario, let me first pray to her and adorn her with flowers). Only here, as she acts to fulfill the expectation of both piety and allure in Mario's image of her, does Tosca finally join her voice with the "Idealized Tosca" motif in the orchestra.

Her devotions completed, Tosca chatters on to Cavaradossi about their romantic plans for the evening, but there is certainly more than a suggestion of artifice in such apparent simplicity and naïveté following so swiftly on the heels of her initial agitation and jealousy. For his part, Cavaradossi remains preoccupied by thoughts of Angelotti and responds only distractedly, *"Stassera?!"* (41; Tonight?!)

Confronted with such indifference, Tosca finds herself trapped by the artificiality of the romantic scene they are enacting. She loves Cavaradossi but cannot simply ask why he is failing to play his part: such a metatheatrical awareness would be an admission that his "Idealized Tosca" is nothing but an illusion. So she must continue with her own script, seemingly oblivious to Cavaradossi's preoccupation. Her dreamy vision of a moonlit night suffused with the perfume of flowers is Cavaradossi's cue for passionate effusion, but Tosca's *"Non sei contento?"* (Aren't you happy?) is met only by a deflating *"Tanto"* (42; Very).

Tosca's repeated *"Lo dici male"* (43; You say it badly) reveals her genuine sense of hurt at Cavaradossi's apathy, though her recourse is more consciously playful chatter about the delights of "*la nostra casetta*" (43; our little house) with an *allegro moderato* vocal line underscored by sprightly syncopated strings colored by woodwinds and harp punctuation. While Cavaradossi remains silent, Tosca raises her poetic rhetoric to ever greater heights of effusion until, at last, she compels a response with the cry "*Arde in Tosca un folle amor*" (48; A mad love burns in Tosca). Cavaradossi's "*Ah! M'avvinci ne' tuoi lacci mia sirena*" (Ah! my siren, you enthrall me in your snares) seems suitably passionate, exploding on a *forte* high B-flat to top the A-flat of Tosca's "*amor*." Yet, for all its ostensible fervor, the musical phrase is decidedly perfunctory.

Microcosmic Empowerment

Cavaradossi's abrupt "*Or lasciami al lavoro*" (50; Now leave me to my work) clearly comes as an unexpected foreshortening of the scene. Tosca conceals her dismay, however, choosing instead to redirect the proceedings by playing the part of the jealous lover. Catching sight of Cavaradossi's portrait of Mary Magdalene and recognizing the face as that of the beautiful blonde Marchesa Attavanti, Tosca launches into what must be considered a theatrical parody of her earlier doubts and suspicions.[12] Shrieking and sobbing in a veritable frenzy, Tosca tears "a passion to totters, to very rags, to spleet the ears of the groundlings."[13] She can be neither placated nor dismissed, and, at last, Cavaradossi is obliged to fulfill his part with the long-delayed profession of love, "*Qual'occhio al mondo può star di paro all'ardente occhio . . . tuo nero?*" (57-8; What eye in the world can equal your dark, ardent eye?)

Tosca has seized directorial control of the love scene. She has compelled Cavaradossi's response, and there is thus more than a hint of irony in her rapturous "*Oh come la sai bene l'arte di farti amare*" (60; Oh, how well you know the art of making yourself beloved). She demands that Cavaradossi repaint the Magdalene with dark eyes like her own and accepts her lover's "*Mia gelosa*" (60-1; My jealous one) with unmitigated pride. As the duet crescendos to its climax, the soaring unison vocal lines and sprightly apreggio orchestration subvert any sense of contrition for Tosca's jealous outburst and undercut the scripted bathos in her words: "*Certa sono del perdon se tu guardi al mio dolor*" (63; I am certain of forgiveness if you behold my sorrow).

At last, Tosca extracts from Cavaradossi the unqualified outpouring of love for which she has longed from the first. In a great *andante passionale con grande espressione* reprise of the original love motif, modulated up to the key of F, Cavaradossi cries, *"Mia vita, amante inquieta, dirò sempre: 'Floria, t'amo!'"* (64-5; My life, my uneasy lover, I will always say: "Floria, I love you!") Finally reassured of Cavaradossi's love, Tosca can now depart. She returns to her girlish coquette role, one moment pulling away from his embrace, the next kissing him in front of the Madonna with a coy *"È tanto buona"* (67; She is so good). Even her last *"Ma falle gli occhi neri"* (67-8; But make her eyes dark) becomes only playfully confident teasing. The irony, of course, is that while Tosca seems empowered within the microcosm of her love scene, she remains alienated from the macrocosmic political context in which it occurs: Cavaradossi intones the words she wants to hear merely to speed her departure and his own return to the business of Angelotti's escape.

The destructive personal consequences of this alienation in turn are manifested at the end of the act when Tosca returns to the church in search of her lover, only to be confronted by Scarpia. By conflating the first two acts of Sardou's play, Puccini and his librettists impose a unity of place that links Tosca's interactions with both Cavaradossi and Scarpia. The scenes with her lover and her nemesis are strikingly juxtaposed to highlight the parallelism in both men's manipulation of Tosca.

La Tosca's Confrontation with Scarpia

In Sardou's play, the scene with Scarpia takes place at Queen Marie-Caroline's victory ball in the Palazzo Farnese. La Tosca enters with all the pomp and brilliance befitting her diva status and holds court, dispensing favors and exchanging banter with the nobles who shower her with admiration: *"Elle entre en grande toilette par la seconde porte à droite, entourée de galants et donnant sa main à baiser à Capréola, Trivulce, Attavanti et à tous les petits monsignori qui se disputent cet honneur"* (64; She enters in full dress by the second door at the right, surrounded by gallants and extending her hand to be kissed by Capréola, Trivulce, Attavanti and all the lesser nobles who contend for that honor). She meets Scarpia almost as an equal, laughing off his pursuit of Angelotti with the insolent declaration that, should such an unhappy man knock at her door, she would immediately open it to him.

La Tosca's violent reaction to the disingenuous presentation of the Marquise Attavanti's fan by Scarpia—offered as evidence of Cavaradossi's betrayal—is designed to be delightfully comic in its melodramatic jealousy, a burlesque of the tempestuous diva. Confronting the marquise's husband, she demands, *"Où est-elle, votre femme, que je lui casse son évantail sur la figure?"* (80; Where is she, your wife, so I can break her fan across her face?)

Her singing of the victory cantata is abandoned without hesitation as La Tosca impetuously determines to surprise the faithless lovers in their nest: *"Dites à la reine que je suis malade . . . enrouée . . . que je ne peux pas chanter. . . . Dites ce que vous voudrez! Bonsoir!"* (84; Tell the queen that I am sick . . . hoarse . . . that I cannot sing . . . . Say what you wish! Goodnight!) When Scarpia orders her to remain until after her performance, La Tosca agrees, but is consumed with impatience. She snaps at the composer Paisiello, *"Oui, oui, je suis prête. . . . Dépêchons, dépêchons!"* (86; Yes, yes, I'm ready. . . . Let's hurry!); and she fumes as the queen makes her grand entrance, *"Allons, finira-t-elle par s'asseoir, cette reine?"* (88; Come on! Will that queen ever finally sit down?) At last, when word arrives that the royalist forces have suffered a crushing defeat, La Tosca queries with barely suppressed delight before she dashes from the salon, *"Alors, on ne chante plus? Ah! quelle chance! . . . Je me sauve!"* (91; So there will be no more singing? Ah, what luck! . . . I escape!)[14]

Tosca's Return

In the opera, however, there is no such spoof of Tosca the diva, only the searing disillusionment felt by Tosca the human being upon discovering Cavaradossi's apparent betrayal. Returning to the church, she is stunned by the Sacristan's intelligence that Cavaradossi has slipped away, despite his earlier assurances that he would be working until evening. Sorrow, disbelief, and denial combine in Tosca's fragmented *"Ingannata? No . . . no . . . tradirmi egli non può."* (111-2; Deceived? No, no, he can't betray me.) Believing herself alone and unobserved, Tosca indulges in none of the theatrical hysterics of her earlier *scena* with Cavaradossi. Instead, she is a soul genuinely adrift, murmuring her desolate monotone *quasi piangendo*. She is oblivious to Scarpia, only mechanically accepting the holy water he proffers.

For his part, Scarpia mercilessly exploits her suffering as he presents the marchesa's fan with solicitous guile. Musically, Tosca's recognition of the Attavanti crest echoes her previous recognition of the marchesa's portrait; but instead of her prior eruption of jealous rage, there is only the almost inarticulate despair of "*Presago sospetto*" (119; Prophetic suspicion) on a heartbroken series of low Ds and C-sharps.

Tosca sheds any vestiges of role-playing to reveal her inner soul in an *andante mesto* suffused with a simple nobility born of genuine suffering. She sings "*con grande sentimento, trattenendo a stento le lagrime, dimentica del luogo e di Scarpia*" (119; with great feeling, holding back her tears with difficulty, oblivious of the place and Scarpia). The numbing grief contained in the narrow range of her mournful "*Ed io venivo a lui tutta dogliosa*" (And I was coming to him full of sorrow) gives way at last to Tosca's writhing struggle for full expression of her inner torment with "*l'innamorata Tosca è prigioniera . . . dei regali tripudi, prigioniera!*" (119-21; the loving Tosca is a prisoner . . . of the royal celebrations, a prisoner!)

Her vocal line, marked *sostenuto molto con grande passione*, is stripped of legato phrasing and infused with an almost unbearable tension by the introduction of sobbing sixteenth-note pairings and plaintive orchestral doubling. Finally, as Tosca gives voice to her agonized repetition of "*prigioniera*" (121), the vocal line drags itself up to a desolate high A before plummeting to low F-sharp.

Grief mingles with revulsion and anger as Tosca turns her thoughts from her own loss to Cavaradossi's imagined rendezvous, her declamatory outbursts building to the terrible cry, "*Tu non l'avrai stassera. Giuro!*" (126; You shall not have him tonight. I swear it!)[15] Her vow brings a feigned rebuke from Scarpia, but Tosca replies through her tears, "*Dio mi perdona. . . . Egli vede ch'io piango!*" (127; God forgives me. . . . He sees that I'm weeping!) Even in her sorrow, Tosca affirms her faith in the ultimate justice of Heaven, in a cosmic order of mercy and forgiveness. Her vocal line lunges *con grande passione* to a suspended series of Fs, which are in turn engulfed by the orchestra's reprise of the "*Floria, t'amo*" motif, cuttingly subverted by mocking horns as Scarpia escorts Tosca from the church.[16]

Example 5.1

© Casa Ricordi - BMG Ricordi SpA, used by permission

Patriarchy vs. Matriarchy

Tosca's declaration of faith signals that the spheres of the personal, the political, and the providential are inextricably interwoven. In the world of the opera, two antithetical political orders, two irreconcilable visions of life vie for dominance: the oppression of Scarpia's patriarchal dictatorship, which, at first, seems omnipotent, and the hope of salvation embodied in the queen's matriarchal reign, which glimmers like a candle in the darkness.

In contrast to Sardou's *La Tosca*, Puccini portrays Queen Marie-Caroline as an idealized personification of mercy and forgiveness.[17] Thus, when Scarpia confronts Tosca with his insidious bargain for Cavaradossi's life in the second act, she tries to go to the queen for clemency; and even Scarpia cannot deny that the appeal would succeed were he not to preempt her royal pardon by having Cavaradossi summarily executed.

Although the queen is never seen onstage, her realm is evoked by the strains of an elegant gavotte and Tosca's neoclassical cantata celebrating the royalist triumph over Napoleon. The glory of the queen and the glory of God become one in victory; but Scarpia closes his windows to shut out the music.[18] With his brutality, his sadism, his dehumanizing sexual lust, Scarpia is the antithesis of everything the queen represents. All the aberrant evil that mars the world of the opera is embodied in Scarpia, and, thus, Tosca's second act confrontation with him takes on enhanced symbolic significance. When she stabs Scarpia, Tosca's personal act of violence becomes, as well, a political blow against a usurping patriarchal order, a blow which brings the justice of Heaven to earth.

Act II

In Sardou's play, La Tosca becomes an active player in Mario's scheme to help Angelotti. Arriving at her lover's villa in the third act, she forces a full explanation from him and then joins in the intrigue. With this empowerment comes new understanding of Scarpia's manipulation:

> LA TOSCA: *Ah! je comprends: c'est un piège!*
> MARIO: *Un piège?*
> LA TOSCA: *Ces soupçons sur toi ... C'est lui!*
> MARIO: *Scarpia?*
> LA TOSCA: *Il me lançait sur la piste, l'infâme!*

MARIO: (effrayé) *Il t'a vue partir?*
LA TOSCA: *Il a dû me suivre!*

(107-8; LA TOSCA: Ah! I understand: it is a trap!
MARIO: A trap?
LA TOSCA: These suspicions of you. . . . It is he!
MARIO: Scarpia?
LA TOSCA: He set me on the trail, the wretch!
MARIO: (*alarmed*) He saw you leave?
LA TOSCA: He must have followed me!)

Puccini, in contrast, shows nothing of Tosca's encounter at the villa, nothing of her conversation with Cavaradossi. The only hint of how she came to possess the secret of Angelotti's hiding place comes in Cavaradossi's virtually inaudible warning when Tosca first enters Scarpia's chamber in the Palazzo Farnese halfway through the second act: "*Di quanto là vedesti, taci, o m'uccidi*" (182; Be silent about how much you saw there, or you kill me).

Torture

After Cavaradossi is removed to the torture chamber, Scarpia spins out an affectedly polite line of conversation about Tosca's visit to the villa. His imperturbable solicitude, however, is subverted by the unspoken menace in his movements as he circles Tosca like a spider ensnaring her in an invisible web. Tosca replies "*con calma studiata*" (185; with studied calm) that her jealousy was foolish and that Cavaradossi was alone, but her poised facade quickly cracks under Scarpia's insinuating scrutiny. The explosion of Tosca's vocal line to a vehement, unaccompanied high A for "*Solo! sì!*" (188; Alone! Yes!) tellingly captures the brittleness of her bravura.

Scarpia insidiously exploits Tosca's emotional strain by describing the agonies which await Cavaradossi, while the orchestra sounds the *andante sostenuto* phrases of the "Torture" motif like the ominous rumblings of a distant juggernaut. Transfixed with mounting terror, Tosca writhes under the psychological assault. Cavaradossi's physical torture is a direct result of his republican ideals and deeds, but Tosca's emotional torture has no such grounding. Her interrogation is not a judicial process but a grotesque psychological rape which chillingly foreshadows the physical violation for which Scarpia lusts. With a shriek of denial that carries her to an accented high C over *fortissimo*

orchestration, she cries "*non è ver*" (192; it is not true). There is no
escape. A groan of pain from Cavaradossi reaches her ears; Tosca capitulates and agrees to reveal Angelotti's hiding place.

Her suffering has only begun, however, for she is quickly placed in
an untenable position by the very man whose life she is trying to save.
Cavaradossi orders her to be silent, and Tosca tries to play the part he
demands. The torture resumes, convulsive orchestration underscoring
the torment in Tosca's lunging "*ah! mostro, lo strazi, l'uccidi . . . ah!
. . . l'uccidi*" (197; ah! monster, you torture him, you are killing him
. . . ah! you are killing him). Scarpia relishes her suffering with demonic
delight, appropriating Tosca's tempestuous vocal melody for his own
words of torment, just as he turns her own capacity for love into an
instrument of torture. For Scarpia, her agony is no more than part of the
script he is directing: "*Mai Tosca alla scena più tragica fu!*" (198; Tosca
was never more tragic on the stage!)

As the implacable "Torture" motif sounds again, Scarpia sadistically
orders the interrogation chamber doors flung open, exhorting the executioner on, assaulting Tosca with a frenzied, orgiastic inquisition. She
tries evasion and denial but finally can endure no more. Her very being
seems to shatter with a primal cry of heart-wrenching despair: "*Ah! Più
non posso! Ah! . . . che orror! . . . Ah! . . . cessate il martir! . . . è troppo
soffrir! . . . Ah! non posso più . . . ah! non posso più!*" (203-5; Ah! I can
bear no more! Ah! what horror! Ah! stop the torment! It is too much to
suffer! Ah! I can bear no more! I can bear no more!)

Example 5.2

© Casa Ricordi - BMG Ricordi SpA, used by permission

Degradation of Tosca

Tosca begs Cavaradossi to permit her to speak, but he is as unyielding as Scarpia. Both men remain locked in their own struggle for dominance, and each demands that Tosca play the role he has scripted for her. At last Tosca sobs to Scarpia, "*Che v'ho fatto in vita mia?!*" (207; What have I done to you in my life?!) She has done nothing. Her existence is enough. She is "Woman" and, hence, an object of his lust, a victim of degradation.[19]

Equally chilling, however, is the abuse Tosca endures at the hands of Cavaradossi after she finally reveals to Scarpia that Angelotti is hiding in the garden well. Her lover is carried, bleeding and unconscious, into the room; Tosca "*corre a lui, ma è presa da orrore alla vista di Cavaradossi tutto insanguinato, e s'arresta cuoprendosi gli occhi colle mani, vergognosa della sua debolezza si avvicina a Cavaradossi cuoprendolo di baci e lagrime*" (211-2; runs to him, but is seized with horror at the sight of Cavaradossi all covered with blood and stops, covering her eyes with her hands; ashamed of her weakness, she approaches Cavaradossi, covering him with kisses and tears).

As the orchestra echoes the melody of Cavaradossi's romantic "*Qual'occhio al mondo*" from Act I, Tosca desperately tries to cling to her lover's idealized image of her. When he demands, "*Tosca, hai parlato?*" (Tosca, did you talk?), she lies, "*No, amor*" (213-4; No, love). Her pretense is futile. Scarpia triumphantly sends Spoletta to arrest Angelotti, and Cavaradossi rewards Tosca's love with a curse: "*M'hai tradito! . . . Maledetta!*" (214-5; You betrayed me! Cursed woman!) Cavaradossi's power struggle with Scarpia remains paramount. After word arrives of Napoleon's victory over the royalist forces, Cavaradossi's incendiary exultation is met by Scarpia with a death sentence.[20] Tosca's desperate pleas go unheeded by both men.[21]

Bargaining

After Cavaradossi is dragged from the room, Tosca tries to regain some control over the situation in which she is trapped. Coldly demanding, "*Quanto?*" (226; How much?), she assumes a posture calculated to negate the passive weakness of her feminine role to this point: "*appoggiando i gomiti sul tavolo, colle mani si sorregge il viso*" (226; leaning her elbows on the table, propping her face on her hands). Scarpia simply laughs. She cannot bargain with him like a man, but only as a woman.

His price is her abject surrender to his lust. As he pursues her, Tosca "*inorridita corre alla finestra*" (234; horrified, runs to the window); her voice rises in inarticulate terror from A-flat to B-flat and, finally, to high B in a pattern which compellingly echoes the emotional disintegration of "*Ah! Più non posso!*" during the torture scene. Tosca finds herself driven to the brink of utter oblivion, self-annihilation offering the only apparent escape from her suffering: "*Piuttosto giù m'avvento!*" (234; I'll sooner throw myself down [from the window!])

Only the strength of her love restrains Tosca. She might escape Scarpia in death, but she could not save Cavaradossi. Nor can she find salvation through the intercession of others: "*le balena l'idea di recarsi presso la Regina e corre verso la porta*" (235; the idea flashes into her mind to go to the queen, and she runs toward the door). Scarpia does not deny the queen's clemency, but demoniacally adds, "*Va pure. Ma è fallace speranza: . . . la Regina farebbe grazia ad un cadavere!*" (235-6; Go then. But it is a false hope: the queen would grant pardon to a corpse!) As Scarpia's relentless hectoring recommences, Tosca has nowhere left to look but within herself. Physically exhausted, emotionally enervated, spiritually adrift, she sinks into prayer, trying to understand what has become of her.[22]

Vissi d'Arte

Her aria "*Vissi d'arte*" marks a stunning turning point in Tosca's existence.[23] With bewildered innocence captured in the translucent opening phrases of the vocal line, underscored by *pianissimo* strings and marked *andante lento appassionato, dolcissimo con grande sentimento*, Tosca looks back on a life devoted to love and art: "*Vissi d'arte, vissi d'amore, non feci mai male ad anima viva*" (242-3; I lived for art, I lived for love, I never did wrong to a living soul). She has fulfilled her role of "Woman." She has been a ministering angel; she has laid flowers on the church altar; she has given jewels for the robes of the Madonna and has lifted her voice in praise of God. She has, indeed, lived her life as an icon of idealized nineteenth-century femininity.

Puccini emphasizes Tosca's crisis of identity in this moment by counterpoising a lush orchestral echo of the "Idealized Tosca" motif from Act I with the fragmented phrases of Tosca's own vocal line as she tries to reconcile her past conduct with her present plight: "*Sempre . . . con fè sincera la mia preghiera ai santi tabernacoli salì*" (243-4; Always . . . with sincere faith my prayers ascended at the holy altars).

Searching for meaning in an existence which now seems incomprehensible, Tosca treads round and round in a spiritual maze that seems to have no exit. Thus, she can only repeat her initial melodic line for the second verse of her aria, her voice weaving through the underscoring orchestration until it crescendos at last to a *forte molto allargando* high B-flat before a sobbing denouement: *"Nell'ora del dolor perchè, perchè . . . Signor, ah . . . perchè me ne rimuneri così?"* (246-7; In the hour of sorrow, why, why, Lord, ah, why do you requite me thus?)

Her cry might seem the voice of existential nihilism, but Tosca's suffering is born of gender politics not cosmic indifference. Given the essential disempowerment of the feminine role Tosca has embraced, her victimization is an inevitable result.

Anagnorisis

Tosca's helplessness serves only to fire Scarpia's lust. She kneels at his feet to plead, *"Vedi . . . le man giunte io stendo a te! . . . Ecco . . . vedi . . . e . . . mercè . . . d'un tuo detto, vinta aspetto."* (249; You see . . . my clasped hands I extend to you! There, you see . . . I wait defeated for a word of mercy.) But there is no mercy: broken and humiliated is exactly how Scarpia desires her. Tosca accedes to his insidious bargain, agreeing to submit to his lust in exchange for Cavaradossi's freedom. As Scarpia is drawing up her safe-conduct pass, however, Tosca experiences a moment of overwhelming anagnorisis.

Finally, Tosca understands that salvation will come only by accepting and affirming her own true self, by casting aside the roles the men in her life have forced upon her, by empowering herself as an individual and shattering the icon of passive victimization. Out of suffering comes redemption as Tosca sees the knife lying on Scarpia's dinner table and resolves to kill her persecutor. Helpless acceptance of oppression is replaced by a new will to seize control of her personal destiny. Her psychological rebirth transcends the capacity of articulate speech, but the unbearable tension in the orchestral "Anagnorisis" motif, with its startling dissonance at the moment Tosca silently stares at the knife, searingly captures her momentous transformation (261-3).

Scarpia rushes to claim his prize, and Tosca plunges the knife into his chest in what seems an almost ritualistic act of violence. A lifetime of repression and torment finds volcanic release in her cry, *"Questo è il bacio di Tosca! Ti soffoca il sangue? Ti soffoca il sangue? Ah! . . . E ucciso da una donna!"* (264-6; This is Tosca's kiss! Is your blood choking you? Is your blood choking you? Ah! And killed by a woman!)

Tosca is freed by her action, arising like a phoenix from the ashes of her earlier existence. She is purified rather than tainted by the slaying. Not for Tosca the monstrous torment of Lady Macbeth or the retreat into insanity of Lucia. Tosca has become an agent of divine justice; she will trust in God to judge and to forgive her, to accept her for what she is and to sanctify her deeds. With true religious faith, Tosca forgives Scarpia for his sins against her, just as she prays that Heaven will forgive her own: *"Or gli perdono!"* (269; Now I forgive him!)[24]

As the orchestra reprises the "Anagnorisis" motif, Tosca washes the blood from her hands and, symbolically cleansed of guilt, removes the safe-conduct pass from the dead man. There is a sense of disbelief in her final unaccompanied words as Tosca recognizes the ultimate vulnerability of Scarpia and the entire hierarchy he embodied: *"E avanti a lui tremava tutta Roma!"* (271; And before him all Rome trembled!)[25]

Although the orchestra provides fragmentary reprises of both Scarpia's "Stalking" motif and Cavaradossi's *"Qual'occhio al mondo,"* Tosca can no longer be contained within either of these melodic captions. At last, the orchestra returns instead to an ironic, dying echo of the "Scarpia" chords from the opening of the opera as the reborn Tosca ritualistically lays the old order to rest, affirming the justice of Heaven on earth by placing two candles beside Scarpia's body and laying a crucifix on his chest in a symbolic enactment of the Last Rites.

Act III

When Tosca arrives at the Castel Sant'Angelo in Act III to rescue her lover, the orchestra heralds her entrance with a surging reprise of Cavaradossi's *"Floria, t'amo"* melody (292-3). Yet, there is no romantic dialogue, no tearful reunion. The comfortable script that guided the lovers through Act I has become untenable. Tosca must convey to Cavaradossi the fundamental transformation she has undergone and reach out to him for a new kind of love.

As she hands Cavaradossi the safe-conduct pass, Tosca launches with precipitous haste into a violent narration of the events leading to Scarpia's slaying. Her monologue, underscored by a kaleidoscopic reprise of orchestral motifs associated with the events of the second act, emphasizes the ultimate futility and destructiveness of the stereotypic role of "Woman" she had adopted, not only with Scarpia but, implicitly, with Cavaradossi himself: *"Fur vani scongiuri e pianti. Invan, pazza d'orror . . . alla Madonna mi volsi e ai Santi."* (295-6; Tears and supplications were futile. In vain, insane with horror, I turned to the Madonna and the saints.)

The strains of the "Anagnorisis" motif underscore Tosca's recollection of sighting the dagger, but her voice rises alone for the climactic *"Io quella lama gli piantai nel cor"* (300-1; I drove that blade into his heart). With her dramatic rise to high C before a plunging descent, Tosca defiantly proclaims her action and poses a challenge for Cavaradossi.[26] He must cast aside his passive, idealized image of her and accept Tosca as she is. The old melodic captions are no longer adequate. A new melody is needed.[27]

At first, however, Cavaradossi responds only with monotone amazement: *"Tu? . . . di tua man l'uccidesti"* (301; You? . . . with your own hand you killed him). Tosca picks up his noncommittal vocal line for her own reply, *"N'ebbi le man tutte lorde di sangue"* (301; My hands were all soiled with blood). She provides no further commentary or emotional coloring for the events she recounts, waiting instead for Cavaradossi's reaction. But her lover seems bewildered, trying to reconcile his image of Tosca from Act I with her stunning revelation of violent action as he murmurs, *"O dolci mani mansuete e pure, o mani elette a bell'opre e pietose, a carezzar fanciulli, a coglier rose, a pregar"* (301-2; O sweet hands, gentle and pure, O hands chosen for good and pious works, to caress children, to gather roses, to pray). Love, he decides, gave such gentle hands the strength to kill.

Love alone clearly cannot fully explain her deed, however. Although Cavaradossi tries at first to ignore the implications of Scarpia's slaying and return to the image of *"o dolci mani"* (304), Tosca can no longer accept such a passive role. Freeing her hands, she interrupts him, outlining her plan for escape, implicitly inviting him to join in a new vision of love: *"Non ti par che le cose aspettan tutte innamorate il sole?"* (308-9; Doesn't it seem to you that all things in love await the sun?) At last, Cavaradossi casts aside his icons and embraces the living being who can give new meaning to his existence: *"Amaro sol per te m'era il morire, Da te la vita prende ogni splendore."* (309-10; Death was bitter to me only because of you. Life takes its every splendor from you.)

Tosca picks up Cavaradossi's dynamic new vocal melody as she joyously shares his vision, while evocatively exotic coloring in the orchestration subtly suggests a palpable transformation of the world through the power of love: "[*Amor*] *vago farà il mondo riguardare*" (312-3; [Love] will make the world lovely to look at). At last, however, even the earth itself vanishes in a mythic *Liebestod* which prophetically foreshadows the lovers' deaths at the end of the opera: "*Finchè congiunti alle celesti sfere dileguerem*" (313; Until, joined with the celestial spheres, we will dissolve).

Love Triumphant

In their new love, Tosca and Cavaradossi find salvation, and the temporal concerns of escape become inconsequential. Thus, Cavaradossi interrupts Tosca's instructions about the mock firing squad to ask, "*Parlami ancor . . . come dianzi parlavi*" (317; Speak to me again . . . as you spoke just now); and Tosca responds with a hymn of love. Their voices joining triumphantly in soaring, unaccompanied unison, Tosca and Cavaradossi are transfigured by their complete and perfect love for each other: "*Trionfal . . . di nova speme l'anima freme in celestial crescente ardor. . . . Ed in armonico vol . . . già l'anima va all'estasi d'amor.*" (319-20; Triumphal in new hope, the soul trembles with growing celestial ardor. . . . And in harmonious flight the soul goes already to the ecstasy of love.)[28]

Example 5.3

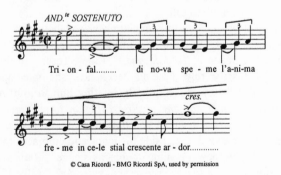

Cavaradossi is led away to his staged execution, but not even the unforeseen horror of his actual death can negate the lovers' transcendence. Despite Tosca's agony of grief as she throws herself on

Cavaradossi's lifeless body, there is no crushing psychological collapse, no emotional disintegration, no return to her earlier role of victim.[29] When Spoletta rushes to apprehend Tosca, "*essa balzando in piedi lo respinge così violentemente da farlo quasi cadere riverso nella botola della scala*" (334; leaping to her feet, she pushes him back so violently as to make him nearly fall back down the stairs), it is a gesture as symbolic as Scarpia's death, an act of self-affirming defiance which reduces Spoletta to impotent absurdity.

Tosca rushes to the castle parapet, not to escape Spoletta, but to embrace her destiny. With her final blazing cry, "*O Scarpia, avanti a Dio!*" (334-5; O Scarpia, before God!), Tosca ascends into the pantheon of tragic heroines, celebrating her individual identity, embracing the righteousness of Heaven and her own place in the divine order of creation.[30] So she rises *in excelsis*, her high B-flat on "*Dio*" borne aloft by the *tutta forza* orchestral melody of Cavaradossi's "*E lucevan le stelle*" (288; And the stars were shining). Suffering and despair are musically transfigured in a triumphant moment of tragic joy as Tosca launches herself into eternity.

Example 5.4

PREVIEW

One of the undisputed cornerstones of the current operatic repertoire, *Madama Butterfly* fuses the emotional quintessence of romanticism and the austere majesty of classical tragedy. With the composition of this opera, Puccini brought his development of the tragic heroine to its dramatic culmination.

Madama Butterfly celebrates the spirit of the individual and the human need for faith, love, and devotion—even as it depicts a hostile world in which those needs are often unfulfilled.

Puccini imbues the character of Butterfly with a nobility and sense of heroic Free Will—even within a preordained destiny—that is utterly lacking in any of the opera's sources.

Absolute Love—an eternal, joyously shared bond between two people—is the very reason for Butterfly's existence. In the first act of the opera, this love infuses Butterfly with profound serenity in her wedding to Pinkerton and gives her the inner strength to endure the curses of her family. Even after Pinkerton's departure and the passing of years, Butterfly still struggles to keep faith and hope alive, to believe that her husband shares her love and will return.

Only in the final act, when she sees Pinkerton's new American wife, does Butterfly accept that all hope is gone. Then, with a nobility of spirit incomprehensible to her craven husband, Butterfly brings her destiny to fulfillment, embracing death once her belief in a love that gave meaning to her existence can no longer be sustained.

CHAPTER 6

Madama Butterfly

Operatic Tragedy

One of the undisputed cornerstones of the current operatic repertoire, *Madama Butterfly* (1904)[1] fuses the emotional quintessence of romanticism and the austere majesty of classical tragedy. With the composition of this opera, Puccini brought his development of the tragic heroine to its dramatic culmination. In later years, the composer turned his attentions to exploring alternative artistic paths—melodrama in *La Fanciulla del West* (1910) and *Il Tabarro* (1918); pathos for *La Rondine* (1917) and *Suor Angelica* (1918); comedy with *Gianni Schicchi* (1918). Never again, however, would he attempt a subject with the tragic power of *Madama Butterfly*.[2]

Madama Butterfly celebrates the spirit of the individual and the human need for faith, love, and devotion—even as it depicts a hostile world in which those needs are often unfulfilled. Absolute Love—an eternal, joyously shared bond between two people—is the very reason for Butterfly's existence. As the heroine of Victor Hugo's Romantic drama *Angelo, Tyran de Padoue* declares, "*Croire à son amour, c'était une idée nécessaire à ma vie*" (To believe in his love was an idea necessary to my life).[3] Without that love, life becomes meaningless and absurd, and only death remains: "*Il mio destino è questo: o morte, o morte o amor*" (My destiny is this: either death or love).[4] These words of Ponchielli's Gioconda caption Butterfly's own destiny just as surely as if they had been pronounced by the ancient oracle at Delphi.

Thus the tragedy of *Madama Butterfly* unfolds, weighted with an almost unbearable tension between the inevitability of a fated doom and the heroic struggles of the woman enmeshed in destiny's snares. As the *Illustrated London News* affirmed after *Madama Butterfly*'s 1905 Covent Garden premiere,

> Puccini's new opera, entirely remodelled since it was first produced and condemned at La Scala more than a year ago, is a tragedy, as complete a tragedy as our operatic stage knows. By its side works like "Faust," "Romeo and Juliet," "Rigoletto" seem almost tawdry in their dramatic aspect, for while they leave us conscious of beauty that is merely sensual at their most dramatic moments, "Madame Butterfly" has something of the deliberate movement and inevitable *dénouement* of a Greek tragedy. In saying this we do not write of the libretto only, although it is a work of more than common merit, as might, indeed, be expected from Signori Illica and Giacosa. . . . Puccini's music conveys the tragedy as surely as the printed word, and conveys it in manner that we have not hitherto associated with the composer, even while recognizing that his achievements have been many and notable, and that he stands for what is best in modern Italian music. Now he seems to discover new paths, to express himself after his own convention, but with an utter absence of conventionality, to treat his work in a spirit of freshness that never suggests affectation, to give a setting that seems to direct and intensify every moment of action upon the stage.[5]

Sources

Inspired in large part by Pierre Loti's immensely popular novel *Madame Chrysanthème* (1887),[6] the source story *Madame Butterfly* was first published as a novella by John Luther Long in 1898 and then dramatized by David Belasco in 1900.[7] Today, both of these versions are often more offensive than captivating, due to their pervasive Eurocentrism and tone of patriarchal condescension: "Chrysanthemum and Butterfly share certain evident similarities. Childlike, affectionate and gay, they appear almost as caricatures of the typical geisha as viewed through

Western eyes, a kind of Japanese version of Little Dora the Child Bride."[8]

As David Belasco set about reshaping Long's novella for stage performance, he shortened and rearranged the original story, turning it into what he called *Madame Butterfly: A Tragedy of Japan.* The plot is compressed in order to accelerate the inevitable catastrophe, and much of the childish frivolity of the novella is jettisoned.[9] Yet, while Belasco's Butterfly certainly inspires pity, she never truly attains the heights of tragic heroism for which the author had aimed.[10] The very speed of Belasco's one-act play denies Butterfly the dramatic space needed for full audience understanding and empathy. She remains a fundamentally reactive figure whose inner spirit is obscured by the retention of pidgin English dialogue that inevitably marginalizes her as a pathetic "American wannabe."

It was, perhaps, a fortunate happenstance that Puccini, who did not speak English, could not understand what was being said on stage when he first saw Belasco's play performed in London during the summer of 1900. Instead, he felt the power of the dramatic situation and the potential of Butterfly herself on a more visceral level.[11] Together with his librettists, Luigi Illica and Giuseppe Giacosa, Puccini infused the character of Butterfly with a nobility and sense of heroic Free Will—even within a preordained destiny—that is utterly lacking in any of the earlier sources. Out of the sparks of the original tale thus came the blazing tragedy of *Madama Butterfly.*

Act I

As she approaches the charming little hilltop house overlooking Nagasaki harbor, Butterfly's arrival for her wedding to Pinkerton is accompanied by a virtual paean of love set to a shimmering orchestration colored by strings and harp.

Butterfly's voice is heard offstage, soaring above the happy chatter of her friends in an ecstatic, poetic affirmation of the destiny she welcomes, of the love which is the source of ultimate meaning in the numbered days of human life: *"Amiche, io son venuta . . . al richiamo d'amor . . . d'amor venni alle soglie ove . . . s'accoglie . . . il bene di chi vive e . . . di chi . . . muor."* (Friends, I have come at love's call . . . I came to the threshold where the good of those who live and those who die is welcomed.)[12] The imagistic effusion which characterizes Puccini's heroine, as well as the lyrical melodic expanse of the "Love" motif heralding her arrival, convey a sense of spiritual sublimity impossible to imagine in the pidgin English of the source stories.

Example 6.1

© Casa Ricordi - BMG Ricordi SpA, used by permission

Celestial love seems to come to earth as the wedding party appears on the hilltop, buoyed up beneath a sea of brilliant paper parasols; Butterfly repeats, "*son venuta al richiamo d'amor*" (58), her voice floating *in excelsis* to an optional high D-flat.

The very glory of this entrance scene heightens the dramatic irony of Butterfly's impending doom, for the audience already knows that Pinkerton does not share Butterfly's Absolute Love. Sharpless had been struck by the love he heard in Butterfly's voice when she visited the consulate, and he warned Pinkerton not to trifle with her heart; but Pinkerton dismissed him with a laugh and a toast to the day he would wed a real American wife.

Interviews

Having arrived at the hilltop, Butterfly greets Pinkerton with a choreographed deference that suggests not only the esteem in which she holds her husband-to-be, but also her comfortable dexterity in negotiating expected social conventions. With firm command, she orders her friends to kneel in honor of "*F. B. Pinkerton*" (59)[13] and then proceeds with the ritual greetings and compliments. Puccini's understated, measured scoring emphasizes the "public face" Butterfly is maintaining at this moment, but it also hints at the sense of spiritual purpose which guides the young bride: an orchestral foreshadowing of the "Conversion" motif anticipates the revelation that, in following her destiny, Butterfly has determined to embrace both a new life and her husband's Christian religion.

At fifteen years of age, Butterfly is chronologically still a child—as Pinkerton notes with lusty delight and Sharpless observes with shocked disapproval. But, like Shakespeare's Juliet, Butterfly possesses a spirit far beyond her years. Responding to Sharpless' questions about her relations, Butterfly frankly unfolds the story of her family's fall from grace, painting a richly hued melodic picture of the poverty which drove the women to become geishas.

When asked about her father, who committed suicide at the emperor's order, however, Butterfly responds only with an abrupt "*Morto*" (68; Dead). The following silence is filled with the foreboding strains of the "Suicide" motif in the orchestra, and the audience is reminded that, for all her present happiness, death is an inescapable part of Butterfly's destiny.

Example 6.2

Butterfly quickly returns to the "public face" of the geisha as she responds with child-like coyness to Sharpless' question about her age. No such play-acting, however, can obscure the mature strength of will with which Butterfly suppresses the malicious gossip of her relatives. As the commissioner and other officials arrive for the wedding ceremony, Butterfly's friends and family begin to bicker about Pinkerton's worth and snipe at the bride's beauty.

Butterfly treats these outbursts with indignant contempt, decisively quelling the turmoil by once again ordering everyone to kneel before Pinkerton. She may affect a "*voce infantile*" (90; child-like voice), but "*al cenno di Butterfly tutti si inchinano innanzi a Pinkerton ed a Sharpless*" (at Butterfly's signal, all bow toward Pinkerton and Sharpless.)[14]

Absolute Love

Butterfly's love gives her this profound serenity and inner strength. She loves Pinkerton absolutely, and she believes that love is shared and reciprocated. Her husband-to-be gives her no indication of his duplicity; only Sharpless and the audience know the truth. Thus, as Pinkerton takes Butterfly by the hand, leading her toward their little house and away from the rest of the guests in the garden, the melody of her entrance music sounds in the orchestra: Butterfly has every reason to believe that she has answered love's call.

With her new life opening before her, Butterfly displays to Pinkerton the few small tokens of her past which she has brought: handkerchiefs, pipe, sash, brooch, mirror, fan. At the slightest indication of displeasure from Pinkerton, she instantly discards a rouge pot, demonstrating that she will sacrifice any part of her past to her love. Significantly, only her father's hara-kiri sword is different. Despite Pinkerton's curiosity, she refuses to show it to him with so many people around; and, as she carries it into the house, the "Suicide" motif sounds in the orchestra, again foreshadowing Butterfly's own doom.

When Butterfly returns, Pinkerton asks about some small statuettes, which, she explains, are the spirits of her ancestors. Although she brings these relics with her, Butterfly understands that her Absolute Love demands a complete dedication of heart and mind and spirit. In a radical departure from Long's source story, Puccini's Butterfly reveals that she has, of her own free will, secretly gone alone to the mission in order to convert to Christianity: "*Colla nuova mia vita posso adottare nuova religione. . . . È mio destino. Nella stessa chiesetta in ginocchio con voi Pregherò lo stesso Dio.*" (98-101; With my new life I can adopt a new religion. . . . It is my destiny. In the same little church, kneeling with you, I will pray to the same God.)[15] Her vocal line is simple and understated in its expression of faith and devotion, and the exquisite melody foreshadowed in Butterfly's first greeting of Pinkerton blossoms with serene abandon: "*Io seguo il mio destino*" (99; I follow my destiny).

Butterfly knows that her destiny will bring with it suffering—the loss of her family, heritage, and past. The pain she feels is clear in her effortful, monochromatic *"E per farvi contento potrò forse obliar la gente mia"* (101-2; And to make you happy perhaps I will be able to forget my own people). But no amount of suffering can sway Butterfly from her fated course, and she throws herself into Pinkerton's arms with the climactic cry, *"Amore mio"* (102; My love). The thunderous reprise of the "Suicide" motif that follows her declaration of love, however, underscores a sense of impending catastrophe.

The dramatic irony of Butterfly's belief in Absolute Love is heightened after the wedding ceremony when the guests offer their congratulations to *"Madama Butterfly."* Believing herself to be Pinkerton's true partner in heart and spirit, Butterfly quickly corrects them: *"Madama F. B. Pinkerton"* (105). The audience, however, is keenly aware that her marriage, and all that she believes it stands for, is a sham. Indeed, in this context, the very title of the opera is infused with poignant symbolism.

Disowned and Happy

The festivities of the wedding party are interrupted by the sudden arrival of Butterfly's enraged uncle, the bonze, who denounces her for abandoning their ancient religion. Horrified by the revelation of her action and the path she has chosen, Butterfly's friends and family disown her.[16] Butterfly is wounded, but she endures their denunciations and departure with silent tears, knowing that they were inevitable. Belief in Pinkerton's love outweighs everything else.

Thus, when her husband declares that all her relatives and all the bonzes of Japan are not worth one tear from her beautiful eyes, Butterfly replies with the innocent faith of a child: his words fall so soothingly on her heart that she almost ceases to suffer from her family's rejection. Her vocal line is sweet and caressing, but it is underscored by an ominous *piano* echo of the "Suicide" motif.

As the first strains of the duet which closes the first act fill the air with the enchantment of love, Butterfly finds herself *"Rinnegata . . . e . . . felice"* (130; Disowned . . . and . . . happy). While Pinkerton remains in the garden, she enters the house to dress for her wedding night. Though the curses of her people still ring in Butterfly's ears, she is aglow with the ecstasy of first love, revealing a complex nexus of emotions ranging from eagerness and impatience to be with her husband to shyness and delight at his looks and smiles, from sorrow at the recollection of her family's curses to final happiness and peace.

Pinkerton, for his part, is oblivious to all these feelings. For him, Butterfly is not even a real woman, but a "*giocattolo*" (134; plaything) whose graceful little squirrel-like movements inflame his desire. There is very little true connection between Butterfly and Pinkerton, and Puccini emphasizes the spiritual distance that separates them through the use of intertwining but distinct vocal lines.

Words of Love

When Butterfly emerges once more into the garden, Pinkerton greets her with the caressing, albeit condescending, *dolcissimo* phrases requisite for his role of ardent lover: "*Bimba dagli occhi pieni di malìa . . . ora sei tutta mia*" (137-8; Child, with your eyes full of enchantment, now you are all mine). His confident advances contrast with Butterfly's happy but bashful response as she diverts his compliments about her white bridal attire, likening herself to the "*piccola Dea della luna*" (139; little goddess of the moon). Her vocal line, with its delicate descending triplets, seems to embody the very footsteps of the goddess who descends at night "*dal ponte del ciel*" (139; from the bridge of heaven).

Butterfly's mythical imagery suggests a vastness of love which cannot be expressed in Pinkerton's more prosaic terms of desire. Her husband readily encourages her, however, borrowing from her own poetic vocabulary to speak of the goddess capturing earthly hearts. His easy appropriation of Butterfly's love imagery is probably no more motivated by sincerity than was his appreciation of the practiced compliments with which she first greeted him, but he repeats her words with such apparent conviction that Butterfly feels her love is shared and returned. Her vocal line, colored by an emotional fluidity of tempo, thus soars with consummate joy as if following the path of the moon goddess up "*negli alti reami*" (140; into the exalted realms).

The poetry of love is all very well and good for Pinkerton, but only if it leads to more tangible results; he presses to know whether the goddess of the moon knows the words to satisfy ardent desire. Butterfly's yearning, passionate response is tinged with prescience: to embrace a love of such magnitude may ultimately mean death. Her triplet-laden vocal line faintly recalls the musical embodiment of the goddess' footsteps, but the delicate whimsy of that conceit is now weighted with fearful, volcanic premonition. Exploding first to top G-sharp and then to high A, Butterfly's music remains anxiously suspended in the upper part of the vocal range as she replies to Pinkerton's question: "*Le sa. . . . Forse dirle non vuole per tema d'averne a morir*" (141-2; She knows them. . . . Perhaps she does not want to say them for fear of having to die for them).

Joy and Fear

Only when Pinkerton promises that love brings not death but celestial joys does Butterfly cast aside her fears. Initiating a new *andante mosso ma sostenendo*, she proclaims Pinkerton—and the love that she believes they share—as the center of her existence: "*Adesso voi siete per me . . . l'occhio del firmamento*" (144-5; Now you are, for me, the eye of the firmament). As she talks of Pinkerton's good looks, his easy laugh, and his sense of freedom, her words suddenly become prosaic. But beneath her words, surging waves of sumptuous orchestration carry the vocal line on their crests, revealing a profundity of feeling beyond articulate expression. As she falls silent, an orchestral echo of the bonze's "Curse" motif recalls how much she has already sacrificed to her love.

With ethereal *pianissimo* phrases, Butterfly begs Pinkerton to love her too, with a "*piccolino*" (148; little) love such as the Japanese people feel: "*una tenerezza sfiorante e pur profonda come il ciel, come l'onda del mare*" (150; a lightly touching tenderness, and yet deep as the sky, as the wave of the ocean). Pinkerton readily agrees, though his non sequitur, "*Mia Butterfly! . . . come t'an ben nomata*" (151; My Butterfly, how well they named you), pointedly underscores his complete incomprehension of her poetic plea.

Once more, there is foreshadowing in Butterfly's terrified response. The jagged, lunging phrases of her vocal line and the tumultuous underscoring—in which a hint of the "Curse" motif emphasizes how completely Butterfly has tied her destiny to Pinkerton—color her distraught, "*Dicon ch'oltre mare se cade in man dell'uom . . . ogni farfalla da uno spillo è trafitta ed in tavola infitta*" (152-4; They say that over the ocean every butterfly that falls into the hands of man is pierced with a pin and stuck to a board).

In a moment of pointed dramatic irony, Pinkerton ignores Butterfly's image of suffering and death, focusing with typical self-absorption only on his own possession of his bride. Just as a pin keeps the butterfly from escaping, so now he has caught Butterfly herself. Believing that he truly means never to let her go, Butterfly ecstatically affirms that she will be his "*per la vita*" (155; for life).

With passionate ardor, Pinkerton now urges Butterfly to come to bed. As Butterfly sees in the myriad stars of the heavens the happy eyes of a cosmos which reflects and celebrates the love she believes she shares with Pinkerton, her vocal line returns to the melody of the "Love" motif. Answering love's call, she has met her destiny. For a brief moment, her vocal line joins in unison with that of Pinkerton; but her husband cannot sustain such romantic effusion. His thoughts are firmly focused on the nuptial bed, and his vocal line quickly breaks down to offer harmonic support and only intermittent doubling of the rapturous melody which carries Butterfly heavenward toward the sphere of divine love and a final radiant high C.[17]

Act II

When the second act of the opera opens, three years have passed; Butterfly is struggling to maintain her belief that Pinkerton will return as promised. A brief orchestral prelude concisely reveals how Butterfly's light-hearted daily routine has become burdened by isolation and loneliness. For the first time, the mournful, downward-thrusting phrases of the "Doubt" motif are heard, illuminating Butterfly's inner struggle to keep faith and hope alive.

Butterfly scorns Suzuki's prayers to the gods of Japan, poignantly affirming her own spiritual path by insisting that the American God is quicker to answer supplicants' prayers, although "*egli ignori che noi stiam qui di casa*" (172; He does not know that we live here). From the beginning, the Christian religion has been inseparable from the love she believes she shares with Pinkerton; and so the pervasive "Doubt" motif, which frames her melancholy thoughts of an oblivious God, suggests the gnawing uncertainty about Pinkerton's love that has begun to torment her.

Example 6.3

Again and again the "Doubt" motif sounds as Butterfly and Suzuki count the remains of the money Pinkerton left to sustain them so long ago. Even when Butterfly insists, "*Ma torna*" (175; But he is coming back), the monochromatic brevity of her vocal phrase and the *forte* revoicing of the "Doubt" motif in the orchestra drain the conviction from her words. She insists that Pinkerton would not have had Sharpless pay their rent, nor would he have put locks on the doors to safeguard his bride from the world, if he did not intend to return. However, Butterfly's carefully measured phrases convey a sense of practiced repetition, a catechism of faith that must be often repeated lest it no longer be believed.

When Suzuki reminds her that no foreign husband has ever returned to his nest, the "Doubt" motif once more crashes in the orchestration. Butterfly tries desperately to silence Suzuki and to block out all weakness of spirit; Pinkerton promised to return when the robins made their nests again, and Butterfly eagerly repeats his words as proof of his intentions. The delicate rising phrases of her *pianissimo* vocal line with its gossamer underscoring, however, seem more indicative of Butterfly's sublimity of feeling than of Pinkerton's brash ardor. The words of the promise may be his, but the love that infuses the music is Butterfly's alone.

Un Bel Dì

Butterfly sees in Suzuki's tears a lack of faith which she will resist with all her strength. Her aria "*Un bel dì*" must surely be only the most recent affirmation of faith Butterfly has spoken to herself over the years. Envisioning every detail of Pinkerton's promised return, her words express absolute confidence, and yet her vocal line is pointedly lacking in the expansive joy such confidence should bring.[18] After the first shimmering G-flats, which begin her *andante molto calmo*, Butterfly's dreamy vocal line sinks relentlessly over the ensuing measures: "*Un bel dì, vedremo levarsi un fil di fumo sull'estremo confin del mare. E poi . . . la nave appare.*" (184; One beautiful day, we will see a thread of smoke rise on the farthest margin of the sea. And then, the ship appears.)

Visionary imagery becomes merely narrative—a narrative richly descriptive in its fluid rhythms and tonalities, a narrative colored by bursts of emotionality, but a narrative that conveys, more than anything, an inescapable tone of practiced recitation. Butterfly describes the entrance of Pinkerton's ship into the harbor and her husband's climb up the hillside to their little house.

She imagines that when he calls for her, she will remain hidden at first "*un po' per celia . . . e un po' per non morire al primo incontro*" (188; a little to tease, and a little so as not to die at the first meeting). On the word "*morire*," Butterfly's vocal line suddenly explodes with a *con forza* return to the original melody of "*Un bel dì*" doubled by *ff con molta passione* orchestration.

The dramatic irony of this moment is crushing, and even Butterfly seems to sense the looming presence of death overshadowing her dream of love: as she turns her thoughts to the terms of endearment Pinkerton will once more bestow on his wife, her vocal line sinks again under the burden of inner doubt.

Butterfly is determined never to yield to such doubt, however, and so she launches a final blazing declaration of faith: "*Tienti la tua paura, io con sicura fede l'aspetto*" (190; Hold onto your fear—I with secure faith await him). Driven ever higher by sheer strength of will, this desperate cry aims for the gloriously soaring culmination of the love music heard at Butterfly's first entrance and again at the end of Act I. But the radiant D-flat and C of those earlier days of joy are now reduced to a sustained top B-flat, which provides no traditional psychological or musical resolution to the aria. As the orchestral postlude repeats, once more, the sinking phrases that began "*Un bel dì*," the wheel of hope and doubt on which Butterfly is pinned seems simply to have completed yet another revolution.

Sharpless Arrives

Still, Butterfly clings to her faith. When Sharpless arrives and greets her as "*Madama Butterfly,*" she immediately insists, "*Madama Pinkerton*" (192). She is delighted to see the consul, however, and sets about observing the various amenities due to such an honored guest. Yet, a pronounced psychological ambivalence becomes evident when Sharpless pulls from his pocket a letter he has received from Pinkerton.

Although Butterfly ostensibly fails to notice the letter, her Japanese hospitality suddenly takes on a feeling of procrastination. First commenting on the blue sky and then offering him something to smoke, Butterfly interrupts the consul three times as he tries to show her the letter. When Sharpless finally succeeds in announcing that the letter is from Pinkerton, Butterfly inquires only after the lieutenant's health.

Fearing to hear what the letter may hold, she tries to delay the inevitable while, at the same time, seeking reassurance from Sharpless. With affected lightness, she asks the consul when robins nest in America: that is when Pinkerton promised to return, and, although they have already nested three times in Japan, she hopes they may nest less frequently overseas. When Sharpless confesses that he has no knowledge of ornithology and tries to return to the letter, Butterfly interrupts him once more to confide how the marriage broker Goro has tried to get her to take other husbands, including the wealthy Prince Yamadori.

Her ramblings might seem no more than conversational chatter, except for the return of the melancholy "Doubt" motif in the orchestra as Butterfly's words trail off; in her own indirect way, she is reminding Sharpless of Pinkerton's promise and her own faithfulness, as if his understanding might somehow affect the fate which awaits her.

Yamadori Pays Court

When Yamadori arrives to pay court, the audience is reminded of the easy command which Butterfly exerts over much of her life. Just as she chose to embrace Christianity along with her love for Pinkerton, just as she crushed the gossiping of her relatives, so she now dexterously deflects the prince. The extended lyrical phrases of her gently mocking greeting offer a parody of her suitor's sighing affection.

Yamadori's promise of worldly riches to relieve her present financial distress falls on deaf ears. Wealth means nothing in a life dedicated to love, and so Butterfly declares *con serietà, "Già legata è la mia fede"*

(214; My wedding vow is already made). When Goro insists that as an abandoned wife she may consider herself divorced, Butterfly responds with dignity that such is not the law of her country, the United States of America.

Knowing from his letter that Pinkerton has already remarried, Sharpless murmurs to himself, "*Oh, l'infelice*" (216; Oh, the unhappy woman). But does Butterfly perhaps hear him? Dignity is suddenly replaced with nervous acceleration as Butterfly demands a confirmation from Sharpless that in America a husband cannot divorce his wife simply by abandoning her. Sharpless replies, "*Vero. . . . Però*" (218; True. . . . However), but his qualifier is ignored. Butterfly choses to acknowledge only what she wants to hear. With a comical impersonation of the divorce judge throwing a feckless husband in prison, Butterfly decisively ends the discussion and, without pausing for breath, moves on to order tea from Suzuki.

Letter Scene

Sharpless informs Yamadori, out of Butterfly's hearing, that Pinkerton is indeed returning, but that he does not want to see his abandoned bride. Thus, when Yamadori makes his departure, the audience is left to await the delivery of this mortal blow to Butterfly herself.

Sharpless sits with Butterfly to read the letter:

> *"Amico, cercherete*
> *quel bel fior di fanciulla. . . .*
> *Da quel tempo felice*
> *tre anni son passati . . .*
> *E forse Butterfly*
> *non mi rammenta più. . . .*
> *Se mi vuol bene ancor,*
> *se m'aspetta . . .*
> *A voi mi raccomando*
> *perchè vogliate con circospezione*
> *prepararla . . . al colpo. . . ."*

> ("My friend, seek out
> that beautiful flower of a girl. . . .
> Since that happy time
> three years have passed . . .
> And perhaps Butterfly
> remembers me no more. . . .

If she still wishes me well,
if she waits for me . . .
I am entreating you
in order that you be willing, with circumspection,
to prepare her . . . for the blow. . . .")[19]

Butterfly interrupts him at every phrase, her fragmented interjections blending joy at hearing from Pinkerton with an almost palpable fear of what may come next. Before Sharpless can conclude the letter, she leaps to the joyful, but misguided, assumption that Pinkerton is at last returning.[20]

Only when Sharpless asks what she would do if Pinkerton were never to return is Butterfly at last forced to confront her own deepest fears. The consul's unaccompanied question is followed by a short, violent orchestral chord which seems to strike like the thrust of a hara-kiri sword. Standing "*immobile, come colpita a morte*" (immobile, as if mortally stricken),[21] Butterfly makes clear, after a deathly pause, that with the end of faith, with the end of love, comes the end of life itself.

Her vocal line is broken into desolate fragments, while the funereal rumblings of the orchestration evoke the destiny which is implacably carrying Butterfly toward death: "*Due cose potrei far: tornar . . . a divertir la gente col cantar . . . oppur . . . meglio, morire*" (232-3; Two things I could do: return to entertaining the people with singing . . . or else, better, to die).

When Sharpless suggests with great effort that she accept Yamadori's marriage proposal, Butterfly tearfully orders Suzuki to bring the consul's shoes so that he may leave at once. On the verge of utter collapse, she clutches her heart and murmurs, "*Oh, mi fate tanto male, tanto male, tanto, tanto*" (235-6; Oh, you give me so much pain, so much pain). Alarmed, Sharpless tries to support her, but Butterfly quickly regains her self-control: "*Ho creduto morir. . . . Ma passa presto come passan le nuvole sul mare.*" (236; I thought I would die. . . . But it passes swiftly as the clouds pass over the ocean.) If Pinkerton has truly forgotten her then there is only death; but with a final rending cry of "*Ah! m'ha scordata?*" (236; Ah! has he forgotten me?) Butterfly rushes from the stage, the orchestra sweeping into a climactic voicing of the motif associated with Butterfly's child.

Dolore

Even if Pinkerton has abandoned his wife, Butterfly believes that his child will bring him back once more. From offstage she cries, "*E questo?*" (237; And this one?); only a fleeting, distorted echo of the "Doubt" motif in the orchestra clouds the triumphant pride with which Butterfly brings her child in to Sharpless. This little boy, with his blue eyes and golden curls, will bring Pinkerton back to her "*per le terre . . . e pei mari*" (241-2; by lands and oceans). Her words are confident, but Butterfly's fragmented phrases during this scene, the unstable, shifting motifs in the underscoring orchestration, and even the strained chromatic ascent of the vocal line for "*per le terre . . . e pei mari*" all bespeak a woman near the limits of emotional endurance.

As she tells her son about what Sharpless has said and what the future will hold for them without Pinkerton, her monologue becomes both an unspoken plea for the consul's intervention and a tragic affirmation of a destiny which holds nothing between the extremes of love and death. Butterfly's tortured vocal line drags itself through nightmarish images of miserable beggary until she thinks of returning to the life of the geisha to support her child; the "Suicide" motif sounds in the orchestra, and the geisha's song is transformed into a grotesque dance of spiritual death.

For Butterfly, returning to the geisha existence brings not only dishonor and humiliation, it marks the abandonment of everything which gave meaning to her life, to go on living "even after the *dream* of life is—all—over."[22] Butterfly rejects such a barren, soulless future. In mounting frenzy she makes her choice, her voice building with terrible resolve over mounting orchestration to a climactic top B-flat that becomes a haunting echo of the ascendant faith in the love music of Act I: "*Morta! morta! Mai più danzar! . . . Piuttosto la mia vita vo'troncar!*" (246-7; Dead! dead! Never more to dance! I would rather end my life!)[23]

Tearfully preparing to depart, Sharpless asks the little boy's name. Her vocal line rising with clarion power and underscored by a *forte* orchestral brass echo of "*Un bel dì*," Butterfly tells the child to answer that his name is "Dolore" (249; Sorrow), but to tell his father, "*il giorno del suo ritorno Gioia, Gioia . . . mi chiamerò*" (250; the day of your return, I will be called Joy).

The importance of her child in supporting Butterfly's faith also explains her blind rage when, after Sharpless departs, Suzuki drags in

Goro. The marriage broker has been spreading stories about how in America children such as Dolore are accursed and outcast. In a fury, Butterfly threatens to kill Goro with her father's hara-kiri sword. Driving the broker away, she returns to her child; her vocal line rising and falling with the tumultuous waves of hope and fear surging within her, Butterfly promises Dolore that soon Pinkerton will return and carry them away to America.

Flower Duet

As if in testament to her faith, a cannon sounds in the harbor. A ship has arrived, and as the orchestra returns to the melody of *"Un bel dì,"* Butterfly breathlessly reads the name of the ship through a telescope: *Abraham Lincoln.*[24] Joy and relief flood Butterfly's vocal line; the pain of doubt vanishes as she cries out, *"Trionfa il mio amor! il mio amor; la mia fè trionfa intera: Ei torna e m'ama!"* (264-5; My love triumphs! My love, my faith triumphs utterly: he is coming back, and he loves me!) For the audience, Butterfly's misplaced joy is almost unbearably painful.

Nonetheless, an echo of the "Love" motif leads in turn to the exuberant "Flower Duet," as Butterfly and Suzuki adorn the little house with blossoms for Pinkerton's return. When Butterfly looks at herself in the mirror, however, she recognizes that she is no longer the same woman she was as a new bride; the pain and doubt she has endured are etched in her face. Yet, out of suffering she hopes joy will come, just as her tears watered the flowers in the garden.

Dressing once more as she was on her wedding night, Butterfly prepares for her vigil. Together with Suzuki and Dolore, she waits, looking out through a hole in the shoji for Pinkerton to come climbing up the hill from the harbor. As night slowly falls, however, the atmospheric strains of the "Humming Chorus" fill the air, melodically recalling the unheeded warnings of Pinkerton's letter.

Act III

At the beginning of Act III, dawn is breaking, but Pinkerton has not come. Butterfly still insists, *"verrà vedrai,"* (310; he will come, you will see), and an orchestral echo of the motif associated with her child is heard. With the passing of the long night, the joy and relief Butterfly felt at sighting the *Abraham Lincoln* are replaced by grief and unspoken resignation.

Carrying her sleeping boy into another room, Butterfly sadly sings him a lullaby which poignantly reveals her own inner suffering and, through a verbal play on the name "Dolore," emphasizes her maternal bond: "*Tu sei con Dio ed io col mio dolor*" (311; You are with God, and I with my sorrow). Juxtaposed with her insistence that Pinkerton will return, this lullaby—its translucent vocal line spun from the melody of the "Child" motif—suggests that Butterfly understands her husband's return will be because of his son and not his wife.[25]

Pinkerton Returns

When Pinkerton finally arrives with his American bride and Sharpless, it is only to take the child away with him. Through her tears, Suzuki reluctantly agrees to break the news to Butterfly. Stung at last with remorse, Pinkerton characteristically choses to flee rather than face his abandoned Japanese wife. Before he can escape, however, Sharpless bitterly reproaches him. With tragic solemnity reminiscent of a Greek chorus, Sharpless laments the heroic woman who has so long kept her faith, but who has now begun to foresee what is to come.

Pinkerton rushes out, and Butterfly's voice is heard calling for Suzuki from inside the house. Butterfly senses, even without being told, that Pinkerton has returned. Yet, as she rushes into the room, searching everywhere for her "hidden" husband, there is no happiness in her fragmented, agitated vocal line or in the ominous orchestral underscoring: "*È qui . . . è qui*" (338; He is here, he is here). There is no return to the joy of her love music or even to the hope associated with her child. Instead, Puccini's scoring provides a chilling musical evocation of alienation and loss.

Seeing Suzuki crying and Kate Pinkerton in the garden, Butterfly understands that all hope is gone. As Sharpless approaches to speak to her, Butterfly murmurs in a deathly monotone, "*non ditemi nulla . . . nulla . . . forse potrei cader morta sull'attimo*" (341; tell me nothing, nothing . . . perhaps I might fall dead at the instant). When Suzuki finally acknowledges that Pinkerton is alive but will return no more, Butterfly looks at Kate and cries, "*Ah! è sua moglie!*" (345; Ah! she is his wife!) In a moment, however, her grief is internalized once more, her vocal line flattening to a *piano*, monotone series of low Ds as, *con voce calma*, she embraces her destiny: *"Tutto è morto per me! tutto è finito!"* (345; All is dead for me! All is finished!)

Before death can come, however, Butterfly must make one last terrible sacrifice: she must give up her child. Without even being asked, she understands *"Voglion prendermi tutto! il figlio mio!"* (345-6; They want to take everything from me! My son!)[26] Her suffering is overwhelming, but with supreme effort, Butterfly accepts this final blow.

Her vocal line weighted with an ineffable fusion of grief and heroic majesty, she offers a last benediction to Kate: *"Sotto il gran ponte del cielo non v'è donna di voi più felice. Siatelo sempre, non v'attristate per me."* (348-9; Beneath the great bridge of heaven, there is no woman happier than you. Be so always, do not sadden yourself for me.) Finally, with a foreboding musical phrase that transfigures the vision of *"s'avvia per la collina"* (187; he sets out for the hill) from *"Un bel dì,"* she tells Kate that she will give up her child if Pinkerton will climb the hill and come for him in half an hour.

Butterfly's Death

When Kate and Sharpless depart, Butterfly collapses in grief as Suzuki tries to comfort her. At last, Butterfly gathers her strength and resolutely orders the tearful Suzuki to close the shoji and go play with Dolore. The "Suicide" motif sounds in the orchestra as Butterfly, left alone, takes down her father's hara-kiri sword and prepares for death. Just at that moment, however, Suzuki thrusts the child into the room. Butterfly drops the sword and rushes to embrace her son one last time, smothering him with kisses during a nearly hysterical seven-fold repetition of *"Tu?"* (357; You?).

Butterfly may have the strength to seize her destiny, but she is still a mother, and the loss of her child is an almost unbearable culmination of her trials. *"Con grande sentimento affannosamente agitato"* (357; With great feeling, painfully agitated), Butterfly bids a final farewell to the boy. Her vocal line, broken by propulsive dotted rhythms and crashing orchestral punctuation, builds to the desolate cry, *"muor Butterfly"* (358; dies Butterfly). She can no longer believe herself to be *"Madama F. B. Pinkerton,"* and so she will die simply *"Butterfly."*

Trying to rationalize events which defy such demythifying treatment, Butterfly tells Dolore that she must die so that he can live happily beyond the ocean. But, ultimately, such inadequate justifications give way to an ecstasy of love and loss that surges against the limits of

expressive power in Butterfly's sweeping *sostenendo* phrases: "*O a me,
sceso dal trono dell'alto Paradiso, guarda ben fiso, fiso di tua madre la
faccia! . . . che te'n resti una traccia . . . guarda ben! . . . Amore, addio!
addio! piccolo amor!*" (359-60; O you, descended from the throne of
exalted Paradise, look well at your mother's face, that a trace of it may
linger with you . . . look well! Farewell, my love! Farewell, little love!)

Example 6.4

© Casa Ricordi - BMG Ricordi SpA, used by permission

Symbolically entrusting the dreams of her new life to her son,
Butterfly blindfolds him and sits him down to play with a small
American flag. Taking the hara-kiri sword, she then goes behind a small
screen:

> *Si ode cadere a terra il coltello, mentre il gran velo bianco
> sparisce come tirato da una mano invisibile. Butterfly
> scivola a terra, mezza fuori del paravento: il velo le cir-
> conda il collo. Con un debole sorriso saluta colla mano il
> bambino e si trascina presso di lui, avendo ancora forza
> sufficiente per abbracciarlo, poi gli cade vicino. In questo
> momento si ode fuori, a destra, la voce affannosa di
> Pinkerton.*

> (The knife is heard to fall to the ground, while the great
> white veil disappears as if pulled by an invisible hand.
> Butterfly slips to the ground, half outside the screen: the
> veil encircles her neck. With a weak smile she lifts her hand
> toward the child and drags herself close to him, still having
> sufficient strength to embrace him—then she falls beside
> him. At this moment the agonized voice of Pinkerton is
> heard outside, offstage right.)[27]

The distorted melodic phrases of "*s'avvia per la collina*" from "*Un
bel dì*" explode from the orchestra as Pinkerton calls again and again
from offstage, "*Butterfly!*" (362). Pinkerton is at last returning, not for

the joyous reunion of Butterfly's dreams, but for the final moment of her death: "*Pinkerton e Sharpless si precipitano nella stanza accorrendo presso Butterfly che con debole gesto indica il bambino e muore. Pinkerton si inginocchia, mentre Sharpless prende il bimbo e lo bacia singhiozzando.*" (Pinkerton and Sharpless rush into the room and over to Butterfly who, with a weak gesture, points to the child and dies. Pinkerton kneels, while Sharpless takes up the child and kisses him, sobbing.)[28]

With a nobility of spirit incomprehensible to her craven husband, Butterfly has brought her destiny to fulfillment. She has embraced death once her belief in a love that gave meaning to her existence could no longer be sustained. And so hers is the terrible personal triumph of the tragic hero who can cry,

> It was Apollo, friends, Apollo,
> that brought this bitter bitterness, my sorrows to
> completion.
> But the hand that struck me
> was none but my own.[29]

PREVIEW

In creating *Turandot*, Puccini transformed Gozzi's fairy-tale source play about a comically willful feminist into a true *fiaba*, a fable for all the ages. The operatic Turandot is an individual who must choose whether to live her life by a desiccating code of vengeance and hatred or by the regenerative values of love and forgiveness.

Puccini also adds to the original story the character of Liù, a faithful slave who embodies the ennobling power of love, which Turandot must come to recognize. The very sympathy that Liù elicits from the audience, however, creates a dramatic crisis of response toward the aloof Turandot, whose capacity for love remains concealed in the subtext of the score until the very last scenes of the opera.

In the first act, Turandot's image of beauty and cruelty is developed primarily at second-hand. Then, in Act II, Turandot reveals her own tortured soul, her obsession with the terrible fate of her ancestor, the Princess Lo-u-Ling, who was abducted, raped, and murdered by a conquering prince. The thirst for sanguinary justice drives Turandot to send her own suitors to their deaths: acting out an unending ritual of punishment and revenge, Turandot makes the princes of today pay for the crimes of antiquity.

Only after Liù's death in the final act does Turandot finally recognize the ultimate futility of such vengeance. She embraces the power of love, and the nightmarish world of Peking is transformed in the rosy light of a new dawn.

CHAPTER 7

Turandot

Romantic Realism

One of Giacomo Puccini's greatest gifts as a dramatic composer was his ability to reveal the transcendent, the heroic, the extraordinary qualities within ordinary people. While earlier composers focused on illuminating the essential humanity of exalted characters, Puccini revealed how such essential humanity could exalt individuals from any walk of life. His artistic vision was a unique fusion of romanticism and *verismo*; his heroines are women who, after nearly a century, still speak to their audiences with an immediacy and indefinable contemporaneity that is unsurpassed in the operatic canon.

Source Play

In his final opera, however, Puccini suddenly turned to a new genre, perhaps finding in the fantasy world of the *fiaba*, the fairy-tale fable, a universalized caption for the theme of love's transfiguring power, which he had so deftly portrayed in the stories of heroines from Manon to Madama Butterfly. The play that attracted Puccini's attention was Carlo Gozzi's, *Turandot, Fiaba Chinese Teatrale Tragicomica* (1762),[1] written in the aftermath of a feud between Gozzi and his primary literary rival, Carlo Goldoni.

In the eighteenth century, Goldoni had advocated a revisionist style of comedy in which more realistically drawn characters and ordered plots would replace the stock character types and erratic improvisations of the venerable *commedia dell'arte* style. In response, Gozzi set out to demonstrate the theatrical vitality of *commedia dell'arte* through a series of *fiabe*.

Inspired by the Persian tales which had gained great popularity in Europe, Gozzi's *Turandot* is a comic parody of feminism which, today, seems fundamentally and irredeemably antiquated. Motivated by pride and a determined sense of self-superiority, the Princess Turandot vows never to be subjugated by a sex she despises on principle. As she warns the Unknown Prince, Calaf, at their first meeting,

> *Principe, desistete*
> *dall'impresa fatale. Al cielo è noto,*
> *che quelle voci, che crudel mi fanno,*
> *son menzognere. Abborrimento estremo*
> *ch'ho al sesso vostro, fa, ch'io mi difenda,*
> *com'io so, com'io posso, a viver lunge*
> *da un sesso, che abborrisco.*

> (Prince, desist
> from this fatal enterprise. By heaven it is well-known
> that those voices, which portray me as cruel,
> lie. Extreme loathing
> that I have for your sex makes me defend myself,
> as I know how to, as I am able, so as to live far
> from a sex I abhor.)[2]

To keep herself from male domination, Turandot poses three riddles to all would-be suitors and sends those who cannot answer to the executioner. In the world of the play, however, Turandot's antipathy toward men is only a comic aberration, no more than a willful perversion of woman's true nature designed to elicit laughter. Throughout the play, Turandot struggles against her own love for Calaf. Hence, even before the Riddle Scene, she wonders to herself, "*E questo solo/ ha forza di destar compassione/ in questo sen?* (risoluta) *No, superarmi io deggio.*" (251; Does this one alone have the power to awaken compassion in this breast? (*resolute*) No, I must get hold of myself.)

Later, Turandot's slave Zelima asks in disbelief, "*Come mai,
signora,/ un sì amabile oggetto, un sì bell'uomo,/ sì generoso, tanto
innamorato/ può destarvi nel seno odio, e puntiglio?*" (259; How ever,
Madame, is so attractive an object, so handsome a man, so generous, so
in love, able to awaken hatred and spite in your breast?) And Turandot
replies,

> *Non tormentarmi . . . sappi . . . ah mi vergogno
> a palesarlo . . . ei mi destò nel petto
> commozioni a me ignote . . . un caldo . . . un gelo. . . .
> No, non è ver. Zelima, io l'odio a morte.
> Ei della mia vergogna nel divano
> fu la cagion. Per tutto il regno, e fuori
> si saprà, ch'io fui vinta, e riderassi
> dell'ignoranza mia.*

> (259-60; Do not torment me . . . but know . . . Ah, I am
>   ashamed
> to reveal it . . . he awakened in my bosom
> feelings unknown to me . . . a heat . . . a chill. . . .
> No, it is not true. Zelima, I hate him to the death.
> He who was the cause of my humiliation in the Divan.
> For all the kingdom, and beyond,
> will know that I was defeated and laugh
> at my ignorance.)

Her misguided feminism leads her to deny the power and fidelity of
Calaf's love: "*Io so, che tutti perfidi/ gli uomini son: che non han cor
sincero,/ nè capace d'amor*" (260-1; I know that all men are treacher-
ous: that they do not have honest hearts, nor the capacity for love). She
refuses to acknowledge Calaf's sincerity even when, having
successfully answered her riddles, he offers to forfeit his life if she can
discover his name and the name of his father before the next day.

Turandot accepts the challenge, and after a number of intrigues
involving her slave Adelma, discovers and vengefully announces the
names. Spurned and banished by Turandot, Calaf tries to stab himself;
only then does the princess recognize her folly. In the comic tradition,
an aberrant figure like Turandot must be chastened and reintegrated
into "normal" society. Thus, in the final monologue of the play, the
feminist princess is a changed woman, repenting her foolishness and
seeking pardon:

Ciel, d'un abborrimento sì ostinato,
che al sesso mascolino ebbi sin'ora,
delle mie crudeltà, perdon ti chiedo.
(si fa innanzi) *Sappia questo gentil popol de' maschi,*
ch'io gli amo tutti. Al pentimento mio,
deh, qualche segno di perdon si faccia.

(305; Heaven, for so obstinate a loathing
that I had for the masculine sex until now,
for my cruelty, I ask pardon.
(*coming downstage*) Know this, kind gentlemen,
that I love you all. To my repentance,
please, give some sign of pardon.)

Turandot through the Modern Mind

Puccini was drawn to this play by its affirmation of love's transforma-
tive power, but the composer's own artistic exploration of this theme
required a radical reworking of the surrounding story by the librettists
Giuseppe Adami and Renato Simoni.[3] As Puccini instructed Simoni,
"*Semplificarlo per il numero degli atti e lavorarlo per renderlo snello,*
efficace e sopratutto esaltare la passione amorosa di Turandot che per
tanto tempo ha soffocato sotto la cenere del suo grande orgoglio. . . . In
fine: una Turandot attraverso il cervello moderno, il tuo, d'Adami e
mio." (Simplify it as to the number of acts and work to render it graceful, effective, and above all exalt Turandot's amorous passion, which she
has smothered for so long beneath the ashes of her great pride. . . . In
short: a Turandot through the modern mind, yours, Adami's and mine.)[4]
    When reconceived "through the modern mind," Turandot becomes
an individual who must choose whether to live her life by a desiccating
code of vengeance and hatred or by the regenerative values of love and
forgiveness. Gozzi's comically willful feminist becomes a complex
human being, subtly revealed in the rich psychological subtext of
Puccini's score. Thus, in *Turandot* (1926),[5] Gozzi's fairytale becomes a
true *fiaba*, a fable for all the ages.

Act I

From the first curtain, Puccini depicts the legendary world of Peking as
a symbolic realm in which beauty and peace are consumed by hatred and

violence. The initial exoticism of the dazzling sunset and picturesque Chinese crowd which fills the massive square near the walls of the Imperial City quickly gives way to a grotesque, surreal nightmare of blood-lust.[6]

A mandarin announces that the Prince of Persia has failed to answer Turandot's riddles and is condemned to death. In an instant, the tranquil crowd is transformed into a frenzied mob, howling for the executioner, torture, and death. This cruelty is, in turn, reflected in the savagery of the guards who thrust the mob back, heedless of the frightened and confused cries which burst forth from the fallen, from mothers and children.

Liù

Yet, as the executioner's men sharpen a huge sword on an immense whetstone, Puccini introduces a scene of tenderness, devotion, and love which is sharp contrast to the horror of Turandot's Peking: in the midst of the melee, the exiled Tartar king Timur and his faithful slave Liù arrive. The mob ignores Liù's calls for pity and aid when the old king collapses to the ground, but suddenly a young man rushes to Timur's side—it is his son, Calaf, who reveals that, like his father, he too has been wandering incognito.

While Gozzi's Timur is little more than a plot expediency, appearing late in the play just in time to be tortured by Turandot, Puccini reconceives the old man as a profoundly affecting father, a man whose love for his son is ultimately matched by his paternal devotion to Liù. For Timur, Liù is far more than a mere slave. His deep attachment to the young woman who has been his constant guide and sole protector in bitter exile is unquestionable; for her part, Liù treats the unhappy king with all the love she might bestow on her own father, or, in this case, on the father of the man she loves. As Liù explains to Calaf "*con dolcezza estatica*" (with ecstatic sweetness),[7] she has shared Timur's suffering "*Perchè un dì . . . nella reggia, mi hai sorriso*" (Because one day . . . in the palace, you smiled at me).[8]

The character of Liù is completely new to Puccini's *Turandot*. In the original play, there is a former servant who knows Calaf's identity, but he is the clownish Barach, an erstwhile tutor of the prince. By creating Liù, Puccini offers a dramatic embodiment of the ennobling power of love, which Turandot herself must come to recognize.[9]

Thus, in the final act of the opera, when Liù embraces torture and death rather than reveal the secret of Calaf's identity, the slave tells Turandot that she is guided by *"Tanto amore segreto, e inconfessato, grande così che questi strazi son dolcezze per me, perchè ne faccio dono al mio signore. . . . Perchè, tacendo, io gli do, gli do il tuo amore."* (334-5; Such love, secret and unconfessed, so great that these torments are sweetness to me because I offer them to my lord. . . . Because, keeping silent, I give him, I give him your love.)

Problems of Sympathy

Liù's affinity with such earlier Puccini heroines as Mimì or Madama Butterfly is clear, and the composer devoted some of his most sublime music to this fragile yet heroic woman. But the very sympathy which Liù elicits from the audience creates a dramatic crisis of response toward the aloof Turandot, whose capacity for love remains concealed in the subtext of the score until the very last scenes of the opera.

Calaf, too, is placed in a tenuous dramatic position; his unwavering love for Turandot seems almost anti-heroic at times because it means ignoring the devotion and sacrifice of Liù. To be sure, Liù never expects Calaf to return her love, and throughout the opera he treats her with constant kindness and gratitude. He tries vigorously, though in vain, to protect her from Turandot's tortures. And yet, although Calaf denounces Turandot as *"Principessa di morte"* (353; Princess of death) after Liù's suicide, he then seizes the princess in his arms and presses an ardent kiss on her lips.

While the kiss at this moment certainly embodies romanticism's fascination with the fusion of love and death, the result is that Turandot's complicity in Liù's suicide and Timur's heart-rending grief are apparently forgotten. With a fairytale, such endings can be accepted as a matter of conventional form; but, when the fairytale has been so profoundly humanized in the remaking, such a transition from pathos to joy is no longer a simple matter.

Puccini himself seems to have recognized this troubling ambivalence of audience response, laboring with his librettists for months to bring the opera's story to a satisfactory conclusion. The resulting text is certainly far from inspired, though as fully realized music-drama the opera's denouement might have succeeded. With the composer's death, however, it was left to Franco Alfano to complete the score from Puccini's notes, and his workman-like rendering of the final scenes fails to approach the level of sublimity necessary for such a delicate finessing of audience sympathy.

Turandot Appears

As in the original play, the first appearance of Turandot herself is delayed until after the wheels of the story have been well set in motion. She is seen only briefly in the first act and utters not a word. Moved to pity by the sight of the hapless Prince of Persia being led to his doom, the people of Peking cry out for mercy, but their cries are short-lived. The stentorian tones of the "Turandot" motif sound in the onstage brass, heralding the entrance of the princess on the imperial balcony (70-1).

Example 7.1

Illumined in a shaft of moonlight, the princess *"appare quasi incorporea, come una visione. Il suo atteggiamento dominatore e il suo sguardo altero fanno cessare per incanto il tumulto. . . . Turandot ha un gesto imperioso: è la condanna."* (appears almost incorporeal, like a vision. Her commanding attitude and haughty look make the tumult magically cease. . . . Turandot makes an imperious gesture: it is the death sentence.)[10]

The Prince of Persia is led away, but Calaf remains, *"immobile, estatico come se la inattesa visione di bellezza lo avesse fatalmente inchiodato al suo destino"* (immobile, ecstatic, as if the unexpected vision of beauty had fatally rivetted him to his destiny).[11] Enraptured, he determines to accept the challenge of the riddles, despite the pleas of his father, despite the implorations of Liù, despite the urgings of the semi-comic court officials Ping, Pang, and Pong.[12]

For nearly half of the opera, Puccini and his librettists deftly allow the image of the beautiful Turandot to be developed primarily at second-hand. The mythic aura of her beauty is established far more powerfully by the willingness of Calaf and the Prince of Persia to die for her than by the reality of Turandot's brief appearance on the balcony.[13]

Equally compelling is the aura of Turandot's cruelty, a cruelty mirrored in the actions of her people. Ping, Pang, and Pong lament, *"Tutto andava secondo l'antichissima regola del mondo. Poi nacque Turandot."* (156-8; Everything went according to the most ancient rule of the world. Then Turandot was born.) They dream of the day Turandot will be conquered by love and all can sing: *"Gloria all'ebbrezza e all'amore che ha vinto, e alla China la pace ridà"* (202-3; Glory to the rapture and the love that has won and given peace back to China).

By the middle of the second act, when Turandot speaks for the first time, her image is firmly established. But the woman herself remains an enigma, the ultimate riddle which Calaf—and the audience—must come to understand.

Act II

In the second scene of Act II, the people of Peking assemble at the Imperial Palace to hear Turandot pose her riddles to the Unknown Prince, Calaf. Atop a vast staircase sits Turandot's father, the emperor, like *"un dio che apparisca di tra le nuvole"* (217; a god who appears from among the clouds); and even he expresses horror at the oath which forces him to permit his daughter's reign of terror. Yet, when the princess actually enters to take her place before the emperor's throne, the "Turandot" motif is sounded not by arrogant brass, but by the gentle voices of children. The simplicity and warmth of this introduction suddenly melts the ice from Turandot's identifying motif, suggesting for the first time that the true nature of the princess may be quite different from her image.

In Questa Reggia

The dramatic groundwork is thus skillfully laid for Turandot's opening aria, *"In questa Reggia"* (231; In this palace). There is no counterpart for this moment of shattering psychological revelation in the original play. While Gozzi depicts a Turandot motivated by frivolous feminist pride, Puccini and his librettists illuminate the tortured soul of a woman obsessed by the terrible fate of her ancestor, the Princess Lo-u-Ling, who was abducted, raped, and murdered by a conquering prince.

The thirst for sanguinary justice drives Turandot to send her own suitors to their deaths: offering herself as the marriage-prize to the victor, she poses three riddles, and the executioner awaits those who cannot answer correctly. Acting out an unending ritual of punishment and revenge, Turandot makes the princes of today pay for the crimes of antiquity.

Her hatred is focused with unwavering precision, falling only on those men who try to possess her. She takes the place of Lo-u-Ling; her hapless suitors become the attackers who are now destroyed by their own lust. There is no distinction in her mind between true love and the act of violence which claimed Lo-u-Ling's life. The man who desires to wed her thus becomes simply another incarnation of the criminal. Unlike Lo-u-Ling, however, Turandot has the power of life and death.

Invocation

Turandot's aria begins with an invocation of the past underscored by minimal orchestration: "*In questa Reggia, or son mill'anni e mille*" (231; In this palace, a thousand thousand years ago). The anguish Turandot feels at the memory of Lo-u-Ling's terrible, haunting cry is powerfully highlighted in the princess' driving vocal phrase, with its agitated dotted rhythms: "*un grido disperato risonò*" (231; a desperate cry resounded). *Forte* orchestral doubling gives strength to Turandot's words, while a striking harmonic overlay a fifth above the vocal line reverberates like the anguished cry from the past which has found new voice in Turandot herself.

As if embodying the journey of that solitary cry down through the centuries, the heavily accented phrases of "*E quel grido, traverso stirpe e stirpe*" (And that cry, through descendant and descendant) fall without accompaniment a full octave from top A before a soft, almost mournful, conclusion on "*qui nell'anima mia si rifugiò*" (231; took refuge here in my soul).

The horror of the past takes hold of Turandot's heart, but the result is an unsettling sense of enervation. The princess is no Fury, and it is clear as the aria progresses that Turandot must steel herself to play her role, ruthlessly suppressing her own humanity in order to perpetuate her endless cycle of retribution. It is an act of will which must recall Lady Macbeth's "Come, you spirits/ That tend on mortal thoughts, unsex me here,/ And fill me from the crown to the toe topful/ Of direst cruelty!"[14]

The assumption of her role requires a virtual act of self-hypnosis by Turandot. Her haunting, unaccompanied "*Principessa Lo-u-Ling*" (232) rises like a vision from the mists of antiquity as Turandot drifts into incantatory memory: "*ava dolce e serena che regnavi nel tuo cupo silenzio in gioja pura*" (232; sweet and serene ancestor who reigned in your dark silence in pure joy). With *forte* declamation, she proclaims as her own guiding principle Lo-u-Ling's defiance of male domination: "*e sfidasti inflessibile e sicura l'aspro dominio, oggi rivivi in me*" (232-3; and defied, unyielding and firm, harsh domination—today you live again in me). But the joy and sweet serenity that this life brought to her ancestor are notably lacking in Turandot's distorted imitation, in her existence of vengeance and willful denial of self.

Past Horrors

As the chorus murmurs the words to this all-too-familiar history, Turandot, "*Come cosa lontana*" (233; Like something far away), lets her mind drift to the chaos of the ancient battle. The past merges ritualistically with the present: "*E Lo-u-Ling la mia ava trascinata da un uomo, come te, come te, straniero, là nella notte atroce, dove si spense la sua fresca voce*" (234-5; And Lo-u-Ling my ancestor dragged away by a man—like you, like you, foreigner—there in the horrible night where her innocent voice died). Lo-u-Ling's cry of terror becomes a cry of terrible retribution as Turandot hurls her words down upon Calaf, her vocal line building over mounting orchestration to a savage top B extended by a fermata before a declamatory denouement: "*io vendico su voi, su voi quella purezza, quel grido e quella morte! Quel grido e quella morte!*" (236-7; I avenge on you, on you that purity, that cry and that death! That cry and that death!)

Example 7.2

© Casa Ricordi - BMG Ricordi SpA, used by permission

The surging flood of righteous triumph which engulfs Turandot is captured in the sweeping melodic phrases of the expansive orchestration, while the princess gives herself up to the role of loveless avenger: *"Mai nessun m'avrà"* (237; No one will ever possess me). Yet, at the very height of her exultation, Turandot incongruously warns Calaf, *"Straniero! Non tentar la fortuna! Gli enigmi sono tre, la morte è una!"* (239; Stranger! Do not tempt fortune! The riddles are three—death is one!) Perhaps Turandot has provided similar warnings to earlier suitors, reflecting her profound unease with the bloody role she has taken upon herself; or perhaps something akin to Calaf's love-at-first-sight stirs within her heart.

In either case, her warning falls on deaf ears, and Calaf replies, *"Gli enigmi sono tre, una è la vita"* (239-40; The riddles are three—one is life). Life and death hang in the balance—for Calaf as he faces the trial of the riddles, and, ultimately, for Turandot herself when she must choose to embrace regenerative love or cling to her devastating hatred. Puccini captures this counterpoising in the clash of Turandot and Calaf's musical phrases: the princess' warning in the key of E-flat major mounts to a top G; the prince responds in the key of F-sharp major, his vocal line reaching high A-sharp; finally, they repeat their lines together in the key of A-flat major, their voices rising to a climactic high C before a declamatory unison denouement.

Three Riddles

Turandot's choice of riddles in the ensuing scene is in itself psychologically revealing. In Gozzi's play, the three riddles have no subtextual significance for Turandot, the answers being the Sun, the Year, and the Lion of the Adriatic.[15] In the opera, on the other hand, the answers to Turandot's riddles strongly suggest the princess' subconscious longing for a partner who can understand and share the mysteries of the true love which lies in her heart: "Hope," which is eternally reborn; "Blood," which burns with passion; and "Turandot," who is the ice which kindles fire.

The first riddle is heralded by onstage trumpets, and Turandot echoes their clarion call with her *"Straniero, ascolta"* (242; Stranger, listen). As she poses the enigma, *"Nella cupa notte vola un fantasma iridescente"* (242; In the dark night flies an iridescent phantom), her vocal line is rigid and detached; her declamatory phrases, with their suspended top Gs, are offset by ominous orchestral punctuation.

Yet, for the concluding phrases, "*Ed ogni notte nasce ed ogni giorno muore*" (244; And every night it is born and every day it dies), Turandot's voice drops to low E, her melody doubled by mournful reeds. Melancholy replaces foreboding, subtly hinting that the cycle of hope and disillusionment is one with which Turandot has personal familiarity.

Calaf correctly answers the riddle, and Turandot is clearly taken aback by this unforeseen turn of events. "*La sua altera superiorità la riprende*" (Her haughty superiority overtakes her again),[16] yet, both the music and staging for her next riddle reveal that Turandot's facade of detached coldness has been badly shaken. The stage directions note that the princess rapidly descends halfway down the great staircase; her conscious motivation may be "*affascinare e stordire il Principe*" (to enchant and daze the prince),[17] but, unconsciously, Turandot is drawing ever closer to the man who may understand her in a way she never thought possible.

Despite Turandot's aggressive posing of the second riddle, nervously agitated orchestration betrays the princess' inner confusion and makes the climactic high B-flat in the final phrase of the riddle seem all the more willful in its defiance. Indeed, by the time Turandot launches into her third and last riddle, the ambivalence of her feelings is transparent. On the surface is frustration and contempt: Turandot reacts to the murmuring of the crowd by imperiously commanding the guards, "*Percuotete quei vili*" (255; Strike those wretches), and descends on Calaf as if "*sulla sua preda*" (257; on her prey).

Beneath the surface, however, the hope and passion alluded to in her first riddles surge through her. She has come down from her great height on the staircase to an equal level with Calaf. She has unconsciously abandoned her exalted station before the celestial throne of the god-like emperor to take the place she longs to occupy in the mortal realm beside Calaf, and for all her ostensible ferocity there is an amorous sensuality in her proximity to the young prince, "*quasi con la bocca sul viso di lui*" (with her mouth nearly on his face).[18]

Under the stress of Turandot's inner tension, the musical and poetic structures of the third riddle become blurred. The expansiveness of the princess' imagery in the earlier riddles gives way to choppy, telegraphic phrases over heightened orchestral accompaniment. The formalized recitation of the riddle quickly breaks down into direct address as Turandot sneers, "*Su, straniero, il gelo che dà foco, che cos'è?*" (258-9; Come, foreigner, what is the ice which gives fire?) But the fever of love that inspires Calaf is coursing through Turandot's own veins, despite her almost desperate efforts to deny it. Her vocal line rising *poco allargando* to a *fortissimo* top A-flat, Turandot's voicing of the final enigma conveys neither the aggressive defiance of the second riddle nor the aloofness of the first. Instead, there is emotional tumult and ineffable longing.

Turandot's Confusion

When Calaf emerges victorious after the last riddle, Turandot is overcome by confusion and uncertainty. Despite the feelings which Calaf has begun to awaken in her heart, she is terrified of sharing Lo-u-Ling's fate. Turandot must confront the reality that her riddles have been answered, and she must yield herself to the Unknown Prince as his bride: the indomitable avenger has suddenly become vulnerable. Torn between fear and nascent love, Turandot symbolically tries to return to the security of her exalted detachment from human passion: she breathlessly reascends the staircase[19] and pleads with the emperor to intervene and nullify the contest. Coming out of the populace's paean of imperial glory, Turandot's supplication has a child-like innocence in its simplicity and confusion: *"Figlio del cielo! Padre augusto! No! Non gettar tua figlia nelle braccia dello straniero!"* (265-6; Son of heaven! August father! No! Do not cast your daughter into the arms of the foreigner!)

Example 7.3

Fi - glio del cie - lo! Pa-dre au-gu-sto! No! Non get-tar tua

fi-glia nel-le brac-cia del-lo stra - nie - ro!

© Casa Ricordi - BMG Ricordi SpA, used by permission

She accuses the prince of mocking her and cries out with growing vehemence, *"No, non guardarmi così, non sarò tua. Mai nessun m'avrà!"* (270-1; No, do not look at me like that. I will not be yours. No one will ever possess me!) Finally, she gives voice to a terrible fragmentary reprise of the "Turandot" motif, her vocal line rising to a pair of rending high Cs, underscored by *fortissimo* orchestration and full chorus, as she demands, "*Mi vuoi nelle tue braccia a forza? riluttante, fremente!*" (272-3; You want me in your arms by force? Unwilling, trembling!)

In these phrases, Lo-u-Ling's cry of terror echoes down over the centuries. But just as Turandot's warning of "*morte*" at the end of "*In questa Reggia*" was matched by Calaf's hope of "*vita*," so now the princess' fear of becoming another victim of male lust is matched by Calaf's vision of her as a woman transformed by the power of true and ardent love: "*Ti voglio tutta ardente d'amor*" (274; I want you ardent with love).

Calaf is not a predator, but a man; he has not competed to win a dehumanized prize, but to be worthy of a woman's supreme love. As proof of his intentions, he offers to forfeit both Turandot's love and his life if she can discover his true identity by the next day. His gesture leaves the princess in stunned silence for the duration of the act. The protective walls of her avenging hatred are crumbling about her, but she remains fundamentally ambivalent about leaving the ruins of her self-imposed emotional fortress to embrace the love Calaf offers. Only Liù's gesture of supreme love and self-sacrifice at the end of the opera can give her the full understanding she needs in order to act.

Act III

Turandot has commanded her people to discover the Unknown Prince's name. Calaf himself is unmoved by threats or enticement until the mob seizes Timur and Liù. The helpless pair are dragged into the imperial gardens, and the familiar strains of the "Turandot" motif announce the princess' arrival. Significantly, however, the motif now highlights Turandot's fundamentally divided sense of identity: the melody is first voiced by the brass, but is then taken up by the gentler tones of strings and woodwinds.

Similarly, while Turandot's words remain relentlessly taunting— "*Sei pallido, straniero*" (326; You are pale, foreigner)—her vocal line is fragmentary and submerged in an expansive orchestral melody that has previously been associated with the arrival of Liù and Timur in Peking. Weighted with both majesty and sorrow, this theme evokes the strength of Liù's love and devotion in a world of cruelty and torment and thus foreshadows both Liù's self-sacrifice and the triumph of love over vengeance within Turandot herself.

Example 7.4

Sei pal - li - do, stra - nie - ro!.........

corni

Meno largo

© Casa Ricordi - BMG Ricordi SpA, used by permission

Liù's offering of her own life out of love for Calaf comes as a shattering revelation to Turandot. As Timur raises his voice in a cry of unending agony over the lifeless body of the faithful Liù, "*Sul volto di Turandot passa una espressione di tormento*" (An expression of torment passes over Turandot's face).[20] The princess listens in silence, but her silence is far more eloquent than any words could be. At this moment, Turandot finally recognizes the ultimate futility of vengeance and retribution. The pursuit of revenge for the death of one innocent woman has now resulted in the death of another. In Liù's face, Turandot must see the death mask of Lo-u-Ling. The princess' handmaidens try to shield her eyes from this horror with a veil, but for Turandot such symbolic defense comes too late.

Once Liù's cortege has made its mournful departure, Calaf confronts Turandot with the consequences of vengeance. Tearing the veil from her face, he cries, "*guarda, crudele, quel purissimo sangue che fu sparso per te*" (354; look, cruel one, at that purest blood which was shed for you). Turandot tries weakly to maintain her unapproachable facade, but there is no real emotional conviction in her "*Tu stringi il mio freddo velo, ma l'anima è lassù*" (355; You press my cold veil, but my soul is up there on high).

Nor do her protestations that the prince's embraces are a profanation ring true anymore; at last, as one contemporary French critic noted after the opera's Paris premiere, Calaf has converted "*cette prêtresse de la vengeance à une religion plus douce, celle de l'amour*" (this priestess of vengeance to a sweeter religion, that of love).[21] Even the final fragmentary echoes of "*In questa Reggia*" are transformed by Calaf's ardor as the prince kisses Turandot with the passionate cry "*il bacio tuo mi dà l'eternità*" (359-60; your kiss gives me eternity).

Del Primo Pianto

"*Il contatto incredibile l'ha trasfigurata*" (The incredible contact has transfigured her),[22] but now Turandot must struggle to redefine herself in a context of love rather than hatred. The "icy princess" is no more, and Turandot weeps, "*La mia gloria è finita*" (364; My glory is ended). In her agitated final monologue, "*Del primo pianto*" (366; Of the first tears), Turandot at last gives voice to the ambivalent emotions Calaf inspired in her from the first moment she saw him: "*C'era negli occhi tuoi la luce degli eroi! C'era negli occhi tuoi la superba certezza. . . . E t'ho odiato per quella. . . . E per quella t'ho amato.*" (368-9; There was in your eyes the light of heroes. There was in your eyes proud certainty. And I hated you for that. . . . And for that I loved you.)

Now she is conquered, conquered by "*questa febbre che mi vien da te*" (370-1; this fever that comes to me from you). Turandot must still recognize, however, that love is not a battle of the sexes with one victorious and the other defeated. To be conquered by love is not to lose oneself, but to discover the transcendent glory of the human heart. Thus, Calaf reveals the purity of his love by renouncing any power over Turandot; in revealing his name to her, Calaf places his life in the princess' hands. Turandot need only announce his identity to the city and triumphantly claim her prize, Calaf's death. Once again, the power of the executioner is hers, but now Turandot realizes that such power is dross.

Calling forth her father and the people of Peking, Turandot announces the stranger's name, her voice floating to a celestial high B-flat: "*Il suo nome è Amore*" (381-2; His name is Love). Humanity has triumphed over inhumanity. Love has vanquished hatred, and, like Turandot herself, the nightmarish world of Peking is transformed. In the rosy light of a new dawn, the Chinese people raise their voices in a great hymn of joyful praise: "*O sole! Vita! Eternità! Luce del mondo è amore!*" (382-3; O Sun! Life! Eternity! Love is the light of the world!) And at the top of the vast imperial staircase, Calaf and Turandot are united, symbolically raised by love as close to heaven as mortals can reach: "*i due amanti si trovano avvinti in un abbraccio, perdutamente, mentre la folla tende le braccia, getta fiori, acclama gioiosamente*" (the two lovers find themselves clasped together, lost in an embrace, while the people extend their arms, throwing flowers with joyous acclamation).[23]

APPENDIX

IL TROVATORE SOURCE PREVIEW

Highlights in the Development of Dramatic Character

For all its enduring popularity in Spain, Antonio García Gutiérrez's *El Trovador* is merely a well-constructed melodrama. In its twisting story of love and vengeance, characters are only superficially explored. Verdi and his librettists further concentrate the play's high-*frisson* plot, while introducing significant changes in the character of Leonora.

Leonora's opening *scena* in Act I, with her aria *"Tacea la notte placida"* (The peaceful night was silent), has no precise correlation in the source play, and Julian Budden traces its inspiration back to Verdi's own *Ernani*.

In Act II of the opera, Leonora is going to enter a convent; in the original play, however, Doña Leonor has actually taken her vows as a nun. Thus, the operatic heroine is not subject to the struggle of conscience which subsequently besets Doña Leonor after she is carried off by her beloved troubadour, Manrico.

Without this inner struggle, Leonora is reduced to a largely passive role in the third act of the opera. In the source play, Doña Leonor takes a much more active part, even participating in a dialogue where Verdi provides Manrico with a *cabaletta*.

Finally, Verdi adds Leonora's Act IV aria *"D'amor sull'ali rosee"* (On rosy wings of love), a prayer which has no corresponding moment in García Gutiérrez's scene outside the prison tower.

Il Trovatore Plot Synopsis

Act I (The Duel)

Scene 1: Aliaferia Palace

To pass the night hours, Ferrando, the captain of the guard, tells Count di Luna's retainers the dreadful story of the count's brother: when the boy was still an infant, a gypsy had been found beside his cradle. The gypsy was driven away, but the child soon fell dreadfully ill. The count's father had the gypsy tracked down and burned at the stake as a witch; but her daughter abducted the count's infant brother, and a child's skeleton was found smoldering on the very pyre where the witch had been burned. The count's father never gave up the hope that his son was still alive and, on his deathbed, made di Luna promise to continue the search. Ferrando insists that, although the witch's daughter was never found, he would recognize her if he ever saw her. The retainers are horrified by the thought of the witch's evil spirit roaming the earth. At the midnight bell, they all disperse with fright.

Scene 2: Gardens of the Aliaferia Palace

Leonora, a noble lady-in-waiting in the court of the Princess of Aragon, tells her confidante, Ines, of her love for a mysterious Black Knight upon whom she had bestowed the victor's laurel at a great tournament and who has come in the guise of a troubadour to sing songs of love beneath her balcony. Ines foresees disaster, but Leonora insists that she will live by the side of her beloved, or die for him.

They enter the palace, and Count di Luna arrives in the darkened garden to voice his love for Leonora. Before he can proceed, the troubadour's serenade is heard. Leonora rushes out to embrace her beloved but mistakenly approaches the count. Outraged, the real troubadour, Manrico, denounces her. Leonora pleads for forgiveness, while Manrico and di Luna confront each other with rage. The two men depart for a duel, while Leonora falls unconscious to the ground.

Act II (The Gypsy)

Scene 1: Gypsy Camp in the Biscay Mountains

While the other gypsies work, Azucena stares into a fire and sings of a victim burned at the stake. Manrico, who believes himself to be her son, lies near Azucena. Having spared di Luna's life in the duel, Manrico was later wounded by di Luna's men during the civil war that is sweeping the land. Azucena has nursed him back to health and now recounts her mother's terrible death and last cry, "Avenge me!" Azucena is the daughter of the witch in Ferrando's story, and she recalls how she abducted di Luna's brother only, in the horror of the moment, to cast her own child into the fire by mistake.

Surprised, Manrico asks about his true identity, but Azucena insists that she was just delirious and that Manrico is, of course, her own son. Word arrives that Manrico has been named commander of the garrison at Castellor but that Leonora, believing Manrico dead, is preparing to enter a convent. Despite Azucena's pleas, Manrico sets off to stop her.

Scene 2: Convent Courtyard

Waiting to abduct Leonora and make her his bride, the Count di Luna reveals the great passion that is consuming him.

Leonora arrives and bids a gentle farewell to her weeping friends. Before she can enter the convent, the count steps forward. Suddenly, Manrico, too, appears, and Leonora voices her wonderment and joy while the two rivals once more confront each other. Manrico's men disarm the count, and the troubadour drags Leonora away with him.

Act III (The Gypsy's Son)

Scene 1: Count di Luna's Military Camp outside Castellor

The count's thoughts of separating Leonora from Manrico are interrupted by the capture of Azucena, who was wandering the countryside in search of her son. As di Luna questions her, Ferrando recognizes the old gypsy. She is condemned to death and taken off to be burned at the stake.

Scene 2: Inside the Fortress of Castellor

Manrico declares his eternal love for Leonora as they prepare for their wedding. Suddenly, word arrives that Azucena is about to be executed, and Manrico rushes off with his men to rescue her.

Act IV (The Execution)

Scene 1: Outside the Aliaferia Palace

Manrico has been captured and imprisoned with Azucena. Leonora arrives in the night outside the prison tower, determined to win Manrico's freedom, even at the cost of her own life.

The Count di Luna appears, and Leonora begs him to pardon Manrico. He refuses with jealous fury. At last, Leonora offers herself to him in exchange for the troubadour's life. The count agrees, and Leonora secretly takes the poison she has concealed in her ring.

Scene 2: Inside the Prison

Azucena is terrified at the prospect of being burned at the stake. Manrico comforts her, and she finally drifts off to sleep thinking of their mountain homeland.

Leonora enters and urges Manrico to flee. Outraged at the thought of the price she has paid di Luna to gain his freedom, Manrico curses her. Fainting from the poison, Leonora reveals the truth and dies in her lover's arms.

Furious at being deceived, the Count di Luna sends Manrico to the executioner's block and drags Azucena to the window to see the axe fall. Azucena reveals that Manrico was really the count's brother and then collapses with the terrible cry, "O Mother, you are avenged!"

La Forza del Destino Preview

Highlights in the Development of Dramatic Character

*L*a *Forza del Destino* is a radical reconception of the Spanish play, *Don Alvaro, o la Fuerza del Sino* by Angel de Saavedra, Duke of Rivas. While Verdi and his librettist retain many of the sprawling play's theatrical trappings, they abandon its meticulous plotting and dramatically alter the characterization of Leonora.

To emphasize Leonora's inner torment in Act I, Verdi adds the monologue "*Me pellegrina ed orfana*" (Wanderer and orphan), as well as her plea to Alvaro to delay their elopement. Further, Verdi brings down the curtain with a symbolically weighted appeal by Leonora for pity from Heaven.

While in Saavedra's play Doña Leonor does not actually appear in the Inn of Hornechuelos, Verdi brings her on-stage in Act II.i. Alienated from those around her and pursued by her vengeful brother (a consolidation of the two brothers found in Saavedra's play), Leonora prays in vain for peace.

In Act II.ii, Leonora pleads with Padre Guardiano to be permitted to take refuge in a hermit's cave. Saavedra makes clear that Doña Leonor chooses the cave over a convent due to her fear of being identified and shamed, but Verdi's heroine claims the voice of Heaven spoke to her.

The momentary peace that Leonora finds among the holy brotherhood inside the church of the Madonna degli Angeli in Act II.iii is also new to the opera; the entire scene is absent from Saavedra's play.

Finally, in Act IV Verdi concludes this new emphasis on the search for peace with the addition of Leonora's prayer "*Pace, pace, mio Dio*" (Peace, peace, my Lord) and the celestial *terzetto finale,* which replaces the original suicide of Don Alvaro in Saavedra's play.

La Forza del Destino Plot Synopsis

Act I

The scene opens at the home of the Marquis di Calatrava in Seville. The marquis bids an affectionate goodnight to his daughter, Leonora, and departs, unaware that she has resolved to elope that very evening with her beloved Don Alvaro. The marquis opposes any union between the two because of Alvaro's Incan ancestry.

Alvaro arrives filled with passionate anticipation. Torn between her affections for father and lover, Leonora begs Alvaro to delay their departure one more day. Taken aback, Alvaro offers to free Leonora from her pledges to him, but she insists nothing will ever divide them.

At that moment, the marquis returns with his men and denounces Alvaro as a vile seducer. Alvaro proclaims the innocence and purity of his love for Leonora and surrenders to her father. He throws down his pistol, which accidentally discharges, mortally wounding the marquis, who curses his daughter with his dying breath.

Act II

Scene 1: Inn at the Village of Hornachuelos

The gypsy Preziosilla entertains a crowd at the inn with fortune-telling and songs of the glory of war. Leonora has been mysteriously parted from Alvaro in the confusion following the marquis' death; now, some months later, she arrives at the inn, alone and disguised in male attire. To her horror, she recognizes her brother Carlo, incognito as a student. He has come to avenge his father's death by killing his sister and Alvaro. The chanting of a passing group of pilgrims is heard, and everyone joins in the prayer. Then Leonora slips into her room, while her brother tells the rest of the crowd about his "friend's" ongoing search for the guilty lovers.

Scene 2: Church of the Madonna degli Angeli outside Hornechuelos

Having fled from the inn unnoticed by Carlo, Leonora arrives at the monastery of Hornachuelos and asks Fra Melitone to speak with the Father Superior, Padre Guardiano. Revealing her true identity to Guardiano, she begs to be allowed to live out her life as a solitary hermit in a nearby mountain cave. Guardiano agrees.

Scene 3: Inside the Church of the Madonna degli Angeli

Guardiano has the monks assemble to pray for this new penitent and for the protection of her secret identity through the threat of divine malediction. Leonora joins the monks' prayer to the Madonna, then departs for her lonely retreat as Guardiano blesses her.

Act III

Scene 1: Wood near Velletri, Italy

Several years have passed, and Alvaro laments the misery of his life without Leonora, whom he believes to be dead. Hearing the sound of a scuffle in the distance, he rushes off and saves the life of Carlo, who is now in disguise as a soldier. Not knowing each other's true identity, the two swear eternal friendship.

Scene 2: Military Camp near Velletri

The Spanish and Italian forces win the battle against the Germans, but Alvaro is wounded. Lest he die on the operating table, Alvaro makes Carlo swear to destroy, unopened, a packet of letters. Carlo's suspicions are aroused by his friend's violent reaction to the name of Calatrava, and he determines to examine the packet. Recalled by his sense of honor, however, Carlo leaves the packet unopened and looks instead through Alvaro's other possessions. He finds a portrait of Leonora and, realizing his friend's identity, vows revenge.

Scene 3: Still near Velletri

After Alvaro has recovered, Carlo confronts and insults him, provoking a duel. They are interrupted, however, by a passing patrol. The scene fills with soldiers, conscripts, and camp followers, all haggling over their looted goods or lamenting their fate. Preziosilla leads a song in celebration of the madness of war, and the crowd begins a wild dance. At this moment, Fra Melitone arrives from Spain to minister to the troops. Appalled by the depravity of the camp, he denounces the revellers. Preziosilla finally restores order and concludes with another rousing song.

Act IV

Scene 1: Courtyard in the Monastery of the Madonna degli Angeli
Several more years have passed. Melitone is feeding beggars who flock to the monastery, but he soon loses patience with their importuning and their praise of brother Raffaele. Carlo arrives, still in pursuit of revenge. He has discovered that the mysterious Raffaele is, in fact, Alvaro. Confronting Leonora's lover once more, Carlo taunts and insults him for his "base" Incan ancestry until Alvaro accepts a duel.

Scene 2: Outside a Hermit's Cave in the Mountains
Leonora emerges from the cave lamenting her inability to find peace after all these years. Hearing the sound of someone approaching, she invokes the monks' earlier malediction and retreats to the cave. The sound of swordplay is heard, and then Alvaro enters. He has mortally wounded Carlo and calls for the unknown hermit in the cave to come hear the dying man's confession.

Leonora rings the bell to summon Padre Guardiano before emerging to warn the intruder to leave this holy ground. The long-parted lovers recognize each other, but any reunion is forestalled as Alvaro tells Leonora of her brother. Leonora rushes off to Carlo's side, but, unforgiving to the end, he stabs her.

Alvaro voices an anguished imprecation, but Padre Guardiano and Leonora urge him to weep and pray for forgiveness. At last, Alvaro yields and feels the peace of absolution. Leonora bids him a tender farewell, promising to wait for him in heaven, and, as she expires, Guardiano declares that she is ascended to God.

*A*IDA S*OURCE* P*REVIEW*

Highlights in the Development of Dramatic Character

Rather than being adapted from an established source play, *Aida* was developed in ongoing consultation with the composer from an original scenario by Mariette. Not surprisingly, therefore, *Aida* evidences less large-scale dramatic revision than many of Verdi's other operas. Nonetheless, a number of notable changes are to be found in the characterization of Aida, particularly during the Nile Scene in the third act of the opera.

By adding the *romanza* "*Oh patria mia*," (Oh my homeland) to his original draft of the score, Verdi creates a far more complex dramatic exploration of Aida's internal conflicts than is found in Mariette's scenario: Aida's love for her country is now foregrounded for the first time, completing the nexus of her romantic, filial, or patriotic emotional bonds.

Later, when Amonasro arrives and demands that Aida trick her beloved Radamès into revealing the secret plans for Egyptian troop movement, Mariette's heroine evinces no hesitation in acceding to his wishes. Verdi's Aida, in contrast, recoils in horror and submits only after a full-scale psychological assault by her father.

Mariette's Aida believes she still has a future with Radamès away from Egypt and so makes no effort to obscure her intentions in getting him to betray his country. In the opera, by contrast, Aida knows that fulfilling her father's wishes means the end of her hope for love with Radamès. When the Egyptian arrives, therefore, Verdi's Aida goes through the carefully scripted motions of a love scene, using deception to trick Radamès into revealing his military secret.

Aida Plot Synposis

Act I

Scene 1: Royal Palace in Memphis

The High Priest Ramfis tells Radamès, a young Egyptian captain, that Ethiopian troops are threatening Thebes and that the goddess Isis has named a new commander for the Egyptian armies. When Ramfis goes to announce the warrior's name to the king, Radamès dreams of being chosen. He has fallen in love with Aida, an Ethiopian captive in the Egyptian court, and, as a glorious commander, he could effect her release from slavery.

The Princess Amneris, daughter of the Egyptian king, sees Radamès in his reverie and probes his thoughts, trying to discover whether her love for him is returned. Amneris fears a rival for the young captain's affections, and the tender glance which Radamès bestows upon Aida when she first appears does nothing to alleviate the Egyptian princess' suspicions. Amneris greets Aida with calculated gentleness, asking why she is unhappy. Aida insists that her distress is for her suffering country, but Amneris is not satisfied. While the princess turns aside to voice her suspicions, Radamès expresses his fear that Amneris might discover the truth, and Aida confesses that her tears are really the result of ill-fated love.

The king and his court enter to receive news of the Ethiopian invaders and their warrior-king, Amonasro. At his name, Aida murmurs to herself, "My father!" The Egyptians prepare for war, naming Radamès commander of the armies and calling for him to return victorious. Aida herself joins in the cry. Yet, once the court has departed, she is consumed by guilt and self-recriminations. Victory for Radamès means death or enslavement for her father, her family, and her people; but victory for Ethiopia means death for her lover. Unable to find a resolution to this terrible dilemma, Aida prays for peace in death.

Scene 2: Inside the Temple of Vulcan

The priests anoint Radamès as supreme commander of the army and ask the favor of the gods in bringing victory to Egypt.

Act II

Scene 1: Amneris' Apartments in the Royal Palace at Thebes

While being entertained by the dancing of her Moorish slaves, Amneris prepares for the return of Radamès and the victorious Egyptian army. When Aida appears, however, Amneris dismisses her entourage. Feigning friendship and concern, Amneris lies, telling Aida that Radamès has been killed in battle. Aida is overwhelmed with grief, and Amneris' suspicions are confirmed. Announcing that Radamès is alive, the Egyptian princess threatens to destroy Aida. Swallowing her own royal pride, Aida humbles herself and pleads for mercy, but Amneris is relentless in her animosity. The princess orders her slave to follow her to the gates of the city where she will welcome the returning hero, and Aida once more prays for peace in death.

Scene 2: Outside the Gates of Thebes

The Egyptian court and populace view the triumphal procession of the victorious army and the presentation of the spoils of war. The king hails Radamès and promises to grant him any wish. First, the prisoners are brought in, and Aida involuntarily voices a cry of recognition upon seeing her father. Amonasro, however, quickly whispers to his daughter that his true rank must not be betrayed; he craftily tells the court that the Ethiopian king has been killed in battle and pleads for the release of the captives. Aida and the rest of the prisoners join with him, but Ramfis and the priests demand that these dangerous captives be put to death. When Radamès intervenes, the king agrees to free all the prisoners except for Aida and Amonasro, who remain as hostages. The king then announces that Radamès will marry Amneris and one day rule Egypt with her. Aida and her lover are horrified, but Amneris exults as the crowd rejoices.

Act III

It is night near the banks of the Nile, and, in the moonlight, the Temple of Isis can be seen amidst the palm trees. A boat arrives carrying Amneris, who has come with Ramfis to pray through the night in preparation for her forthcoming wedding. They enter the temple, and Aida appears. She is to meet Radamès and fears he may be coming for a final farewell. Her mind turning to the peace she might find in death beneath the dark waters of the Nile, Aida then thinks of the beautiful homeland she would never see again.

Amonasro appears. He knows Aida's secret feelings for Radamès and promises that throne, homeland, and love can all be hers. If Aida can coax from her lover the route the Egyptian army will travel, Amonasro and his men can ambush and destroy the enemy. Aida refuses with horror at the thought of such a betrayal; her father curses her, invoking the spectral image of her dying mother and slaughtered people. Aida capitulates. She pleads to be returned to her father's love and promises to extract the information from Radamès despite the terrible personal cost of her actions.

Radamès arrives, promising that after another victory he will be able to gain the king's blessing for a marriage with Aida. Aida, however, scorns his plan and questions the sincerity of his love until Radamès finally agrees to flee with her to Ethiopia. As they prepare to depart, she asks what road they should take to avoid the Egyptian army, and Radamès reveals that his troops will pass through the Nàpata gorge. Amonasro triumphantly steps from his hiding place and reveals his true identity to the stunned Egyptian. The Ethiopian king tries to persuade Radamès to flee with them, but the young man is overcome with remorse at his unintentional act of treachery. Amneris and Ramfis, having heard the commotion, come out of the temple, and Amonasro lifts his dagger to kill the princess. Radamès blocks his way, however, and then surrenders to Ramfis while Amonasro drags Aida away.

Act IV

Scene 1: Outside the Palace's Subterranean Judgment Chamber

Amneris desperately tries to save Radamès' life, offering to intervene on his behalf with the king if he will foreswear his love for Aida. Learning that Aida escaped when her father was killed and that she is still alive, Radamès refuses Amneris' offer. The spurned princess cries that she will be avenged. No sooner has Radamès been taken into the Judgment Chamber, however, than Amneris repents her jealous rage and prays that Radamès be spared. Alone outside the chamber, she hears Radamès refuse to defend himself against the charges of treason. He is sentenced to death, and Amneris curses the priests before collapsing in despair.

Scene 2: Inside the Temple of Vulcan; a Crypt Visible Below

Sealed in a tomb beneath the floor of the Temple of Vulcan, Radamès is lamenting that he will never see Aida again when his lover appears from the shadows. Foreseeing his doom, she hid herself in the crypt to die with him. Radamès tries in vain to move the stone which seals the entrance, but Aida is filled with joy. Delirious, she envisions the angel of death who will lead them to the ecstasy of immortal love. Bidding farewell to worldly suffering and torment, the lovers sink into each other's arms, while, in the temple above, Amneris prays for peace.

La Bohème Source Preview

Highlights in the Development of Dramatic Character

While drawing upon various episodes in Murger's *Scènes de la Vie de Bohème*, Puccini and his librettists freely adapt the original story and interpolate new material to create a truly unique stage work.

Murger's serialized vignettes of bohemian artistic life depict a period of youthful indiscretion, sexual indulgence, and defiance of establishment authority, after which the characters enter into the ranks of middle-class respectability.

Completely transforming the novel, Puccini jettisons virtually all the specific details of the source story and conflates the original character of Mimì with Murger's minor figure Francine, a gentle, consumptive young woman who devotes the final months of her brief life to a blissful interlude of love.

Murger's Mimì laughs at the very idea of wasting her time on a man interested only in platonic love. Her features reveal a brutal lack of sensibility; deceitful and mercenary, she takes on the local prostitutes as her friends and role models. Quickly falling out of love with Rodolphe, she makes his life miserable, except during brief moments of reconciliation. This wantonness is suppressed in the opera, however, and the first two acts establish a new, idealized heroine.

These changes, in turn, necessitate development of third and fourth acts in the opera that have no real parallel in Murger's novel. Mimì's affair with a viscount, which is addressed at some length in the novel, is merely alluded to by Puccini. Even more significantly, Mimì's death is transformed from a ghastly farce into a moving affirmation of love.

La Bohème Plot Synopsis

Act I

It is Christmas Eve in the freezing Paris garret shared by the poet Rodolfo, the painter Marcello, and their friends. Without money for firewood, the two bohemians begin throwing one of the poet's manuscripts into the stove. The philosopher Colline next arrives, having failed to pawn a bundle of books; together, they toss the rest of Rodolfo's manuscript into the fire. The heat is soon gone, but just at that moment the musician Schaunard enters, flush with money from an engagement playing for a wealthy Englishman. He is followed by two messenger boys bearing food, drink, and firewood. The four friends celebrate and prepare to go out into the Latin Quarter for Christmas Eve dinner.

Before they can depart, however, the landlord Benoît pounds on the door, demanding his rent. The bohemians bring him inside and ply him with wine until he indiscreetly begins to boast of his amorous adventures. Feigning outrage that a married man would behave in such a fashion, the friends summarily expel Benoît from the room—without his rent money.

While the others leave, Rodolfo remains behind for a few moments to finish an article he is writing. There is a soft knock at the door, and Rodolfo discovers Mimì in the hallway. On the way to her apartment, the young woman's candle has blown out, and she asks her neighbor to relight it for her. Overcome by the exertion of climbing the stairs, she is seized with a consumptive coughing spell and faints. Rodolfo lifts her to a chair. As she revives, he notes how beautiful she is, but Mimì quickly relights her candle and departs. A moment later she returns, however, realizing she has forgotten her key, which was dropped when she fainted. The draft extinguishes both of their candles in quick succession, leaving them to search for her key in the twilight.

Their hands meet, and Rodolfo takes the opportunity to tell her of his life as a poet, of his hopes and dreams. Mimì shyly reciprocates, speaking of her solitary life embroidering flowers and the enchantment she finds in the poetry of springtime. At last, Rodolfo declares his passion, and Mimì abandons herself to the call of love. As Rodolfo's friends cry for him to join them below, Mimì offers to accompany him to the Christmas Eve festivities, and the two lovers slowly depart.

Act II

The streets of the Latin Quarter are teeming with merrymakers, vendors, children, and students. While Rodolfo buys a small pink bonnet for Mimì, his friends enter the Cafè Momus. Finding it packed to overflowing, they simply bring a table outside. Rodolfo joins them and introduces Mimì. Soon Marcello's beloved, the beautiful and flighty Musetta, arrives on the arm of pompous old Alcindoro. Using every trick in her considerable repertoire, Musetta tries to make Marcello jealous. Having succeeded, she quickly dispatches Alcindoro, pretending that her shoe is pinching and must be immediately replaced. With the old man out of the way, Marcello and Musetta are reunited, and the bohemians make their merry escape, leaving the bill for Alcindoro when he returns.

Act III

On a snowy February morning, Mimì arrives at an inn on the outskirts of Paris where Marcello and Musetta are staying. She asks a maidservant to call Marcello, and the painter soon joins her outside. He has spent the past month painting figures on the facade of the inn, while Musetta has been teaching singing to the visitors. Mimì begs his help, explaining that Rodolfo loves her but is consumed with jealousy. He left her the night before, declaring all was over between them. Rodolfo has been sleeping inside the inn, and, hearing him awake, Marcello promises to help. He urges Mimì to return home, but she hides behind a plane tree and overhears the ensuing conversation between Rodolfo and Marcello.

The painter chides Rodolfo until he at last confesses that his tantrums and rages conceal feelings of guilt; Mimì is dying of consumption, and he is too poor to save her. Stunned, Mimì is overcome with sobs and coughing. Rodolfo and Marcello rush to her aid. Marcello quickly returns to the inn, however, where Musetta can be heard laughing flirtatiously with an unknown stranger. Mimì bids farewell to Rodolfo, telling him that, if he wants, he may keep the bonnet he bought her on Christmas Eve as a remembrance of their love. Rodolfo laments the end of an idyllic relationship, but Mimì gently reminds him of his own jealousy. At last, while Marcello and Musetta emerge from the inn engaged in one of their habitual spats, Rodolfo and Mimì agree to remain together until the spring.

Act IV

Some months have passed. Marcello and Rodolfo are discovered once more in their garret, trying to work but preoccupied with thoughts of their lost loves. Schaunard and Colline arrive with dinner, and some boisterous horseplay commences. At this moment, Musetta enters in alarm. She has found Mimì, alone and dying, wandering in the street. Wanting to die with Rodolfo, Mimì left the viscount who had become her protector. Musetta has brought her back to the garret, but Mimì is too weak to climb the last stairs. The friends quickly bring her into the apartment and lay her gently on a cot. Rodolfo is left alone with Mimì as the others hasten off to buy medicine and summon a doctor, paying for these necessities with Musetta's earrings and Colline's beloved overcoat.

Mimì declares that even now Rodolfo remains the love of her life. The two reminisce about their first meeting and the happy moments they shared, then Mimì sinks back, exhausted. The others return, and Musetta places a warm fur muff on Mimì's freezing hands, saying it is a gift from Rodolfo. While Rodolfo moves to drape the garret window, Mimì gently passes away. As the other bohemians try to contain their sorrow, Rodolfo cries out Mimì's name and collapses beside her lifeless body.

─────────────────── ≈ ───────────────────

Tosca Source Preview

Highlights in the Development of Dramatic Character

In Sardou's melodrama *La Tosca*, plot machinations are paramount, while flamboyant splashes of historical color and spectacle camouflage an essential reliance on static character types. Sardou's heroine is little more than a construct of the "Diva." She manifests no personal growth or developing understanding during the play, whereas Puccini's Tosca undergoes a stunning metamorphosis.

Conflating Sardou's first and second acts, Puccini and his librettists juxtapose Tosca's relationships with her beloved Cavaradossi and her nemesis Scarpia; Sardou's spoof of the tempestuous diva is replaced by Tosca's disillusionment upon learning from Scarpia of Cavaradossi's apparent betrayal.

Sardou's heroine eventually becomes an active player in Cavaradossi's political intrigues; arriving at her lover's villa, she compels a full explanation from him and then joins in the scheme. Conflating Sardou's third and fourth acts into Act II of the opera, Puccini shows nothing of Tosca's encounter at the villa. Her questioning by Scarpia thus seems not the pursuit of justice, but a chilling psychological rape. Further, Puccini adds Tosca's prayer *"Vissi d'arte"* (I lived for art), a critical moment in the journey of self-knowledge which leads to Scarpia's death.

In Act III, Puccini again departs from Sardou's play, creating a narrative for Tosca which reveals the transformation she has undergone and implicitly challenges Cavaradossi to accept and love her for the woman she truly is. Tosca's metamorphosis is complete, and, hence, a heroic tone not found in Sardou's play infuses her final cry, *"O Scarpia, avanti a Dio!"* (O Scarpia, before God!)

─────────────────── ≈ ───────────────────

Tosca Plot Synopsis

Act I

Angelotti, a consul in the former Roman Republic and now an escaped political prisoner, cautiously enters the Church of Sant'Andrea della Valle, where he takes refuge in the private chapel of his sister, the Marchesa Attavanti, who had earlier secreted a bundle of clothes and the chapel key for him. No sooner is he hidden than the Sacristan enters, expressing great interest in the painter Cavaradossi's untouched lunch hamper. Cavaradossi himself then arrives to continue work on his painting of the Mary Magdalene.

The Sacristan comments on the similarity between the features of the painting and those of the mysterious blonde lady who has prayed so piously in the church for the past several days. Cavaradossi acknowledges the inspiration of this beautiful woman but declares that his heart belongs only to the dark-haired opera star Floria Tosca. When the Sacristan wanders off, Angelotti emerges from the chapel. Cavaradossi immediately recognizes him and offers his help, but at that moment Tosca's voice is heard outside. Cavaradossi quickly gives his lunch hamper to the exhausted fugitive, hiding him once more in the chapel until he can send Tosca on her way.

Cavaradossi tries to pacify Tosca as quickly as possible to hasten her departure, while she prolongs her visit with happy thoughts of their coming night together and jealous outbursts aimed at the painter's imaginary lovers and the Marchesa Attavanti, whom she recognizes as the model for the Mary Magdalene. Assuaged at last, Tosca departs. A cannon shot announces that Angelotti's escape has been discovered. Cavaradossi and Angelotti quickly leave for the painter's villa outside Rome.

The Sacristan and boy choristers enter in great excitement, celebrating the defeat of Napoleon by the royalist forces, but their festivities are interrupted by the arrival of Baron Scarpia, chief of the secret police. Scarpia soon finds the Attavanti chapel gates unlocked and Cavaradossi's lunch hamper empty. He also discovers a fan with the Attavanti crest and determines to use it to win Tosca for himself. When Tosca returns to the church to tell Cavaradossi that the state festivities will keep her from meeting him that evening, Scarpia easily convinces her that Cavaradossi has left for a tryst with the Marchesa Attavanti.

Grief-stricken, Tosca vows vengeance, and Scarpia orders his men to follow her to Cavaradossi. As the crowd assembles for the *Te Deum*, Scarpia cries that soon Tosca will be his.

Act II

In his apartments at the Farnese Palace, Scarpia has dinner and awaits news from his spies. Having sent a note to summon Tosca, he eagerly anticipates her submission to his lust. Cavaradossi is brought in under arrest, but Scarpia's men have been unable to find Angelotti at the villa. When Tosca arrives, Scarpia questions her, while the defiant Cavaradossi is sent to the torture chamber. Tosca at first denies any knowledge of Angelotti, but the sound of her lover's screams compels her to reveal that the prisoner is hiding in a well in the villa gardens.

Cavaradossi is brought back into the room. Tosca assures him that she has said nothing, but Scarpia mockingly orders his men to search the well in the garden. Cavaradossi curses Tosca and, as word arrives that the royalist army has been defeated by Napoleon, taunts Scarpia with the cry that liberty is at hand. He is dragged away, and Scarpia informs Tosca that the only way to save Cavaradossi's life is to surrender to his own desires. Tosca pleads and prays in vain. Finally, she agrees. Scarpia explains that a mock execution will be performed and gives orders to his henchman in Tosca's presence. He then writes a safe-conduct pass for Tosca and Cavaradossi. As he rushes to embrace his conquest, however, Tosca stabs him with a knife from his dinner table. Placing a crucifix and candles around his body, Tosca takes the safe-conduct and leaves the darkened room.

Act III

Atop the Castel Sant'Angelo, Cavaradossi laments the loss of his beloved Tosca. When she arrives, telling of Scarpia's murder and the mock execution, they joyfully look forward to a future of love. The execution is performed, but Tosca soon discovers that Scarpia has betrayed her: Cavaradossi is dead. As she sobs over his body, Scarpia's men are heard approaching to arrest her for the baron's murder. Rushing to the ramparts of the castle, Tosca cries, "O Scarpia, before God!" and flings herself from the parapet.

Madama Butterfly Preview

Highlights in the Development of Dramatic Character

Inspired in large part by Pierre Loti's immensely popular novel *Madame Chrysanthème*, the source story *Madame Butterfly* was first published as a novella by John Luther Long and then dramatized by David Belasco. The stage version jettisons much of the childish frivolity in the novella and compresses the tale to accelerate the inevitable catastrophe. Today, however, both of these versions are often more offensive than captivating, due to their pervasive Eurocentrism and tone of patriarchal condescension. In contrast, Puccini and his librettists transform the character of Butterfly into a true tragic heroine.

The first act of the opera has no parallel in Belasco's play, but loosely traces its origins to Long's novella. The call of love which motivates Puccini's Butterfly is entirely missing from the source story, though, as is the dramatic manner in which Butterfly's family disowns her for betraying their religion.

Belasco's play provides the structure for the second and third acts of the opera, although Puccini includes a number of significant variations. Butterfly's aria "*Un bel dì*" (One beautiful day) thus replaces the improvisatory antics found in Belasco's scene. Butterfly's constant interruptions of Sharpless, as he tries to read Pinkerton's letter to her, are not to be found in the play; and Butterfly's impassioned monologue, declaring that death would be better than a return to the geisha life, is a reworking of the mock-tragic scene in Long's novella. Finally, Puccini adds Butterfly's wrenching farewell to her child in the last moments of the opera.

Madama Butterfly Plot Synopsis

Act I

The marriage broker Goro is showing Lieutenant Benjamin Franklin Pinkerton, of the United States Navy, the amenities of a charming hilltop house overlooking Nagasaki harbor. When the American consul, Sharpless, arrives, Pinkerton explains with delight that he has bought the house for nine hundred and ninety-nine years, with the option to cancel every month! He also announces that he is about to marry an enchanting little Japanese girl, Madama Butterfly, though he also plans to marry a real American wife later. Sharpless warns the lieutenant not to trifle with so great a love as Butterfly's, but his admonitions go cavalierly unheeded.

Butterfly's voice is heard in the distance, and soon she appears on the hilltop, surrounded by her friends. At her command, they all bow to Pinkerton. Butterfly exchanges the customary compliments with her fiance and readily answers Sharpless' questions about her background: her family has fallen on hard times, and the women have turned to making their livelihood as geishas; her mother is an honorable woman, but poor; her father is dead; she, herself, is only fifteen years old.

As the officials arrive, the relatives gossip about Pinkerton and his bride-to-be, but Butterfly silences them. Pinkerton then leads her away toward the little house, and Butterfly shows him the few personal possessions she has brought. Her manner is light and happy until Pinkerton asks about the hara-kiri sword. Butterfly refuses to show it to him with so many people around; as she takes it into the house, Goro explains that Butterfly's father committed suicide at the order of the emperor. Returning, Butterfly reveals she has secretly gone to the Christian mission—with her new life, she will also embrace Pinkerton's religion, though it means estrangement from her own people.

The wedding service is performed, and Pinkerton leads the guests in a toast. Suddenly, the enraged cries of Butterfly's uncle, a Buddhist priest, are heard. Bursting on the scene, the bonze denounces Butterfly for abandoning her religion; horrified by her renunciation of them, Butterfly's people disown her. Pinkerton chases them away and comforts his new bride. She goes inside the house to change for their wedding night; when she returns, Butterfly rapturously declares her love for Pinkerton, and he leads her toward the nuptial bed.

Act II

Three years have passed since Pinkerton left Japan, promising to
return to Butterfly when the robins made their nests again. He has not
returned, and Butterfly's maid, Suzuki, prays to the gods of Japan to
relieve her mistress' sorrow. For her part, Butterfly insists that her husband will return, and she imagines with Suzuki the scene when, one
beautiful day, his ship will be spotted on the horizon.

Sharpless arrives with a letter from Pinkerton, but Butterfly's continuous interruptions—extending various hospitalities and then asking
Sharpless about the nesting habits of robins in America—prevent the
consul from reading the contents to her. Goro then arrives with a wealthy
Japanese, Prince Yamadori, eager to make Butterfly his next temporary
bride. With dignity, Butterfly spurns his advances, insisting that she is
already married to Pinkerton and that in America, unlike Japan, a
husband cannot divorce his wife simply by abandoning her. Sharpless
confides to Yamadori that Pinkerton is coming to Nagasaki but is not
returning to Butterfly.

After Yamadori departs, Sharpless reads Pinkerton's letter to
Butterfly. Again, she interrupts him at every phrase, kissing the letter,
commenting, expressing her joy, reminding him of her own faithful
love. In his letter, Pinkerton asks Sharpless to prepare Butterfly for the
blow (that he is returning but has remarried). Butterfly, however, leaps
to the misguided conclusion that Pinkerton is coming back to her. When
Sharpless finally asks what she would do if Pinkerton were never to
come back, Butterfly replies, stricken, that she could either return to the
life of a geisha or else, better, die.

When Sharpless advises her to accept Yamadori's proposal, Butterfly
hastily calls for Suzuki to bring the consul's shoes so that he may depart
at once. Then, with a desperate cry, she rushes into another room, returning with the son she has borne Pinkerton. She implores the consul to tell
her husband of the child, believing that, once he knows of his son,
Pinkerton will return from the far ends of the earth; on that day, the
child's name will be changed from Sorrow to Joy. Sharpless sadly agrees
to carry the message and then departs.

A commotion breaks out as Suzuki drags in Goro. The broker has
been telling people in the town that in America children like Butterfly's
son are outcast and accursed. In a fury, Butterfly threatens to kill Goro
with her father's hara-kiri sword, and the broker flees in terror. Taking

her child in her arms, Butterfly promises that soon his father will return and carry them away to America.

A cannon sounds in the harbor: Pinkerton's ship has arrived. Butterfly and Suzuki joyfully decorate the entire house with flowers and dress the faithful wife in her wedding garments. Then Butterfly, her son, and Suzuki take up their positions at the shoji, looking down the hillside for Pinkerton to appear.

Act III

The entire night passes, and in the morning there is still no sign of Pinkerton. Singing a sad lullaby, Butterfly carries her child into another room.

Sharpless, Pinkerton, and the lieutenant's new American wife, Kate, then arrive. They have come to take Pinkerton's son away with them. Speaking quietly to Suzuki, Sharpless implores her to break the news to Butterfly—for the good of the child. Tearfully, Suzuki agrees. In the meantime, Pinkerton suddenly becomes aware of Butterfly's devotion through the years and is consumed by remorse. He receives no sympathy from Sharpless, however, who recalls that he warned Pinkerton not to trifle with such a loving heart. At last, rather than face his abandoned bride, Pinkerton flees.

Butterfly rushes into the room, sensing that Pinkerton has returned. Failing to find him anywhere, Butterfly sees Kate out in the garden and quickly realizes that she is Pinkerton's new wife. Kate asks if she will give up the child, and Butterfly sadly agrees. She blesses Kate and promises that Pinkerton can take his son if he returns in half an hour.

Butterfly orders Suzuki to go play with the boy, and she then prepares for suicide. She lifts her father's sword to her throat, but, just at that moment, Suzuki pushes the child into the room. Butterfly runs to embrace him. Bidding him an agonized final farewell, she blindfolds her son and sets him down to play with a doll and a small American flag. Going behind a screen, Butterfly then stabs herself. Crawling back to her little boy, she embraces him once more, before collapsing by his side.

Pinkerton's voice is heard calling Butterfly from offstage. The lieutenant and Sharpless rush into the room as Butterfly weakly points toward the child and dies. Pinkerton falls to his knees, while Sharpless picks up the boy and kisses him, sobbing.

TURANDOT SOURCE PREVIEW

Highlights in the Development of Dramatic Character

Suggested by the Persian tales which had gained great popularity in Europe, Gozzi's *commedia dell'arte* fable *Turandot, Fiaba Chinese Teatrale Tragicomica* is a comic parody of feminism. To keep herself from male domination, Turandot poses three riddles to all would-be suitors and sends those who cannot answer to the executioner. This antipathy toward men is only a comic aberration, however; thus, by the end of the play, the feminist princess is changed through the power of love.

The theme of triumphant love drew Puccini to Gozzi's play, but the composer's own artistic vision required a radical reworking of the story. Only the broadest outlines of the play remain, and the character of Turandot herself is completely reimagined.

Thus, in Act I, the new character of Liù is introduced to embody the ennobling power of love, which Turandot must come to recognize. The addition of Turandot's second act aria "*In questa Reggia*" (In this palace) changes the motivation for the princess' deadly games from the frivolous feminist pride of Gozzi's heroine to a tormented obsession with the terrible fate of Turandot's ancestor, the Princess Lo-u-Ling. This psychological change, in turn, lays the groundwork for Turandot's transfiguration in Act III, when the death of Liù compels her to recognize the ultimate futility of vengeance and embrace the regenerative power of love.

Turandot Plot Synopsis

Act I

In the Imperial City of Peking, during legendary times, a blood-thirsty mob has assembled for the execution of the Prince of Persia, the latest ill-fated man to try to win the hand of the beautiful Princess Turandot. She has sworn to marry only if her suitor can successfully answer three riddles she poses; if he fails, the sentence is death.

While the crowd mills about, Timur, the exiled Tartar king, and his faithful slave Liù arrive in the city. Caught in the melee, Timur falls to the ground. Liù's calls for aid go unheeded until a young man steps forward to help. It is Timur's son Calaf (the Unknown Prince), who has been wandering incognito. With father and son reunited, Liù explains that she has been Timur's tireless protector and companion because once in the king's palace Calaf had smiled upon her.

The moon rises, and the people grow restless waiting for the executioner. Moved to pity by the sight of the Prince of Persia, they appeal to Turandot for mercy. The princess appears in a shaft of moonlight on the imperial balcony. Silent and aloof, she motions for the execution to proceed.

Entranced by her beauty, Calaf determines to accept the challenge of the riddles. Despite the entreaties of Liù and Timur, as well as the frantic intervention of the comic court officials Ping, Pang, and Pong, Calaf strikes the ceremonial gong with the cry, "Turandot!"

Act II

Scene 1: Royal Pavilion
Ping, Pang, and Pong lament the bloodshed and cruelty that Turandot has brought to China and dream of the day when she will be transformed by love.

Scene 2: Before the Vast Staircase of the Imperial Palace
The people of Peking assemble for the contest. The aged Emperor Altoum tries to dissuade the Unknown Prince from rushing to certain death, but Calaf holds firm. Heralded by the voices of children, Turandot herself appears and takes her place before the emperor.

She recounts the story of her ancestor, Princess Lo-u-Ling, whose abduction, rape, and murder by a foreign prince in ancient times has led to Turandot's own quest for vengeance. She warns Calaf not to tempt fate, but he is adamant.

Turandot poses the three riddles, and Calaf answers each one correctly. Turandot then appeals to the emperor to set aside the young prince's victory, but Altoum refuses. Turandot confronts Calaf, demanding to know whether he will take her even by force, but he replies that he wants her love. As proof of his feelings, he offers to forfeit his own life if she can discover his true identity by the following morning.

Act III

Scene 1: The Gardens of the Imperial Palace

By Turandot's command, all Peking seeks to discover the Unknown Prince's name this night. Ping, Pang, and Pong alternately attempt to threaten and bribe Calaf into fleeing the city. Calaf refuses.

The mob drags Timur and Liù forward and calls for Turandot. The princess orders the captives tortured. Liù declares that she alone knows the Unknown Prince's identity; then she kills herself, carrying the secret to her grave in order to ensure the triumph of Calaf's love.

Overwhelmed with grief, Timur laments beside the lifeless Liù, and the crowd is struck with fear and remorse. Liù's body is borne from the scene, and Calaf confronts Turandot. He tears the ceremonial veil from her face and passionately kisses her.

At last, Turandot admits her love for Calaf but weeps for the loss of her former glory. Calaf promises her that her glory is just beginning through the power of love. As final proof of his own feelings, he places his life in Turandot's hands, revealing his name to her.

Scene 2: Before the Vast Staircase of the Imperial Palace

As dawn breaks, Turandot announces to the emperor and the people of Peking that she has discovered the stranger's name: it is Love. Turandot and Calaf passionately embrace, and the crowd joyfully voices a hymn of praise to the glory of love.

NOTES

Introduction

1. See, for example, Robert Donington, *Opera and Its Symbols* (New Haven, Conn.: Yale University Press, 1991); Catherine Clément, *Opera, or the Undoing of Women*, trans. Betsy Wing (Minneapolis: University of Minnesota Press, 1988); or Herbert Lindenberger, *Opera: The Extravagant Art* (Ithaca, N.Y.: Cornell University Press, 1984).

2. A number of notable exceptions are found, particularly in the extensive body of scholarly writing devoted to the works of Giuseppe Verdi. Among the contemporary scholars evidencing a more interdisciplinary perspective are Julian Budden, *The Operas of Verdi* (New York: Oxford University Press, 1973); Massimo Mila, *L'Arte di Verdi* (Turin: Giulio Einaudi Editore, 1980); David R. B. Kimbell, *Verdi in the Age of Italian Romanticism* (London: Cambridge University Press, 1981); and Gary Schmidgall, *Shakespeare and Opera* (New York: Oxford University Press, 1990).

3. Beginning in the eighteenth century, when troupes of public fair performers began to congregate in the Boulevard du Temple, Parisian theaters catering to the popular taste have been dubbed "Boulevard" theaters and the authors writing for them "Boulevard" playwrights. René Charles Guilbert de Pixérécourt was the undisputed king of melodrama in the period, writing works such as *Coelina, ou l'Enfant de Mystère* (1800).

4. Peter Conrad emphasizes opera's focus on the inner life of characters, but he couches this understanding in the rather surprising assertion that such psychological development ties opera more closely to the novel than to the dramatic stage. See his *Romantic Opera and Literary Form* (Berkeley: University of California Press, 1977).

5. See Victor Hugo, Préface, *Cromwell*, in *Théâtre Complet de Victor Hugo*, ed. J.-J. Thierry and Josette Mélèze (Monaco: Éditions Gallimard, 1963), 1: 409-54.

6. Victor Hugo, Préface, *Marie Tudor*, in *Théâtre Complet de Victor Hugo*, ed. J.-J. Thierry and Josette Mélèze (Monaco: Éditions Gallimard, 1963), 2: 414.

7. As late as 1917, G. B. Shaw reiterated his long-standing opinion that Verdi "wrote so abominably for the human voice that the tenors all had goat-bleat (and were proud of it); the baritones had a shattering *vibrato*, and could not, to save their lives, produce a note of any definite pitch; and the sopranos had the tone of a locomotive whistle without its steadiness." *Shaw's Music: The Complete Musical Criticism in Three Volumes*, ed. Dan H. Laurence (New York: Dodd, Mead & Company, 1981), III: 694.

8. A particularly rich source of nineteenth-century staging information is found in the holdings of two Parisian archives, the Bibliothèque de l'Arsenal and the Bibliothèque Historique de la Ville de Paris.

Chapter 1: *Il Trovatore*

1. Giuseppe Verdi, letter to Clara Maffei, 29 January 1853, in *I Copialettere di Giuseppe Verdi*, ed. Gaetano Cesari and Alessandro Luzio (Milan: Forni Editore Bologna, 1968), 532.

2. Cammarano died in 1852 leaving the last act of the opera uncompleted. The final versification and adjustments demanded by the composer were executed by Leone Emmanuele Bardare. For a detailed discussion of the opera's genesis, see also Julian Budden, *The Operas of Verdi* (New York: Oxford University Press, 1973).

3. Giuseppe Verdi, letter to Cesarino De Sanctis, 29 March 1851, in Franco Abbiati, *Giuseppe Verdi* (Milan: G. Ricordi & C., 1959), II: 121.

4. Giuseppe Verdi, letter to Cammarano, 4 April 1851, in Abbiati, II: 122-3.

5. As the critic for the *Illustration* rather acidly noted, "*Ce sujet sombre et violent convenait singulièrement, il faut dire, à la nature de son génie. Il aime à peindre les passions furieuses et les actions atroces. Il les recherche, les recueille, et les couve avec amour.*" (This somber and violent subject was singularly suited, it must be said, to the nature of his genius. He likes to paint furious passions and atrocious subjects. He seeks after them, gathers them, and broods over them with love.) Review of *Il Trovatore* by Giuseppe Verdi, *Illustration* (6 January 1855), 10.

6. Review of *Il Trovatore* by Giuseppe Verdi, *Illustrated London News* (19 May 1855), 496.

It is interesting to note, however, that the popularity of *Il Trovatore* wore thin at times from overexposure: "The house was good, but by no means crowded. It is full time that opera-house managers gave this excessively-hackneyed opera some respite. By laying it aside for a season or two it might recover in some measure its lost freshness." Review of *Il Trovatore* by Giuseppe Verdi, *Illustrated London News* (11 May 1861), 437.

7. Letter to Opprandino Arrivabene, 2 May 1862, in *Verdi Intimo: Carteggio di Giuseppe Verdi con il Conte Opprandino Arrivabene [1861-1886]*, ed. Annibale Alberti (Milan: A. Mondadori Editore, 1931), 17.

8. It is important to note that Verdi's pessimism in *Il Trovatore* yielded to a more complex and balanced exploration in his later *oeuvre*. Thus, in *Simon Boccanegra*, a belief in the power of love to end the cycle of human violence is clear when the Doge addresses his people, beseeching them to end the bloodshed which has ravaged Genoa: "*e vo gridando: pace! e vo gridando: amor. . . . e vo gridando: amor!*" (And I cry to you: "Peace!" And I cry to you: "Love". . . . And I cry to you: "Love!"). Giuseppe Verdi, *Simon Boccanegra* (Milan: G. Ricordi & C., 1971), 133.

9. Abbiati, II: 241.

10. Recall Verdi's own objections to this very *coro-cavatina* sequence in his letter to Cammarano of 4 April 1851.

11. This scene does not have a precise correlation with García Gutiérrez's play, and Julian Budden traces its inspiration back to Verdi's own *Ernani* (1844); see *The Operas of Verdi*, II: 75.

12. Giuseppe Verdi, *Il Trovatore* (Milan: G. Ricordi & C., 1968), 33. Subsequent references will be given parenthetically.

13. The humorous incongruity of this melodic inversion of textual meaning recalls the oft-told story of a certain tenor who was singing Enzo in Amilcare Ponchielli's *La Gioconda*. As he began the famous aria "*Cielo! e mar!*" (Heaven! and sea!), he gestured with great dramatic intensity first at the ground and then up to the sky! Amilcare Ponchielli, *La Gioconda* (Milan: G. Ricordi & C., 1980), 147.

14. Review of *Il Trovatore* by Giuseppe Verdi, *Illustration* (6 January 1855), 10. Although the expression "*hurler avec les loups*" translates idiomatically as "to do as the others," in this context the literal "to howl with the wolves" seems more fitting!

15. William Weaver, trans., *Seven Verdi Librettos* (New York: W. W. Norton & Company Inc., 1975), 82.

16. In the original play, Doña Leonor has already taken her vows as a nun before Manrique rescues her from Don Nuño's men, hence her struggle of conscience after being carried off by her beloved troubadour.

17. The operatic convention of a static ensemble was added to the original play. In García Gutiérrez's scene, the curtain falls as Manrique appears and the abductors recognize him. Antonio García Gutiérrez, *El Trovador*, ed. Carlos Ruiz Silva (Madrid: Ediciones Cátedra, 1985), 141. Subsequent references will be given parenthetically.

18. In this context, the frequent performance practice of having the tenor join with Leonora for her melodic reprise is unfortunate: the stasis of her dramatic characterization is blurred by the introduction of a new element into the established vocal pattern.

19. Weaver, 100.

20. It is unfortunate that modern performance practice often cuts this line, along with the first verse of the *cabaletta*, so that the tenor can go directly into the second verse with its famous, interpolated high Cs.

The staging promptbook from the Paris Opéra's French-language premiere of *Il Trovatore* in 1857 ironically indicates an effort to make Leonora's interjected line seem more dramatically plausible by focusing her attention out through the window to where the stake is being prepared for Azucena. The result, however, is only to add to the dramatic absurdity of the scene as Leonora and Manrico crisscross upstage and downstage for their individual lines: "*Pendant le solo de Manrique:* Barbares, affreux délire, *etc., etc., Léonore remonte la scène, jette ses regards au dehors par les fenêtres du fond, et donne les signes du plus grand désespoir.—Elle redescend pour attaquer:* Souffrance extrème, *etc., etc. Pendant ce solo de Léonore, Manrique dans la plus vive agitation court aux fenêtres, puis il redescend attaquer de nouveau:* Supplice infâme qui la réclame." (During Manrico's solo "Barbarous, atrocious delirium" etc., etc., Leonora goes upstage, looking outside through the back windows and showing the signs of great despair. She comes back downstage to begin "Utmost suffering" etc., etc. During Leonora's solo, Manrico runs to the windows with the keenest agitation, then comes back downstage to begin again with "Infamous torment which claims her.") H. Robert Cohen, ed., *The Original Staging Manuals for Twelve Parisian Operatic Premières* (New York: Pendragon Press, 1991), 257.

21. In the source play, Doña Leonor plays a much more active role in the corresponding scene; there is a dialogue with Manrique at the spot where Verdi provides the tenor with his *cabaletta* (171-3).

22. García Gutiérrez's play contains no corresponding prayer in the scene of Doña Leonor outside the prison tower (178-80).

23. Gaetano Donizetti, *Lucrezia Borgia* (New York: Edwin F. Kalmus, n.d.), 211.

24. Giuseppe Verdi, *Rigoletto* (Chicago and Milan: University of Chicago Press and G. Ricordi & C., 1983), 352.

Chapter 2: *La Forza del Destino*

1. Originally premiered in St. Petersburg, Russia, in 1862, *La Forza del Destino* was extensively revised by Verdi before it was performed at La Scala in 1869. The revised version has been the standard performance edition and will be the basis for the present discussion.

2. William Shakespeare, *The Tragedy of King Lear*, in *The Riverside Shakespeare*, ed. G. Blakemore Evans (Boston: Houghton Mifflin Company, 1974), I.ii.118-26.

3. William Shakespeare, *The Tragedy of Julius Caesar*, in *The Riverside Shakespeare*, I.ii.140-1.

4. During its 1831 premiere performance, Victor Hugo's verse drama *Hernani* provoked a riot at the venerable Comédie-Française between audience stalwarts of the established neoclassical tradition of writing and advocates of the emerging romantic movement. The "Battle of *Hernani*," as it came to be known, is now generally regarded as a turning point in theater history.

5. The term "metatheatrical" denotes works manifesting a self-conscious theatricality, a playful awareness of their own status as theatrical performance.

6. Joseph Kerman, "Second Thoughts on *Forza*," *Opera News* 26/7 (1961): 24.

7. Letter to Léon Escudier, 20 August 1861, in "Lettres Inédites de G. Verdi à Léon Escudier," *Rivista Musicale Italiana* 35 (1928): 22.

8. Letter to Andrea Maffei, 20 October 1876, in *I Coppialettere di Giuseppe Verdi*, ed. Gaetano Cesari and Alessandro Luzio (Milan: Forni Editore Bologna, 1968), 624.

For another perspective on Verdi's invention of reality in *Forza* see also George Martin, "Verdi's Imitation of Shakespeare: *La Forza del Destino*," *Opera Quarterly* 3 (1985): 19-29.

9. Giuseppe Verdi, *La Forza del Destino* (Milan: G. Ricordi & C., 1969), 62. Subsequent references will be given parenthetically.

10. For a more extended discussion of how Verdi adapted both Saavedra's play and Schiller's scene in order to create his own artistic vision, see also Julian Budden, *The Operas of Verdi* (New York: Oxford University Press, 1973), II: 496-502.

11. Vincent Godefroy, *The Dramatic Genius of Verdi: Studies of Selected Operas* (New York: St. Martin's Press, 1975), II: 102.

12. In contrast, the response of Saavedra's Doña Leonor to her father leaves more of her anguish subtextual: "(Abatida y turbada.) *Buenas noches, padre mío*." ([*Spiritless and troubled.*] Good night, my father.) Angel de Saavedra, *Don Alvaro, o la Fuerza del Sino*, ed. Ermanno Caldera (Madrid: Taurus Ediciones, 1986), 87. Subsequent references will be given parenthetically.

13. For further discussion of the *Re Lear* connection, see also Budden, II: 450, and Godefroy, II: 104.

14. Note that the famous "Destiny" motif is not heard during these early scenes, but accompanies the marquis' arrival at the finale of Act I (42).

15. In addition to the musical echoes, the dramatic parallels between this scene and Violetta's farewell to Alfredo in the second act of *La Traviata* (1853) are particularly noteworthy. Both Violetta and Leonora find themselves resolved to follow paths which will bring great suffering: one to leave her lover, the other to leave her family. The fundamental difference, however, is that the depth of Violetta's suffering is matched by the height of the joy she has found, albeit fleetingly, with Alfredo; Leonora experiences all of the suffering, but none of the joy of love.

16. In Saavedra's play, there is no such final appeal for pity from Heaven. Instead the curtain falls on the marqués' cursing of Leonor, "*¡Yo te maldigo!*" (100; I curse you!)

17. In the Spanish play, Doña Leonor does not actually appear in the tavern scene; she remains safely behind her closed chamber door. Further, Saavedra employs two brothers as the instruments of family vengeance, the student Alfonso and the soldier Carlos. Alvaro kills them both. In the opera, these two brothers are consolidated into the single obsessive figure of Carlo.

18. Musically, this denouement provides an ominous foreshadowing of the cycle of hope and disillusionment which Leonora will endure from this moment to the final act of the opera: her feeling of peace during the "*Vergine degli Angeli*" (169-72) prayer with Padre Guardiano and the monks has no more lasting effect than her inspiration by the sounds of the "*Venite, adoremus*" (122).

19. This entire scene is absent from Saavedra's play.

20. In *The Operas of Verdi*, Budden notes of the scoring at the close of this scene, "A final touch of mastery is the descending figure—E flat-D-G—played by lower strings, bassoon, third trombone and bass brass under the concluding bars as if to remind us that, despite appearances, all is far from well, and that Leonora has not escaped her fate" (II: 474-5).

21. Saavedra includes no comparable scene in his play. He does, however, indicate in Doña Leonor's earlier dialogue with Padre Guardián that the last inhabitant of the cave was attacked by bandits and saved only by divine intervention, in the form of a lightening bolt which struck down the attackers (124).

22. In Verdi's original version, the duel took place on stage during a gathering storm, and a *duettino* of reunion between Alvaro and Leonora followed at this point.

23. Uncertain about how to approach this iconoclastic opera, criticism of *Forza* in performance has historically been characterized by a pervasive ambivalence. The reaction of the *Illustrated London News*, even to the revised version, is perhaps typical: "The accumulated horrors of the original book have been slightly modified, and the composer has made some changes in the score. The opera contains some dramatic and effective writing, but the general impression is heavy, and wanting in variety." Review of *La Forza del Destino* by Giuseppe Verdi, *Illustrated London News* (25 June 1880), 615.

24. Contrast this last moment, for example, with the serene dissolution Gilda experiences in Verdi's *Rigoletto* or the ecstatic joy which infuses Violetta at the end of the composer's *La Traviata*.

Chapter 3: *Aida*

1. The genesis of *Aida* has been thoroughly documented by numerous scholars and need not be fully retraced here. In summary, the original scenario was written by the French Egyptologist Auguste Mariette, who sent it to the Parisian impresario Camille Du Locle. Du Locle presented the scenario to Verdi, and, together, they created a working libretto outline. Finally, Verdi and Antonio Ghislanzoni shaped the completed libretto, and Ghislanzoni provided the verses.

Throughout the transformation from scenario to stage, Verdi was actively involved in molding the story to his own vision.

2. William Shakespeare, *The Tragedy of Romeo and Juliet*, in *The Riverside Shakespeare*, ed. G. Blakemore Evans (Boston: Houghton Mifflin Company, 1974), V.iii.111.

3. In Giulio Ricordi's production book from the La Scala premiere, Aida is clearly a woman of color with "olive, dark reddish skin." *Disposizione Scenica per l'Opera Aida* in *Verdi's Aida: The History of an Opera in Letters and Documents*, comp. and trans. Hans Busch (Minneapolis: University of Minnesota Press, 1978), 558.

Her race is a moot point in the opera itself, however. Race is never used to define her, in contrast, for instance, to Jago's captioning of Otello to Roderigo: "*a Desdemona bella, che nel segreto de' tuoi sogni adori, presto in uggia verranno i foschi baci di quel selvaggio dalle gonfie labbra*" (beautiful Desdemona, whom in your secret dreams you adore, will soon tire of the dark kisses of that swollen-lipped savage). Giuseppe Verdi, *Otello* (Milan: G. Ricordi & C., 1969), 31-2.

The only references to Aida's color are both rather ironic: on first seeing Aida in Act I and suspecting her love for Radamès, Amneris murmurs, "*Trema che il ver m'apprenda quel pianto e quel rossor*" (Tremble lest that weeping and blushing reveal the truth to me); and again, when she confronts Aida in Act II, Amneris remarks, "*Ah! quel pallore*" (Ah! that pallor). Giuseppe Verdi, *Aida* (Milan: G. Ricordi & C., 1980), 21 and 94. Subsequent references will be given parenthetically.

Nor is Aida defined by her gender. Her love, her conflicting loyalties, her torment, are not unique to her, but are manifested with varying degrees of subtlety and self-understanding in Radamès as well. As Fabrizio Della Seta notes, Radamès "is very different from Aida as well as Amneris, both of whom are enmeshed in contradictions, but who have a full and tragic awareness of that fact, something Radamès lacks until almost the end of the opera." Fabrizio Della Seta, "'*O cieli azzurri*': Exoticism and Dramatic Discourse in *Aida*," in *Cambridge Opera Journal* (March 1991): 59.

Nor is Aida oppressed by the weight of patriarchal authority. Even the concept of a monolithic patriarchal hierarchy is subverted by the religious and political order in the world of the opera: the hectoring priests of Egypt are in the service of the goddess Isis; the abstract authority of the king is balanced by the active presence of Amneris. Indeed, it is Amneris, concealing her venomous intent beneath the flower of "sisterhood," who torments Aida the most. Aida's only true oppression by the patriarchy comes in the third act when Amonasro denounces her for refusing to aid in his plan to entrap Radamès: "*Non sei mia figlia. . . . Dei Faraoni tu sei la schiava!*" (228; You are not my daughter. . . . You are a slave of the Pharaohs!) But Amonasro demands of Aida only the same unswerving loyalty to Ethiopia that he, his wife, and sons have shown. His rage stems not from Aida's defiance of his paternal authority, but from her betrayal of patriotic love.

Aida cannot even be defined by her status as a slave in the Egyptian court. She may be enslaved, but she is far from being "a slave." Slavery, as her father intimates, is a question of attitude rather than bonds. They may both be enslaved, but while they maintain their defiance and independence of spirit, they will still be free. Thus, symbolically, they both roam unchecked about the Temple of Isis, plotting a new victory over the Egyptians in Act III. Aida is oppressed not by the actual terms of her captivity, but because the circumstances of that captivity place in conflict her loves for family, country, and Radamès.

4. Verdi's musical and dramatic innovations in *Aida* were greeted with mixed sentiments by contemporary critics. Most hailed the opera as a masterpiece, but much attention was focused on the ostensible influence of Wagnerism on Verdi's art and musical composition:

> *Di una sola cosa tutti gli spettatori devono aver portato il convincimento fuori di teatro—ed è che si son trovati per quasi quattr'ore davanti al grandioso—grandiosità di creazione—grandiosità d'interpretazione—grandiosità di estrincazione—grandiosità, non di mole, ma di pensieri—non di proporzioni soltanto ma d'idee. . . . Il* Lohengrin *Italiano—Spieghiamoci un po'. . . Fra l'*Aida *e il* Lohengrin *il punto di contatto, di analogia è questo: che in entrambe non si fa della musica, ma si fa con deliberato proposito un poema in cui la musica non è che uno degli elementi.*

> (After leaving the theater, the spectators must have been convinced of only one thing, and that is that for nearly four hours they found themselves before greatness—greatness of creation—greatness of interpretation—greatness of expression—greatness, not of size, but of thought—not only of proportions, but of ideas. . . . The Italian *Lohengrin*—let us explain a bit . . . There is a point of contact, of analogy between *Aida* and *Lohengrin* which is this: that both are not made as music, but, with deliberate purpose, as poems in which music is only one of the elements.) *Il Pungolo,* 9 February 1872, in *Le Prime: Duecento Anni di Teatro alla Scala,* ed. Giuseppe Pintorno [Milan: Grafica Gutenberg Editrice, 1982]), 80.

5. Julian Budden, *The Operas of Verdi* (New York: Oxford University Press, 1973), III: 166. See also Charles Osborne, *The Complete Operas of Verdi* (New York: Da Capo Press, 1969), 377-82; and Verdi's letter of 26 May 1870 to Camille Du Locle, in Busch, 17.

6. George Martin notes, "although the action is set in Egypt, it really takes place in a never-never land in which Verdi can manipulate the characters as he

wants." George Martin, *Verdi: His Music, Life and Times* (New York: Dodd, Mead & Company, 1983), 465.

7. As the opera unfolds, it becomes clear that the "Aida" motif is actually more specifically associated with Aida's love for Radamès, a love which she ultimately recognizes as the very essence of her being. Verdi's richly symphonic prelude to *Aida* thus symbolically adumbrates the course of Aida's life: the first plaintive strains of her love melody grow in richness and intensity, confront the opposing motif of the Egyptian priests who will condemn Radamès to die, and finally rise in ethereal transcendence with the peace that Aida and Radamès will find together in death.

8. Busch, 558.

9. Her intrusion is highlighted in the directions of the *Disposizione Scenica* (Busch, 561), which indicate that Aida enters from up-left and then crosses to center-stage until she is between Radamès and Amneris.

10. Busch, 563.

11. Busch, 564.

12. In order to preserve the psychological continuity of Aida's forthcoming *scena*, Verdi was prepared to accept the logistical difficulties of clearing the full ensemble during only eight measures of exit music. The *Disposizione Scenica* thus warns, "These exits must occur very quickly, and the chorus must not block the wing but must make room so that the stage will be empty by the end of the few instrumental bars that close the piece." Busch, 565.

13. With typical acerbity, G. B. Shaw offers this perspective on speculation of Wagnerian influence in this scene and in the scoring for *Aida* in general:

> I am, of course, aware that when *Aida* first reached us, it produced a strong impression of Wagnerism. But at that time nothing of Wagner's later than *Lohengrin* was known to us. . . . Everybody then thought that a recurring theme in an opera was a Wagnerian Leitmotif, especially if it stole in to a *tremolando* of the strings and was harmonized with major ninths instead of sub-dominants; so when this occurred in Aida's *scena*, *Ritorna vincitor*, we all said 'Aha! Wagner!' And, as very often happens, when we came to know better, we quite forgot to revise our premature conclusion. . . .
>
> The real secret of the change from the roughness of *Il Trovatore* to the elaboration of the three last operas is the inevitable natural drying up of Verdi's spontaneity and fertility. So long as an opera composer can pour forth melodies like *La donna è mobile* and *Il balen*, he does not stop to excogitate harmonic elegancies and orchestral sonorities which are neither helpful to him dramatically nor demanded by the taste of his audience. But when in process of time the

well begins to dry up; when instead of getting splashed with
the bubbling over of *Ah si, ben mio*, he has to let down a
bucket to drag up *Celeste Aida*, then it is time to be clever,
to be nice, to be distinguished, to be impressive, to study
instrumental confectionery, to bring thought and knowledge
and seriousness to the rescue of failing vitality. In *Aida* this
is not very happily done. *Shaw's Music: The Complete
Musical Criticism in Three Volumes*, ed. Dan H. Laurence
(New York: Dodd, Mead & Company, 1981), III: 571-2.

14. Interestingly, this orchestral figure also echoes the ominous onset of the
storm scene in Verdi's *Rigoletto*, where Gilda waits outside the murderer's
house, hoping to save her lover though, ultimately, it will cost her own life.

15. Busch, 452.

16. Busch, 565.

17. Busch, 576.

18. Gaetano Donizetti, *Lucia di Lammermoor* (Milan: G. Ricordi & C.,
1967), 259.

19. Jean Humbert, "À Propos de l'Égyptomanie dans l'Oeuvre de Verdi:
Attribution à Auguste Mariette d'un Scénario Anonyme de l'Opéra *Aïda*," *Revue
de Musicologie* 62 (1976): 250.

20. Busch, 597.

21. Humbert, 250.

22. Busch, 598.

23. Busch, 598.

24. Verdi was particularly insistent that the psychological and dramatic truth
of this moment be paramount. In an oft-quoted letter to Ghislanzoni of 28
September 1870, he declares, "In such a state of fear and moral depression, Aida
cannot and must not sing a *cabaletta*. . . . After Amonasro has said *Sei la schiava
dei Faraoni* [You are a slave of the Pharaohs], Aida can only speak in broken
phrases." Busch, 69.

25. Humbert, 250-2.

26. *Revue des Deux Mondes* 15 (1876): 461.

27. Busch, 617.

Chapter 4: *La Bohème*

1. For further discussion of the genesis of the opera, see also William
Ashbrook, *The Operas of Puccini* (Ithaca, N.Y.: Cornell University Press, 1985);
Arthur Groos and Roger Parker, *Giacomo Puccini* (London: Cambridge
University Press, 1986); or Joseph Kestner, "Woe to the Vanquished," *Opera
News* 41/19 (1977): 14-7.

2. In contrast to Puccini's opera, character development is not one of the
strengths of Murger's novel. As Camille Bellaigue notes of *Scènes de la Vie de*

Bohème, "*le moindre mérite est sans doute l'analyse ou la psychologie*" (the least merit is without doubt analysis or psychology). Review of *La Bohème* by Giacomo Puccini, *Revue des Deux Mondes* 148 (1898): 470.

3. In the final chapter of Murger's novel, the title of which loosely translates as "You Are Only Young Once," a year has passed since Mimì's death, and Rodolphe and Marcel give a party to celebrate their entrance into respectable society. The poet has written a book which attracted a great deal of attention from the critics; the painter has had two pictures shown at the Salon; Musette is marrying a wealthy bourgeois; and their friends have all made their fortunes. Henry Murger, *Scènes de la Vie de Bohème*, ed. Loïc Chotard (Monaco: Éditions Gallimard, 1988), 393-97. Subsequent references will be given parenthetically.

4. See Murger, 274-301.

5. In Murger's novel, Mimì laughs at the very idea of wasting her time on a man interested only in platonic love. Her features reveal a brutal lack of sensibility; deceitful and mercenary, she takes on the local prostitutes as her friends and role models. Quickly falling out of love with Rodolphe, she makes his life miserable except during brief moments of reconciliation (181-203 and 213-33).

6. Giacomo Puccini, *La Bohème* (Milan: G. Ricordi & C., 1969), vii. Subsequent references will be given parenthetically.

7. See *La Bohème*, 187-8.

8. Giuseppe Verdi, *Aida*, (Milan: G. Ricordi & C., 1980), 301.

9. To avoid the risk of accidents posed by having unattended fires in individual apartments, tenants received lit candles from the concierge to take up with them when they returned to their accommodations. If the candles blew out, they would have to descend to the concierge once more or seek out a neighbor.

10. Albert Carré's promptbook for a production of *La Bohème* at Paris' Théâtre National de l'Opéra-Comique in 1898 reinforces the sense of Mimì's decorum. In the score, when Rodolfo first offers "*un po' di vino*" (57; a little wine), Mimì replies "*Grazie*" (57; Thank you). The staging notes, however, clarify that "*Elle refuse*" (She refuses). Mimì is declining the drink with an implicit "*No*, thank you." Only when pressed a second time to accept the glass does she relent with the admonition, "*Poco, poco*" (57; Just a little, just a little). *La Bohème* by Giacomo Puccini, manuscript promptbook by Albert Carré (Paris: Association des Régisseurs Théâtrales, 1898), 21.

11. On her death bed, Mimì admits that she knew all along Rodolfo had found the key "*assai presto*" (268; quickly enough).

12. As in the printed score, Albert Carré's promptbook highlights the significance of this moment. Mimì has remained seated beside Rodolfo's writing table at downstage-right throughout "*Che gelida manina*" and the first portion of "*Mi chiamano Mimì*." Now, propelled by the strength of her emotions, "*Elle se lève*" (26; She rises).

13. It is significant that the caressing phrases of Rodolfo's ardent "*O soave fanciulla*" (O sweet girl) are juxtaposed with the offstage cry of his friend Marcello, "*trovò la poesia*" (78; he found poetry); as Rodolfo notes in Act II,

"*La più divina delle poësie è quella, amico che c'insegna amare!*" (114; The most divine of poems is the one, my friend, which teaches us to love!)

14. Albert Carré's promptbook makes Rodolfo's intentions clear: as Rodolfo sings "*Sarebbe così dolce restar qui*" (81; It would be so sweet to remain here), he "*la pousse doucement du côté du lit*" (28; pushes her gently to the side of the bed). Mimì, however, "*passe devant lui. Elle va reprendre son châle qu'elle a laissé sur la chaise puis de la cheminée.*" (28; passes in front of him. She goes to take up her shawl, which she left on the chair near the fireplace.)

15. The third and fourth acts of the opera have no real parallel in Murger's novel, a fact Jean-Michel Brèque attributes to the radical reworking of Mimì's character: "*Le création d'une Mimì aussi nouvelle a contraint les librettistes, aux 3e et 4e actes, à élaborer une action dramatique originale, sensiblement différente de celle des* Scènes" (The creation of such a new Mimì compelled the librettists, in the third and fourth acts, to elaborate an original dramatic plot, appreciably different from that of *Scènes*). Jean-Michel Brèque, "La Vie de Bohème selon Puccini: Du Pathétique avant Toute Chose," Avant-Scène Opéra (March-April 1979): 8.

16. It often comes as something of a jolt when certain critics point out that by the standards of conventional morality, Mimì and Rodolfo are living in sin without the benefit of marriage. Although technically true, this thought is rarely in the mind of the spectator in the theater, perhaps because the whole concept of social conventions and morality seems so utterly irrelevant to the opera. While Murger's novel wallows in the illicit nature of sexual liaisons, the opera is focused on love. Puccini's Mimì embodies a pure and absolute love, as untainted by jealousy and suspicions as it is unconfined by social or religious conventions. Her relationship with Rodolfo is blessed by love alone, just as her faith in God is expressed in daily prayer but not regular church attendance (72).

17. Interestingly, Albert Carré's set sketches reveal that, in the Opéra-Comique production, Mimì was the visual focal point for this scene. The tree behind which she concealed herself was at center-stage, while Rodolfo and Marcello carried on their conversation further off to stage-right (63).

18. This plunging orchestral theme is often identified with Mimì's fatal coughing and, thus, provides an ominous foreshadowing of the death which awaits her.

19. In Murger's novel, by contrast, considerable attention is paid to Mimì's relationship with the viscount, and they separate due to the viscount's outrage over Mimì's attachment to a poem she inspired Rodolphe to write (358-93).

20. Symbolically, as Musetta recounts Mimì's desire to die with Rodolfo, the motif of the "*primavera*" dream from "*Mi chiamano Mimì*" sounds in the orchestra (250).

21. Murger's Mimì, by contrast, dies alone in a ghastly hospital ward. She had returned to Rodolphe—softened by the hardships and misfortunes she had endured—a changed woman, but one who elicits pity from the reader without ever aspiring to the heights of tragic heroism. Her passing culminates a grotesque series of mistakes and misunderstandings: returning home one day,

Rodolphe receives a note from a physician friend saying that Mimì had died in the hospital. Rodolphe feels nothing at the news, speculating that perhaps his love had died when he had learned of Mimì's impending fate. Days later, however, he runs into the physician who explains that his note had been a mistake, that Mimì had only been moved to another ward. Rodolphe returns to the hospital only to be informed that Mimì had in fact died earlier that very morning and had been buried in a pauper's grave (358-93).

Chapter 5: *Tosca*

1. Joseph Kerman's excoriation of *Tosca* in his study *Opera as Drama* has been particularly influential. After such memorable turns-of-phrase as "Tosca leaps, and the orchestra screams the first thing that comes into its head, 'E lucevan le stelle'" (15), Kerman concludes, "The more fully one knows the true achievement of the art of opera, the more clearly one sees the extent of Puccini's failure, or more correctly, the triviality of his attempt." Joseph Kerman, *Opera as Drama* (Berkeley: University of California Press, 1988), 16.

2. G. B. Shaw writes of an 1890 London performance of Sardou's *La Tosca*,

> I felt nothing but unmitigated disgust. The French well-made play was never respectable even in its prime; but now, in its dotage and *delirium tremens*, it is a disgrace to the theatre. Such an old-fashioned, shiftless, clumsily constructed, emptyheaded turnip ghost of a cheap shocker as this Tosca should never have been let pass the stage door of the Garrick. I do not know which are the more pitiable, the vapid two acts of obsolete comedy of intrigue, or the three acts of sham torture, rape, murder, gallows, and military execution, set to dialogue that might have been improvized by strolling players in a booth. Oh, if it had but been an opera! It is fortunate for John Hare that he has only the dramatic critics to deal with. *Shaw's Music: The Complete Musical Criticism in Three Volumes*, ed. Dan H. Laurence (New York: Dodd, Mead & Company, 1981), I: 911.

3. See also Bernard Bovier-Lapierre, "Tosca: Subversion Lyrique?" *Avant-Scène Opéra* (September-October 1977): 93-4.

4. There is a certain irony, therefore in commentaries such as William Ashbrook's "A Message of Love," which suggests that Cavaradossi's painting in the first act offers an interpretive key to the opera: "The portrait, then, would seem to contain some message for Tosca. Here it should not be forgotten that the subject of the painting is Mary Magdalene, a fallen woman who found salvation, her former ardent nature being transfigured by a nobler concept of love. Mario, it appears, not only loves Tosca for herself as she now is but hopes his love will

help her to realize some of her unrecognized potential." William Ashbrook, "A Message of Love," *Opera News* 43/8 (1978): 27.

5. For another perspective on Tosca's self-conscious acting, see also Richard Brett and John Potter, "Role-Playing: Tosca as Woman and Actress," *Opera News* 41/9 (1977): 18-20.

6. Aeschylus, *Agamemnon*, in *Oresteia*, trans. Richard Lattimore (Chicago: University of Chicago Press, 1953), 38.

7. John Louis DiGaetani offers a different perspective on Tosca's faith in "Puccini's *Tosca* and the Necessity of Agnosticism," *Opera Quarterly* (Spring 1984): 76-84.

8. Victorien Sardou, *La Tosca*, in *Théâtre Complet* (Paris: Albin Michel, Éditeur, 1934), I: 24. Subsequent references will be given parenthetically.

9. Giacomo Puccini, *Tosca* (Milan: G. Ricordi & C., 1956), 18-9. Subsequent references will be given parenthetically.

10. William Ashbrook, *The Operas of Puccini* (Ithaca, N.Y.: Cornell University Press, 1985), 87.

11. Mosco Carner, *Puccini: A Critical Biography* (London: Barrie & Jenkins, 1979), 402.

12. Compare the melodramatic exaggeration of Tosca's musical expression of jealousy in this scene with the comparative understatement of her suspicions upon her first entrance or the complex, nuanced shadings of her disillusionment after returning to the church later in the act.

Albert Carré's promptbook for a production of *Tosca* at the Théâtre National de l'Opéra-Comique in Paris shortly after the opera's premiere in Rome highlights the exaggeration in Tosca's violent jealousy: "*Elle essaye de monter sur l'échafaudage. Il l'arrête, ayant deposé pinceux et palette. Elle menace avec sa canne. Il la fait redescendre.*" (She tries to climb onto the scaffolding. He stops her, having laid down brushes and palette. She menaces with her cane. He makes her come down again.) *Tosca* by Giacomo Puccini, manuscript promptbook by Albert Carré (Paris: Association des Régisseurs Théâtrales, n.d.), 16.

13. William Shakespeare, *The Tragedy of Hamlet Prince of Denmark*, in *The Riverside Shakespeare*, ed. G. Blakemore Evans (Boston: Houghton Mifflin Company, 1974), III.ii.9-11.

14. Sarah Bernhardt, the creator of Sardou's *La Tosca*, did not number singing among her many talents, so this staging was *de rigueur*!

15. Puccini uses the orchestral motif identified with the fugitive Angelotti to punctuate these lines, however, thus reminding the audience that Tosca's fears are unfounded.

16. On many levels, Tosca's departure from Sant'Andrea della Valle adumbrates her final moments on the parapets of the Castel Sant'Angelo. In Act I, Tosca promises to take meaningful action, but her effort to thwart Cavaradossi's tryst is misguided and ultimately futile; by Act III, on the other hand, she has killed Scarpia, taking truly meaningful action to destroy the evil that poisoned her world. Musically, the suspended Fs of "*Egli vede ch'io piango*" voice a faith that is still instinctive and unconsidered in its implications; in contrast, the

soaring high B-flat which climaxes the final "*O Scarpia, avanti a Dio!*" (334-5; O Scarpia, before God!) sounds Tosca's triumphant understanding of her own identity and place in the universe. In the first act, the power of love seems to be denied by the subversive orchestral echo of the "*Floria, t'amo*" motif; by the end of the opera, however, despair itself is negated in the *fff tutta forza con grande slancio* orchestral transfiguration of "*E lucevan le stelle*" (288; And the stars were shining).

17. Sardou's play offers a reactionary view of female power run amok; Queen Marie-Caroline of Naples and the former harlot, Lady Hamilton, reign over a society of omnipresent corruption and amorality. Baron Scarpia is no more than a minor player, although a particularly dangerous one, and his malignant presence is more than balanced by the noble male freedom fighters Angelotti and Mario. Reprehensible as Scarpia is, he seems himself to be a pawn: "*Ce n'est pas cette femme que je redoute, mais l'autre, l'Hamilton, qui veut qu'Angelotti soit pendu et qui ne me pardonnera jamais que sa proie lui échappe. Un mot de cette Anglaise qui mène tout là-bas, et c'est fait de moi.*" (70-1; It is not this woman [the queen] I fear, but the other, the Hamilton woman, who wants Angelotti hanged and who will never forgive me for her prey escaping her. One word from that Englishwoman who directs everything over there, and it's done for me.)

18. In reviewing the English premiere of *Tosca*, the *Illustrated London News* notes Puccini's use of neoclassical music to evoke a contrast between the queen's realm and Scarpia's: "In the second act there is an ingenious introduction of the stately music of the eighteenth century, in a gavotte and cantata, in which La Tosca is singing. The voices are heard outside the room in which Scarpia is plotting." Review of *Tosca* by Giacomo Puccini, *Illustrated London News* (21 July 1900), 108.

19. Albert Carré's staging notes reinforce this sense of brutal degradation. As Scarpia demands to know where Angelotti is hidden, Tosca falls to her knees: "*Il la traîne par terre. Il la traîne vers la canapé. Elle laisse tombe sa tête sur la canape. Spoletta a reparu. Scarpia remonte et lui fait signe, puis il se rapproche de la Tosca et, au cri de Cavaradossi, il la saisit par les cheveux et tourne son visage vers lui.*" (53-5; He drags her along the ground. He drags her to the sofa. She lets her head fall on the sofa. Spoletta has reappeared. Scarpia crosses up and makes a sign to him, then he draws near to Tosca again and, at Cavaradossi's cry, he seizes her by the hair and turns her face towards him.)

20. Puccini's addition of this connective scene in the opera allows the conflation into a single act of Cavaradossi's interrogation, which occurs in Act III of the play, and Scarpia's assault of Tosca, which takes place in Act IV.

21. In *Seven Puccini Librettos* (New York: W. W. Norton & Company, 1975), William Weaver reconstructs from first edition librettos a fuller indication of the original stage directions for this scene than those that appear in the printed score: "Sciarrone and the policemen seize Cavaradossi and drag him toward the door. With a supreme effort, Tosca tries to hold tight to Cavaradossi, but in vain. She is brutally thrust away" (151).

22. The stage directions indicate, "*Tosca affranta dal dolore si lascia cadere sul canapè*" (242; Overcome by suffering, Tosca lets herself fall onto the sofa), but it has become traditional for sopranos to sing the aria from a prone position on the floor. Gustl Breuer recounts Maria Jeritza's story of how she originated this staging: "'Then, during the final rehearsal Alfred Jerger, the Scarpia, and I got so carried away, that he threw me to the floor with such force that I thought I had broken a few ribs. I lay there, knowing that in a few bars I had to sing '*Nur der Schönheit, weih't mein Leben*' (the German text of '*Vissi d'arte*'). I didn't know how I would get back on my feet, let alone have any breath—with my entire body hurting. Then Professor Arnold Rosé, the famous first violinist of the Vienna Philharmonic, started the first bars of the aria and I just began to sing. I didn't even bother to push back my dishevelled hair from my face. When I had finished I thought to myself, 'All right; now we will face the storm.' But instead, Puccini's voice came from the auditorium, '*Brava, brava, bella Carissima!* You have *done* it! I knew you would invent something . . . it is perfect!'" Gustl Breuer, "Tosca, Jeritza, and Me," *High Fidelity Magazine* (December 1957): 58.

23. In Sardou's play, by contrast, La Tosca evidences no introspective awareness or search for understanding of her own life: "*Ah! Dieu bon, Dieu grand, Dieu sauveur! . . . Qu'il y ait un tel homme et que tu le laisses faire! Tu ne le vois donc pas?. . . Tu ne l'entends donc pas?*" (141; Ah! good God, great God, savior God! That there could be such a man, and that You allow it to be! Do you not see him then? Do you not hear him then?)

24. In contrast, Sardou's La Tosca coldly declares, "*A présent, je te tiens quitte!*" (147; Now we are even!)

25. Puccini insisted that this line be left in the libretto, writing to Giulio Ricordi, "*Perchè ha tolto l'ultimo verso:* 'e avanti a Lui tremava tutta Roma?' *Io l'ho messo e mi gioca bene. È meglio lasciarlo dunque.*" (Why have you removed the final line: 'And before him all Rome trembled?' I put it there and it plays well for me. It is better, therefore, to leave it.) Letter to Giulio Ricordi, July 1898, in *Carteggi Pucciniani*, ed. Eugenio Gara (Milan: G. Ricordi & C., 1958), 167.

26. In Sardou's play, there is no metamorphosis of La Tosca, and therefore no need to challenge Mario to accept her true self. Hence, instead of this narration, La Tosca cries only, "*Ah! si je l'ai tué!* (Avec une joie sauvage.) *Oh! ça, oui, je l'ai bien tué!*" (154; Ah! yes, I killed him! [*With a savage joy.*] Oh! yes, I really killed him!)

27. The significance of this dramatic moment is emphasized in Albert Carré's promptbook, which indicates that, as Tosca recounts the killing of Scarpia, she moves away from Cavaradossi and toward the center of the stage, symbolically compelling her lover to follow her to new ground (74).

28. Giulio Ricordi's objections to the musical fragmentation and ostensible lack of melodic scope in Puccini's construction of this entire scene, as well as the composer's vigorous defense, are documented in Carner, 118-20.

29. Significantly, Puccini deleted Tosca's original despairing reprise of Cavaradossi's "*E lucevan le stelle*" melody from this point in the autograph.

Instead, the motif is reserved for the end of the opera, where despair is negated by the tragic joy of Tosca's final *"O Scarpia, avanti a Dio!"*

30. In contrast, the death of Sardou's La Tosca lacks such heroic resonance: Spoletta shouts, *"Ah! Démon . . . je t'enverrai rejoindre ton amant!"* (Ah! Demon . . . I will send you to rejoin your lover!), and La Tosca replies, *"J'y vais, canailles!"* (161; I'm going there, wretched scum!)

Chapter 6: *Madama Butterfly*

1. When *Madama Butterfly* premiered at La Scala in early 1904, it was a fiasco. Puccini immediately set about revising the score and dividing the original two acts into three; the new version received a triumphant reception later that same year in Brescia. Further cuts and adjustments in the score followed. The present discussion will refer to the three-act performing edition which has become the standard modern score for the opera. For comprehensive detailing of the genesis of the opera, as well as the various changes and alterations Puccini made in his original score, see also Arthur Groos, "Lieutenant F. B. Pinkerton: Problems in the Genesis and Performance of *Madama Butterfly*," in *The Puccini Companion*, ed. William Weaver and Simonetta Puccini (New York: W. W. Norton & Company, 1994); William Ashbrook, *The Operas of Puccini* (Ithaca, N.Y.: Cornell University Press, 1985); and Mosco Carner, *Puccini: A Critical Biography* (New York: Holmes & Meier, 1992).

2. Indeed, *Madama Butterfly* is the only one of these operas to be specifically designated a "tragedy" by the composer, the subtitle of the opera being *"Tragedia giapponese."*

3. Victor Hugo, *Angelo, Tyran de Padoue* in *Théâtre Complet de Victor Hugo*, ed. J.-J. Thierry and Josette Mélèze (Monaco: Éditions Gallimard, 1963), 2: 669.

4. Amilcare Ponchielli, *La Gioconda* (Milan: G. Ricordi & C., 1980), 117. This opera was based on Hugo's *Angelo, Tyran de Padoue.*

5. Review of *Madama Butterfly* by Giacomo Puccini, *Illustrated London News* (15 July 1905), 74.

6. Loti's tale, drawn from his own experiences in Japan, often reads like a travelogue. The eponymous Chrysanthème enters into a mercenary temporary marriage with a French naval officer who quickly discovers that he has no particular affection for his tiny bride. When his ship sails after some months, there is no regret on either side, and his final sight of Chrysanthème is her testing the quality of the money he has paid. While this plot bears only the most passing resemblance to the events in *Madame Butterfly*, critics have noted the influence of Loti's descriptive language and imagery on the subsequent story (see Carner, 410-14).

7. John Luther Long, *Madame Butterfly* (New York: The Century Company, 1904). Subsequent references will be given parenthetically.

Long's novella tells how a carefree young geisha named Cho-Cho-San—or Madame Butterfly—is wed by her family to Lieutenant B. F. Pinkerton of the United States Navy. Although their temporary marriage of convenience is hardly inspired by love, Butterfly does come to love Pinkerton and the unaccustomed freedom of her life with him. Indeed, beneath its trappings of Japanese exoticism, Long's narrative is a coming-of-age tale, chronicling the pains and joys of first love. Thus, when Pinkerton isolates her from her relatives and they in turn disown her, Butterfly proudly declares in her characteristically appalling pidgin English,

> "Nobody speak to me no more—they all outcast me *aexcep'* jus' you; tha' 's why I ought be sawry."
>
> She burst into a reckless laugh, and threw herself like a child upon him.
>
> "But tha' 's ezag' why I am *not*! Wha' 'is use lie? It is not inside me—that sawry. Me? I 'm mos' bes' happy female woman in Japan—mebby in that whole worl'. What you thing?"
>
> He said that he thought she was, and he took honest credit for it. (11)

After Pinkerton leaves Japan, Long's Butterfly, with the charming high-handedness of a child dressing up to play house, lives happily with her new son, Trouble, and her maid, Suzuki. While waiting patiently for Pinkerton's return, Butterfly spurns the marriage proposals of the wealthy Japanese prince Yamadori; but that suitor's cruel remarks about deserted children plant the seeds of doubt in Butterfly's mind: "Though Yamadori came no more, he had brought the serpent to Madame Butterfly's Eden" (45).

Trying to learn some news of Pinkerton, Butterfly visits the American consul, Sharpless, but leaves abruptly when he urges her to accept Yamadori's proposal. Instead, she clings to her dream that Pinkerton will return as he promised—when robins make their nests again—and take his family to "live in his large castle at United States America" (65).

When Pinkerton's ship finally does arrive, Butterfly believes the promise has come true; but at this moment of joy she also recognizes that she is no longer the child she once was: "'I am no longer beautiful! Waiting an' doubting make one soon sad an' old. An' how long we have wait!—how long!'" (70).

After filling their little house with festive flowers, Butterfly, Trouble, and Suzuki wait a week for Pinkerton to appear; then, one morning, they find that his ship has left: "Cho-Cho-San was frightened. The sinking at her heart she now knew to be black doubt. Her little, unused, frivolous mind had not forecast such a catastrophe" (74-5).

Butterfly's adolescent days of mindless frivolity are over. She visits the consul once more and meets Pinkerton's new American wife, Adelaide. Having just visited Butterfly's house to see about taking Pinkerton's child away with them, Adelaide is enchanted by the unknown little Japanese in the consul's office: "'How very charming—how *lovely*—you are, dear! Will you kiss me, you pretty—*plaything*!'" Butterfly's response is a soft, "'No'" (80).

Butterfly at last rejects the role of "plaything" that had defined her life up to this moment. She will no longer be treated as a toy. She has fallen in love. She has suffered. And now she returns, grief-stricken, to her little house to die. Taking out her father's hara-kiri sword, she presses the blade to her neck, but

> something within her cried out piteously. They had taught her how to die, but he had taught her how to live—nay, to make life sweet. Yet that was the reason she must die. Strange reason! She now first knew that it was sad to die. He had come, and substituted himself for everything; he had gone, and left her nothing—nothing but this. (85)

Butterfly's "little, unused, frivolous mind" has turned from game-playing and childish chatter to a striking new understanding of herself and what Pinkerton meant to her life. A path marked by both happiness and sorrow has led Butterfly to maturity, and, ultimately, Butterfly's maternal devotion to her young son gives her a reason to move on with her life:

> The baby crept cooing into her lap. The little maid came in and bound up the wound.
>
> When Mrs. Pinkerton called next day at the little house on Higashi Hill it was quite empty. (86)

8. Michael Teague, "*Madame Butterfly*: The Real Story," *Opera News* 40/19 (1976): 18.

9. David Belasco, *Madame Butterfly* in *Six Plays by David Belasco* (Boston: Little, Brown, and Company, 1929). Subsequent references will be given parenthetically.

The play picks up half way through Long's narrative, as Butterfly, her son Trouble, and her servant Suzuki await Pinkerton's return to Japan. Butterfly's original two visits to the American consul are consolidated and reframed: Sharpless now comes to visit Butterfly's house, bringing news that Pinkerton will not be returning and urging his abandoned bride to accept Prince Yamadori's marriage proposal. While Long's protagonist reacts only with a reproachful "You—thing—those—? *You?*" (65), Belasco provides his heroine with a powerful new affirmation of love:

> I got liddle heart illness. I can't . . . I can't someways give up thinkin' he'll come back to me. You thing tha's all over?

> All finish? (*Dropping her fan. Sharpless nods assent.*) Oh,
> no! Loave don' forget some thin's or wha's use of loave?
> (*She claps her hands—beckoning off.*) Loave's got remem-
> ber . . . (*pointing*) some thin's! (*A child enters.*) (24)

When Pinkerton's new American wife, Kate, arrives to claim the lieutenant's child from this "pretty little plaything" (30), Butterfly replies with a dignity and self-knowledge that were left implicit in Long's novella: "No—playthin' . . . I am Mrs. Lef-ten-ant B. F. —No—no—now I am, only—Cho-Cho-San, but no playthin'" (30). Butterfly effortfully tells her to come back for the child in fifteen minutes. Left alone with Suzuki, Butterfly then bids her faithful servant a weary farewell, "Well—go way an' I will res' now... I *wish* res'—sleep . . . long sleep . . . an' when you see me again, I pray you look whether I be not beautiful again . . . as a bride" (31). Not even her child can redeem the meaninglessness of Butterfly's life now:

> (*She sets the child on a mat, puts the American flag in its
> hand, and, picking up the sword, goes behind the screen that
> the child may not see what she is about to do. A short
> pause—the sword is heard to drop. Madame Butterfly reap-
> pears, her face deathly—a scarf about her neck to conceal
> the wound. Suzuki opens the door, sees the face of her mis-
> tress—backs out of the room in horror. Madame Butterfly
> drops to her knees as she reaches the child, and clasps it to
> her. A hand is thrust through the shoji and the bolt is drawn.
> Kate enters quickly, urging the reluctant Pinkerton to follow
> her.*)

> Lieutenant Pinkerton (*Discerning what she has done*). Oh!
> Cho-Cho-San!

> (*He draws her to him with the baby pressed to her heart. She
> waves the child's hand which holds the flag—saying
> faintly:*)

> Madame Butterfly. Too bad those robins didn' nes' again.
> (*She dies.*) (32)

10. The London *Times* thus reported at the play's British premiere, "in any other than an exotic setting this dramatic episode would be intolerably painful. Redeemed as it is by delicate grace and, above all, by strangeness of detail, the little play proves by no means as distressing as a bald recital may suggest, but tear-compelling merely. A tragedy to be sure, but a toy tragedy" (Carner, 134-5).

11. The popular story, perpetuated by Belasco himself, is that after the performance the composer was so overcome by emotion he embraced Belasco with

tears in his eyes and swore that he must have the rights to set *Madame Butterfly*, a colorful tale which many of Puccini's biographers dispute.

12. Giacomo Puccini, *Madama Butterfly* (Milan: G. Ricordi & C., 1969), 52-5. Subsequent references will be given parenthetically.

The image of answering love's call clearly parallels Mimì in *La Bohème*: "*Donde lieta uscì al tuo grido d'amore, torna sola Mimì*" (Mimì returns alone to the place she happily left at your call of love). Giacomo Puccini, *La Bohème* (Milan: G. Ricordi & C., 1969), 206.

13. Rationales for the consistent inversion of Pinkerton's initials (his name being Benjamin Franklin Pinkerton) abound in operatic criticism. They include attribution to the Italian custom of "reversing Christian and surnames" (Patrick Hughes, *Famous Puccini Operas* [New York: The Citadel Press, 1962], 114); the suggestion that the letters "B. F." might be subject to "a somewhat ambiguous interpretation," e.g. "bloody fool," in English-speaking countries (Carner, 413); and the belief that the initials are a carryover from the original name given to Pinkerton by Illica—"Sir Francis Blummy Pinkerton" (Ashbrook, 112).

14. William Weaver, trans., *Seven Puccini Librettos* (New York: W. W. Norton & Company Inc., 1975), 200.

15. In contrast, Long's Butterfly flirts with Christianity only as a consolation after her husband's actions cause her to be disowned by her family:

> He would provide her a new motive, then, Pinkerton said,—perhaps meaning himself,—and a new religion, if she *must* have one—himself again. . . . Pinkerton expounded what he called the easier Western plan of salvation—seriously, too, considering that all his communications to her were touched with whimsy. This was inevitable—to Pinkerton. After all, she *was* quite an impossible little thing, outside of lacquer and paint. But he struck deeper than he knew; for she went secretly to the church of the missionary who served on the opposite hill, and heard the same thing, and learned, moreover, that she might adopt this new religion at any time she chose—even the eleventh hour.
>
> She went out joyously; not to adopt his religion, it is true, but to hold it in reserve if her relatives should remain obdurate. Pinkerton, to his relief, heard no more of it. (8)

16. In Long's story, Butterfly is disowned in a less dramatic family meeting, not because of her own actions but because Pinkerton has barred the family from visiting them (5-11).

17. While Puccini does provide an optional high C for the tenor at this moment, the A is far more dramatically consistent: Absolute Love carries Butterfly to new heights that Pinkerton never attains. The parallel with the Act I love duet from *La Bohème* is clear.

18. In contrast to the practiced recitation of Puccini's heroine, Long's Butterfly diverts Suzuki from her doubts with some five pages of improvisatory story-telling about what they will do upon Pinkerton's return: "Cho-Cho-San had a fine fancy, and the nesting of the robins could not, at the longest, be much longer delayed now; so she let it riot" (25). Belasco's Butterfly is similarly improvisatory and delighted throughout, although her antics are more abbreviated:

> Suzuki, w'en we see that ship comin' in—sa-ey—then we goin' put flowers aevery where, an' if it's night, we goin hang up mos' one thousan' lanterns—eh-ha? . . . Wael, twenty, mebby; an' sa-ey, w'en we see him comin' quick up path—(*imitates*) so—so—so—(*lifts her kimono and strides in a masculine fashion*) to look for liddle wive—me—me jus' goin' hide behind shoji (*making two holes with her wet finger in the low paper shoji and peeking through*) an' watch an' make believe me gon 'way; leave liddle note—sayin': 'Goon-bye, sayonara, Butterfly'. . . . Now he come in. . . . (*Hides.*) Ah! An' then he get angery! An' he say all kinds of 'Merican languages—debbils—hells! But before he get too angery, me run out an' flew aroun' his neck! (*She illustrates with Suzuki, who is carried away and embraces her with fervor.*) Sa-ey! *You* no flew roun' his neck—jus' me. (*They laugh in each other's arms.*) Then he'll sit down an' sing tha's liddle 'Merican song—O, how he'll laugh. . . . Then I'll dance like w'en I was Geisha girl. (15-16)

19. Weaver, 228-30.

20. In Belasco's play, Butterfly does not interrupt Sharpless at any point during the letter scene, either before or after Yamadori's visit; Sharpless is allowed to read the letter completely before Butterfly joyfully concludes that Pinkerton is returning to her (16-23). Long's story does not even contain a letter sent by Pinkerton, although Sharpless does at one point briefly pretend to have received one in order to allay Butterfly's fears (78).

21. Weaver, 230.

22. Tennessee Williams, *Cat on a Hot Tin Roof* (New York: New American Library, 1985), 44.

23. Butterfly has nothing comparable to this monologue in Belasco's play, although in Long's version she does amuse herself and Suzuki by indulging in a mock-tragic scene of beggary and return to the geisha life (17-22).

24. In Belasco's play, the ship is called by the less ironic name, *Connecticut* (26).

25. In this context, either of the endings Puccini wrote for the lullaby becomes dramatically charged: if Butterfly concludes with the floating G on "*dolor*" (312; sorrow), it shows how growing despair is draining the hope and

faith which once carried her vocal line to the shimmering top notes that culminated her entrance music or the first act love duet; if she takes the optional top B, the vocal line becomes a melancholy shadow of those earlier joyful effusions in the manner of "*Un bel dì.*"

26. Given the social mores of the time, Kate's eager acceptance of her husband's "illegitimate" mixed-race child stretches credibility to the breaking point. As a dramatic stroke necessary to the completion of Butterfly's tragic destiny, however, it is essential.

27. Weaver, 256.

28. Weaver, 256. The manuscript promptbook for a Parisian production of *Madama Butterfly* in the early years of the twentieth century reveals some fascinating variations on the stage directions for the death scene printed in the Italian score:

> *Elle se lève, conduit l'enfant vers le fond . . . et fait sortir l'enfant dans le jardin. Elle referme le shosie, court à la porte E dont elle pousse la verrou, elle en fait autant à la porte D, puis elle penêtre derrière le paravent, tenant dans les mains le sabre. On entend le sabre tomber. Le voile blanc est tiré derrière le paravent. On entend la voix de Pinkerton à droite. Butterfly paraît, le cou enveloppé du voile, elle veut aller ouvrir à droite E, par où s'entend la voix. Elle s'y traîne sur les genoux, se lève pour atteindre le verrou et retombe morte, tandis que le shosie est secoué de l'extérieur.*
>
> (She rises, taking the child upstage, and makes the child go out into the garden. She closes the shoji again, runs to door E which she bolts, as she does also to door D. Then she goes back behind the screen, holding the sword in her hands. The sword is heard to fall. The white veil is pulled behind the screen. The voice of Pinkerton is heard offstage right. Butterfly appears, her neck enveloped in the veil. She wants to go open door E, from where the voice is heard. She drags herself there on her knees, raises herself to reach the bolt, and falls back dead, while the shoji is shaken from outside.) *Madama Butterfly* by Giacomo Puccini, manuscript promptbook by Albert Carré (Paris: Association des Régisseurs Théâtrales, n.d.), 71.

The locks on the shoji doors, of course, come from the source stories, but placing the child out in the garden is a new stroke. Since Pinkerton need not come into the house to collect his son, his shaking of the shoji at the end suggests that he is trying to get back into the house to be reunited with Butterfly herself. Butterfly's love for her husband remains undiminished, and her supreme effort to open the doors and effect a reunion with Pinkerton even at the last moment indicates that she believes her love to be returned. The logical problems with this romantic scenario are manifest, since Pinkerton has already married a second time. But as a symbolic image of Butterfly's Absolute Love, a love which even death cannot vanquish, this staging is powerfully revealing.

29. Sophocles, *Oedipus the King*, in *Sophocles I: Three Tragedies*, trans. David Grene (Chicago: University of Chicago Press, 1954), 68-9.

Chapter 7: *Turandot*

1. Gozzi's play had already provided the source material for over half-a-dozen nineteenth-century operas, as well as an early twentieth-century opera by Ferruccio Busoni. A German adaptation of the play was also enjoying currency, a production in 1911 being directed by Max Reinhardt with incidental music composed by Busoni.

2. Carlo Gozzi, *Turandot*, in *Fiabe Teatrale*, ed. Paolo Bosisio (Rome: Bulzoni Editore, 1984), 250. Subsequent references will be given parenthetically.

3. Extensive discussion of the genesis of *Turandot* is provided by William Ashbrook, *The Operas of Puccini* (Ithaca, N.Y.: Cornell University Press, 1985), and Mosco Carner, *Puccini: A Critical Biography* (New York: Holmes & Meier, 1992).

4. Giacomo Puccini, letter to Renato Simoni, 18 March 1920, in *Carteggi Pucciniani*, ed. Eugenio Gara (Milan: G. Ricordi & C., 1958), 490.

5. At the time of his death from throat cancer in 1924, Puccini had completed the scoring through the death of Liù in the last act. The opera was finished by Franco Alfano, at the commission of Arturo Toscanini, and had its premiere at La Scala in 1926. At the first performance, Toscanini ended the opera after Liù's death scene, indicating to the audience that this was where the maestro had laid down his pen.

6. John Louis DiGaetani offers an extended discussion of *Turandot*'s various symbolic elements, including lighting, in *Puccini the Thinker: The Composer's Intellectual and Dramatic Development* (New York: Peter Lang Publishing, Inc., 1987).

7. William Weaver, trans., *Seven Puccini Librettos* (New York: W. W. Norton & Company, 1981), 404.

8. Giacomo Puccini, *Turandot* (Milan: G. Ricordi & C., 1978), 21. Subsequent references will be given parenthetically.

9. In Gozzi's play, Turandot's slave Adelma, a captured Tartar princess, is in love with Calaf, much as Liù is in the opera. But unlike Liù, she quickly betrays the prince to Turandot, thinking that once the Princess spurns him, Calaf will accept her own love.

10. Weaver, 408.

11. Weaver, 408.

12. For Gozzi, Turandot's Peking is a comic fantasy world through which the audience is guided by the outrageous *commedia dell'arte* figures Pantalone, Tartaglia, Brighella, and Truffaldino. These stock characters, or Masks, are transported by the author's imagination into the court of the Chinese emperor, where they provide a running, and irreverent, commentary. The Masks are retained in Puccini's opera—though in considerably less exaggerated form—as the court officials Ping, Pang, and Pong. During the composition of the libretto for *Turandot*, Puccini wrote to Adami, "*Non abusate coi mascherotti veneziani— quelli debbono essere i* buffoncelli *e i filosofi che qui e lì buttano un lazzo o un parere (ben scelto, anche il momento) ma non siano degli importuni, dei petulanti.*" (Do not abuse the Venetian Masks—they should be the *clowns* and philosophers that here or there throw out a joke or an opinion—well chosen, as also the moment—but they must not be importunate or overbearing.) *Giacomo Puccini Episolario*, ed. Giuseppe Adami (Milan: Arnoldo Mondadori Editore, 1982), 166.

13. Conveying the breathtaking power of Turandot's fairy-tale beauty only adds to the not inconsiderable vocal and dramatic challenges facing the soprano who takes on this role.

14. William Shakespeare, *The Tragedy of Macbeth*, in *The Riverside Shakespeare*, ed. G. Blakemore Evans (Boston: Houghton Mifflin Company, 1974), I.v.40-3.

15. The last of these riddles is, of course, an inside joke between Gozzi and his Venetian audience, since the city of Venice claims the title "Lion of the Adriatic."

16. Weaver, 438.

17. Weaver, 438.

18. Weaver, 438.

19. Weaver, 440.

20. Weaver, 454.

21. Review of *Turandot* by Giacomo Puccini, *Illustration* (7 April 1928), 350.

22. Weaver, 458.

23. Weaver, 462.

PREVIEW

Selected from Cited Criticism
Available in English

Ashbrook, William. *The Operas of Puccini*. Ithaca, N.Y.: Cornell University Press, 1985. Detailed survey.

Budden, Julian. *The Operas of Verdi*. 3 vols. New York: Oxford University Press, 1973. In-depth musicological and historical study.

Carner, Mosco. *Puccini: A Critical Biography*. 3rd ed. New York: Holmes & Meier, 1992. Psychoanalytical approach to biography and operas.

Clément, Catherine. *Opera, or the Undoing of Women*. Trans. Betsy Wing. Minneapolis: University of Minnesota Press, 1988. Feminist overview.

DiGaetani, John Louis. *Puccini the Thinker: The Composer's Intellectual and Dramatic Development*. New York: Peter Lang Publishing, Inc., 1987. Thematic discussion.

Godefroy, Vincent. *The Dramatic Genius of Verdi: Studies of Selected Operas*. 2 vols. New York: St. Martin's Press, 1975. Exploration of genesis, dramatic character, and themes.

Groos, Arthur, and Roger Parker. *Giacomo Puccini*. London: Cambridge University Press, 1986. Detailed survey.

Kimbell, David R. B. *Verdi in the Age of Italian Romanticism*. London: Cambridge University Press, 1981. Detailed musical, dramatic, and historical study.

Martin, George. *Verdi: His Music, Life and Times*. New York: Dodd, Mead & Company, 1983. General survey.

Osborne, Charles. *The Complete Operas of Verdi*. New York: Da Capo Press, 1969. General survey.

SELECTED BIBLIOGRAPHY

Texts and Scores

Aeschylus. *Oresteia*. Trans. Richard Lattimore. Chicago: University of Chicago Press, 1953.

Belasco, David. *Madame Butterfly. Six Plays by David Belasco*. Boston: Little, Brown, and Company, 1929.

Donizetti, Gaetano. *Lucia di Lammermoor*. Milan: G. Ricordi & C., 1967.

———. *Lucrezia Borgia*. New York: Edwin F. Kalmus, n.d.

García Gutiérrez, Antonio. *El Trovador*. Ed. Carlos Ruiz Silva. Madrid: Ediciones Cátedra, 1985.

Gozzi, Carlo. *Fiabe Teatrali*. Ed. Paolo Bosisio. Rome: Bulzoni Editore, 1984.

Hugo, Victor. *Théâtre Complet de Victor Hugo*. Ed. J.-J. Thierry and Josette Mélèze. 2 vols. Monaco: Éditions Gallimard, 1963.

Long, John Luther. *Madame Butterfly*. New York: The Century Co., 1904.

Loti, Pierre. *Madame Chrysanthème*. Paris: Calmann-Lévy, Éditeurs, 1923.

Murger, Henry. *Scènes de la Vie de Bohème*. Ed. Loïc Chotard. Monaco: Éditions Gallimard, 1988.

Ponchielli, Amilcare. *La Gioconda*. Milan: G. Ricordi & C., 1980.

Puccini, Giacomo. *La Bohème*. Milan: G. Ricordi & C., 1969.

———. *Madama Butterfly*. Milan: G. Ricordi & C., 1969.

———. *Tosca*. Milan: G. Ricordi & C., 1956.

———. *Turandot*. Milan: G. Ricordi & C., 1978.

Saavedra, Angel de. *Don Alvaro, o la Fuerza del Sino*. Ed. Ermanno Caldera. Madrid: Taurus Ediciones, 1986.

Sardou, Victorien. *Théâtre Complet*. 15 vols. Paris: Albin Michel, Éditeur, 1934.

Schiller, Friedrich von. *Schillers Werke*. Ed. Hans Heinrich Borcherdt. 42 vols. Weimar: Hermann Böhlaus Nachfolger, 1949.

Scribe, Eugène. *Théâtre Complet*. 24 vols. Paris, 1835.

Shakespeare, William. *The Riverside Shakespeare*. Ed. G. Blakemore Evans. Boston: Houghton Mifflin Company, 1974.

Sophocles. *Oedipus the King. Sophocles I: Three Tragedies.* Trans. David Grene. Chicago: University of Chicago Press, 1954.

Verdi, Giuseppe. *Aida.* Milan: G. Ricordi & C., 1980.

——. *La Forza del Destino.* Milan: G. Ricordi & C., 1969.

——. *Otello.* Milan: G. Ricordi & C., 1969.

——. *Rigoletto.* Chicago and Milan: University of Chicago Press and G. Ricordi & C., 1983.

——. *Simon Boccanegra.* Milan: G. Ricordi & C., 1971.

——. *La Traviata.* Milan: G. Ricordi & C., 1988.

——. *Il Trovatore.* Milan: G. Ricordi & C., 1968.

Williams, Tennessee. *Cat on a Hot Tin Roof.* New York: New American Library, 1985.

Works Consulted

Aston, Elaine. "Outside the Doll's House: A Study in Images of Women in English and French Theatre 1848-1914." Diss. University of Warwick (U.K.), 1987.

Balthazar, Scott Leslie. "Evolving Conventions in Italian Serious Opera: Scene Structure in the Works of Rossini, Bellini, Donizetti, and Verdi, 1810-1850." Diss. University of Pennsylvania, 1985.

——. "Music, Poetry, and Action in *Ottocento* Opera: The Principle of Concurrent Articulations." *Opera Journal* 22/2 (1989): 12-34.

Barbier, Patrick. *La Vie Quotidienne à l'Opéra au Temps de Rossini et de Balzac, Paris/1800-1850.* Paris: Hachette, 1987.

Belasco, David. *The Theatre through Its Stage Door.* New York: Harper & Brothers Publishers, 1919.

Brockway, Wallace, and Herbert Weinstock. *The World of Opera: The Story of Its Development and the Lore of Its Performance.* London: Methuen & Co., Ltd., 1963.

Carlson, Marvin. "French Stage Composition from Hugo to Zola." *Educational Theatre Journal* 23 (1971): 363-78.

——. *The French Stage in the Nineteenth Century.* Metuchen, N. J.: Scarecrow Press, Inc., 1972.

Chahine, Samia. *La Dramaturgie de Victor Hugo (1816-1843).* Paris: Éditions A.-G. Nizet, 1971.

Challis, Bennett. "The Technique of Operatic Acting." *Musical Quarterly* 13 (1927): 630-45.

Chorley, Henry F. *Thirty Years' Musical Recollections.* Ed. Ernest Newman. New York: Alfred A. Knopf, 1926.

Christiansen, Rupert. *Prima Donna: A History.* New York: Viking, 1985.

Clément, Catherine. *Opera, or the Undoing of Women.* Trans. Betsy Wing. Minneapolis: University of Minnesota Press, 1988.

Cohen, H. Robert, and Marie-Odile Gigou. "Notes et Documents (la Conservation de la Tradition Scénique sur la Scène Lyrique en France au XIXe Siècle: les Livrets de Mise en Scène et la Bibliothèque de l'Association de la Régie Théâtrale." *Revue de Musicologie* 64 (1978): 253-67.

―――. *Cent Ans de Mise en Scène Lyrique en France (env.1830-1930).* New York: Pendragon Press, 1986.

Conrad, Peter. *Romantic Opera and Literary Form.* Berkeley: University of California Press, 1977.

Descotes, Maurice. "Du Drame à l'Opéra: les Transpositions Lyriques du Théâtre de Victor Hugo." *Revue de la Société d'Histoire du Théâtre* 34 (1982): 103-56.

Dilla, Geraldine P. "Music-Drama: An Art-Form in Four Dimensions." *Musical Quarterly* 10 (1924): 492-9.

Donington, Robert. *Opera and Its Symbols.* New Haven, Conn.: Yale University Press, 1991.

Draper, F. W. M. *The Rise and Fall of the French Romantic Drama: With Special Reference to the Influence of Shakespeare Scott and Byron.* New York: E. P. Dutton & Company, n.d.

Dupêchez, Charles. *Histoire de l'Opéra de Paris: Un Siècle au Palais Garnier 1875-1980.* Paris: Librairie Académique Perrin, 1984.

Edwards, H. Sutherland. *The Prima Donna: Her History and Surroundings from the Seventeenth to the Nineteenth Century.* 2 vols. London, 1888.

Ellis, Katharine. *Music Criticism in Nineteenth-Century France: La Revue et Gazette Musicale de Paris, 1834-80.* Cambridge: Cambridge University Press, 1995.

Gatti, Carlo. *Il Teatro alla Scala nella Storia e nell'Arte (1778-1963).* 2 vols. Milan: G. Ricordi & C., 1964.

Gautier, Théophile. *Histoire de l'Art Dramatique en France depuis Vingt-cinq Ans.* 4 vols. Paris, 1858.

Grout, Donald Jay. *A Short History of Opera.* 2nd ed. New York: Columbia University Press, 1965.

Gundry, Inglis. "The Nature of Opera as a Composite Art." *Proceedings of the Royal Musical Association* 73 (1946-7): 25-33.

Hogarth, George. *Memories of the Opera in Italy.* 2 vols. London, 1851.

Howarth, W. D. *Sublime and Grotesque: A Study of French Romantic Drama.* London: George G. Harrap & Co. Ltd., 1975.

Kerman, Joseph. *Opera as Drama.* rev. ed. Berkeley: University of California Press, 1988.

La Fenice. Milan: Nuove Edizioni, 1972.

Lindenberger, Herbert. *Opera: The Extravagant Art.* Ithaca, N.Y.: Cornell University Press, 1984.

Loewenberg, Alfred, comp. *Annals of Opera.* 2 vols. 3rd ed. Totowa, N. J.: Rowan and Littlefield, 1978.

Lumley, Benjamin. *Reminiscences of the Opera*. London, 1864.

Matheopoulos, Helena. *Diva: Great Sopranos and Mezzos Discuss Their Art*. Boston: Northeastern University Press, 1991.

Matthews, Brander. "The Conventions of the Music-Drama." *Musical Quarterly* 5 (1919): 255-63.

————. *French Dramatists of the Nineteenth Century*. 3rd ed. New York: Benjamin Blom, 1901.

Meisel, Martin. *Realizations: Narrative, Pictorial, and Theatrical Arts in Nineteenth-Century England*. Princeton, N. J.: Princeton University Press, 1983.

Mila, Massimo, ed. *Il Melodramma Italiano dell'Ottocento: Studi e Ricerche per Massimo Mila*. Turin: Giulio Einaudi Editore, 1977.

Miragoli, Livia. *Il Melodramma Italiano nell'Ottocento*. Rome: P. Maglione & C., 1924.

Moynet, M. J. *French Theatrical Production in the Nineteenth Century*. 1973. Trans. Allan S. Jackson with M. Glen Wilson. Ed. Marvin A. Carlson. Rare Books of the Theatre Series 10. New York: The Max Reinhardt Foundation with the Center for Modern Theatre Research, 1976.

Nuttall, A. D. *Why Does Tragedy Give Pleasure?* Oxford: Clarendon Press, 1996.

Pelz, Mary Ellis, and Gerald Fitzgerald, comps. *Metropolitan Opera Annals Third Supplement: 1966-76*. Clifton, N. J.: James T. White & Company, 1978.

Pintorno, Giuseppe, ed. *Le Prime: Duecento Anni di Teatro alla Scala*. Milan: Grafica Gutenberg Editrice, 1982.

Prod'homme, J.-G. *L'Opéra (1669-1925)*. Paris: Librairie Delagrave, 1925.

Rasponi, Lanfranco. *The Last Prima Donnas*. New York: Alfred A. Knopf, 1984.

Rolandi, Ulderico. *Il Libretto per Musica attraverso i Tempi*. Rome: Edizioni dell'Ateneo, 1951.

Rosenthal, Harold. *Two Centuries of Opera at Covent Garden*. London: Putnam, 1958.

Schlitzer, Franco. *Mondo Teatrale dell'Ottocento*. Naples: Fausto Fiorentino, 1954.

Schmidgall, Gary. *Shakespeare and Opera*. New York: Oxford University Press, 1990.

Seltsam, William H., comp. *Metropolitan Opera Annals: A Chronicle of Artists and Performances*. New York: The H. W. Wilson Company, 1947.

————. *Metropolitan Opera Annals (First Supplement: 1947-57): A Chronicle of Artists and Performances*. New York: The H. W. Wilson Company, 1957.

————. *Metropolitan Opera Annals (Second Supplement: 1957-1966): A Chronicle of Artists and Performances*. New York: The H. W. Wilson Company, 1968.

Shaw, Bernard. *Shaw's Music: The Complete Musical Criticism in Three Volumes*. Ed. Dan H. Laurence. 3 vols. New York: Dodd, Mead & Company, 1981.

Smith, Patrick J. *The Tenth Muse: A Historical Study of the Opera Libretto.* New York: Schirmer Books, 1975.

Tintori, Gianpiero, ed. *La Scala.* Milan: Nuove Edizioni Milano, 1966.

Visetti, Albert. "Tendencies of the Operatic Stage in the Nineteenth Century." *Proceedings of the Musical Association* 22 (1896): 141-51.

Weaver, William. *The Golden Century of Italian Opera from Rossini to Puccini.* London: Thames and Hudson, 1980.

Puccini

Ashbrook, William. "A Message of Love." *Opera News* 43/8 (1978): 26-7.

———. *The Operas of Puccini.* Ithaca, N.Y.: Cornell University Press, 1985.

———. "Puccini and the Soprano." *Opera News* 23/11 (1959): 8-9.

Ashbrook, William, and Harold Powers. *Puccini's Turandot: The End of the Great Tradition.* Princeton, N. J.: Princeton University Press, 1991.

Atlas, Allan W. "Newly Discovered Sketches for Puccini's *Turandot* at the Pierpont Morgan Library." *Cambridge Opera Journal* (July 1991): 173-93.

Avant-Scène Opéra, September-October 1977.

———. March-April 1979.

———. October 1983.

Bellaigue, Camille. Review of *La Bohème* by Giacomo Puccini. *Revue des Deux Mondes* 148 (1898): 464-74.

Berrong, Richard M. "*Turandot* as Political Fable." Opera Quarterly 2/3 (1995): 65-75.

La Bohème by Giacomo Puccini. Manuscript promptbook by Albert Carré. Paris: Association des Régisseurs Théâtrales, 1898.

Brett, Richard, and John Potter. "Role-Playing: Tosca as Woman and Actress." *Opera News* 41/9: 18-20.

Breuer, Gustl. "Tosca, Jeritza, and Me." *High Fidelity Magazine* (December 1957): 56+.

Carner, Mosco. *Madame Butterfly: A Guide to the Opera.* London: Barrie & Jenkins, 1979.

———. *Puccini: A Critical Biography.* 3rd ed. New York: Holmes & Meier, 1992.

———. *Giacomo Puccini: Tosca.* New York: Cambridge University Press, 1985.

Casini, Claudio. *Giacomo Puccini.* Turin: Unione Tipografico-Editrice Torinese, 1978.

Coeuroy, André. *La Tosca de Puccini.* Paris: Librairie Delaplane, 1923.

DiGaetani, John Louis. *Puccini the Thinker: The Composer's Intellectual and Dramatic Development.* New York: Peter Lang Publishing, Inc., 1987.

———. "Puccini's Tosca and the Necessity of Agnosticism." *Opera Quarterly* (Spring 1984): 76-84.

Dry, Wakling. *Giacomo Puccini*. New York: John Lane Company, 1906.

Dyer, Richard. "Puccini, His Sopranos, and Some Records." *Opera Quarterly* (Autumn 1984): 62-71.

Frame, Florence K. "Madame Butterfly: The Dramatists." *Opera News* 40/19 (1976): 20-2.

Ganderax, Louis. Review of *La Tosca* by Victorien Sardou. *Revue des Deux Mondes* 84 (1887): 920-32.

Greenfeld, Howard. *Puccini*. New York: G. P. Putnam's Sons, 1980.

Groos, Arthur. "Madame Butterfly: The Story." *Cambridge Opera Journal* (July 1991): 125-58.

Groos, Arthur, and Roger Parker. *Giacomo Puccini*. London: Cambridge University Press, 1986.

Hecht, Suzanne. "Victorien Sardou et la 'Pièce Bien Faite.'" Diss. Columbia University, 1971.

Hughes, Patrick. *Famous Puccini Operas*. New York: Citadel Press, 1962.

Kestner, Joseph. "Woe to the Vanquished." *Opera News* 41/19 (1977): 14-7.

Madame Butterfly by Giacomo Puccini. Manuscript promptbook by Albert Carré. Paris: Association des Régisseurs Théâtrales, n.d.

Maguire, Janet. "Puccini's Version of the Duet and Final Scene of *Turandot*." *The Musical Quarterly* 74 (1990): 319-59.

Marggraf, Wolfgang. *Giacomo Puccini*. New York: Heinrichshofen Edition, 1977.

Monaldi, Gino. *Giacomo Puccini e la Sua Opera*. Rome: Casa Editrice Selecta, 1925.

Morey, Carl. "Puccini's Ladies." *Opera Canada* 16/2 (1975): 28-9.

Osborne, Charles. *The Complete Operas of Puccini: A Critical Guide*. New York: Atheneum, 1982.

Puccini, Giacomo. *Carteggi Pucciniani*. Ed. Eugenio Gara. Milan: G. Ricordi & C., 1958.

———. *Letters of Giacomo Puccini*. Ed. Giuseppe Adami. Trans. Ena Makin. Philadelphia: J.B. Lippincott Company, 1931.

———. *Giacomo Puccini Epistolario*. Ed. Giuseppe Adami. Milan: Arnoldo Mondadori Editore, 1982.

Review of *Madama Butterfly* by Giacomo Puccini. *Illustrated London News* (15 July 1905): 74.

Review of *La Tosca* by Victorien Sardou. *Illustration* (10 December 1887): 403.

Review of *Tosca* by Giacomo Puccini. *Illustrated London News* (21 July 1900): 108.

Review of *Tosca* by Giacomo Puccini. *Illustrated London News* (29 June 1901): 956.

Review of *Tosca* by Giacomo Puccini. *Illustration* (17 October 1903): 260.

Review of *Turandot* by Giacomo Puccini. *Illustration* (7 April 1928): 350.

Ricci, Luigi. *Puccini Interprete di Se Stesso*. Milan: G. Ricordi & C., 1954.

Salerno, Franco. *Le Donne Pucciniane*. Palermo: Casa Editrice Trimarchi, 1928.

Sartori, Claudio, ed. *Giacomo Puccini: Symposium Collana di Saggi Musicali Diretta da Guido M. Gatti.* Milan: G. Ricordi & C., 1959.

"Taking Title to the Tour: 'Tosca.'" *Opera News* 17/24 (1953): 4-6.

Teague, Michael. "Madame Butterfly: The Real Story." *Opera News* 40/19 (1976): 18-9.

Torrefranca, Fausto. *Giacomo Puccini e l'Opera Internazionale.* Turin: Fratelli Bocca Editori, 1912.

Tosca by Giacomo Puccini. Manuscript promptbook by Albert Carré. Paris: Association des Régisseurs Théâtrales, n.d.

Weaver, William, trans. *Seven Puccini Librettos.* New York: W. W. Norton & Company, 1981.

————. *Puccini: The Man and His Music.* New York: E. P. Dutton, 1977.

Weaver, William, and Simonetta Puccini, eds. *The Puccini Companion.* New York: W. W. Norton & Company, 1994.

Verdi

Abbate, Carolyn, and Roger Parker, eds. *Analyzing Opera:Verdi and Wagner.* Berkeley: University of California Press, 1989.

Abbiati, Franco. *Giuseppe Verdi.* 4 vols. Milan: G. Ricordi & C., 1959.

"*Aïda* Vue des Coulisses de l'Opéra." *Illustration* (30 October 1880): 292.

Atti del Congresso Internazionale di Studi Verdiani 3d. Milan, 1972. Parma: Istituto di Studi Verdiani, 1974.

Atti del 1 Congresso Internazionale di Studi Verdiani. Venice, 1966. Parma: Istituto di Studi Verdiani, 1969.

Avant-Scène Opéra, July-August 1976.

————. December 1989.

Basevi, Abramo. *Studio sulle Opere di Giuseppe Verdi.* Florence, 1859.

Beghelli, Marco. "Per un Nuovo Approccio al Teatro Musicale: l'Atto Performativo come Luogo dell'Imitazione Gestuale nella Drammaturgia Verdiana." *Italica* 64 (1987): 632-53.

Bennett, Rodney M. "Aida as Ethiopian." *Opera* (July 1970): 622-4.

Bollettino dell'Istituto di Studi Verdiani (1969-82).

Budden, Julian. *The Operas of Verdi.* 3 vols. New York: Oxford University Press, 1973.

————. *Verdi.* New York: Vintage Books, 1987.

Busch, Hans, comp. and trans. *Verdi's Aida: The History of an Opera in Letters and Documents.* Minneapolis: University of Minnesota Press, 1978.

Cohen, H. Robert, ed. *The Original Staging Manuals for Twelve Parisian Operatic Premières.* New York: Pendragon Press, 1991.

Conati, Marcello. *La Bottega della Musica: Verdi e la Fenice.* Milan: Il Saggiatore, 1983.

————. *Verdi: The Man and His Music.* Trans. Elizabeth Abbott. New York: G. P. Putnam's Sons, 1955.

Della Seta, Fabrizio. "'*O cieli azzuri*': Exoticism and Dramatic Discourse in Aida." *Cambridge Opera Journal* (March 1991): 49-62.

Díaz-Duque, Ozzie F. "Garcia Gutiérrez y Verdi: Estudio Comparativo de *El Trovador* e *Il Trovatore*." Diss. The University of Iowa, 1980.

Erasmi, Gabriele. "'*Norma*' ed '*Aida*': Momenti Estremi della Concezione Romantica." *Studi Verdiani* 5 (1988-9). Parma: Istituto Nazionale di Studi Verdiani (1989): 85-108.

Friedlaender, Maryla. "Aida and the Cult of Isis." *Opera News* 11/10 (1946): 10-2.

Furie, Kenneth. "'La Forza del Destino': Verdi at His Gloomiest and, So, Most Verdian." *New York Times* (25 February 1996): H31+.

Godefroy, Vincent. *The Dramatic Genius of Verdi: Studies of Selected Operas.* 2 vols. New York: St. Martin's Press, 1975.

Gossett, Philip. "Verdi, Ghislanzoni, and Aida: The Uses of Convention." *Critical Inquiry* (December 1974): 291-334.

Holmes, William C. "The Earliest Revisions of 'La Forza del Destino.'" *Studi Verdiani* 6 (1990): 55-98.

Humbert, Jean. "À Propos de l'Égyptomanie dans l'Oeuvre de Verdi: Attribution à Auguste Mariette d'un Scénario Anonyme de l'Opéra *Aïda*." *Revue de Musicologie* 62 (1976): 229-56.

Hussey, Dyneley. *Verdi.* London: J. M. Dent and Sons Ltd., 1963.

Kerman, Joseph. "Second Thought on Forza." *Opera News* 26/7 (1961): 24+.

Kimbell, David R. B. *Verdi in the Age of Italian Romanticism.* London: Cambridge University Press, 1981.

Lagenevais, F. de. Review of *Aida* by Giuseppe Verdi. *Revue des Deux Mondes* 15 (1876): 448-62.

Lee, M. Owen. "Elemental, Furious, Wholly True." *Opera News* 52/7 (1987): 14+.

Loveday, Lilian Foerster. "A Plan of Action." *Opera News* 27/6 (1962): 9-13.

Martin, George. *Verdi: His Music, Life and Times.* New York: Dodd, Mead & Company, 1983.

———. "Verdi's Imitation of Shakespeare: *La Forza del Destino*." *Opera Quarterly* (Fall 1985): 19-29.

McDaniel, Myrtle Yvette. "An Analysis of the Characterizations of Aida and Amneris." D.M.A. Thesis. Louisiana State University, 1992.

Mila, Massimo. *L'Arte di Verdi.* Turin: Giulio Einaudi Editore, 1980.

———. *Giuseppe Verdi.* Bari: Editori Laterza, 1958.

Moreen, Robert Anthony. "Integration of Text Forms and Musical Forms in Verdi's Early Opera." Diss. Princeton University, 1975.

Osborne, Charles. *The Complete Operas of Verdi.* New York: Da Capo Press, 1969.

[Phillips-] Matz, Mary Jane. "Aida without Tears." *Opera News* 22/4 (1957): 4-8.

———. *Verdi: A Biography.* New York: Oxford University Press, 1993.

Porter, Andrew. "Destination Unknown: or How Should 'Forza' End?" *Opera* 32 (1981): 1108-13.

Prod'homme, J. G. "Lettres Inédites de G. Verdi à Léon Escudier." *Rivista Musicale Italiana* 35 (1928): 1+.

Redmond, James, ed. *Themes in Drama 3: Drama, Dance and Music.* New York: Cambridge University Press, 1981.

Review of *Aida* by Giuseppe Verdi. *Illustrated London News* (1 July 1876): 22.

Review of *Aida* by Giuseppe Verdi. *Illustrated London News* (28 June 1879): 606.

Review of *La Forza del Destino* by Giuseppe Verdi. *Illustrated London News* (29 June 1867): 655.

Review of *La Forza del Destino* by Giuseppe Verdi. *Illustrated London News* (25 June 1880): 615.

Review of *Il Trovatore* by Giuseppe Verdi. *Illustrated London News* (6 January 1855): 10.

Review of *Il Trovatore* by Giuseppe Verdi. *Illustrated London News* (19 May 1855): 496.

Review of *Il Trovatore* by Giuseppe Verdi. *Illustrated London News* (9 May 1858): 462.

Review of *Il Trovatore* by Giuseppe Verdi. *Illustrated London News* (11 May 1861): 437.

Rinaldi, Mario. *Le Opere Più Note di Giuseppe Verdi.* Florence: Leo S. Alschki, 1986.

Robinson, Paul. "Is *Aida* an Orientalist Opera?" *Cambridge Opera Journal* (July 1993): 133-40.

Said, Edward W. *Culture and Imperialism.* New York: Alfred A. Knopf, 1993.

Savigny, M. Review of *Aida* by Giuseppe Verdi. *Illustration* (24 November 1883): 331.

Soffredini, A. *Le Opere di Verdi: Studio Critico Analitico.* Milan: Carlo Aliprandi, 1901.

Stedman, Jane W. "Aida's Ethiopia." *Opera News* 13/16 (1949): 11-13.

———. "Slaves of Love and Duty." *Opera News* 21/15 (1957): 10-3.

Studi Verdiani. 6 vols. Parma: Istituto di Studi Verdiani (1982-90).

Todde, Felice. "Cenni sul Rapporto fra 'El Trovador' di Garcia Gutiérrez ed 'Il Trovatore' di Verdi." *Nuova Rivista Musicale Italiana* (September 1986): 400-15.

Torchi, L. "L'Opera di Giuseppe Verdi e i Suoi Caratteri Principali." *Rivista Musicale Italiana* 8 (1901): 279-325.

Verdi, Giuseppe. *Verdi Intimo: Carteggio di Giuseppe Verdi con il Conte Opprandino Arrivabene [1861-1886].* Ed. Annibale Alberti. Milan: A. Mondadori Editore, 1931.

———. *I Copialettere di Giuseppe Verdi.* Ed. Gaetano Cesari and Alessandro Luzio. 2 vols. 1913. Milan: Forni Editore Bologna, 1968.

————. *Letters of Giuseppe Verdi*. Ed. and trans. Charles Osborne. London: Victor Gollancz Ltd., 1971.

————. *Verdi: The Man in His Letters*. Ed. Franz Werfel and Paul Stefan. Trans. Edward Downes. New York: L. B. Fischer, 1942.

Verdi Newsletter 1-21 (1976-93).

Weaver, William, trans. *Seven Verdi Librettos*. New York: W. W. Norton & Company Inc., 1975.

————, ed. *Verdi: A Documentary Study*. New York: Thames and Hudson, n.d.

Weaver, William, and Martin Chusid, eds. *The Verdi Companion*. New York: W. W. Norton & Company, 1979.

Weiss, Pietro. "Verdi and the Fusion of Genres." *Journal of the American Musicological Society* 35 (1982): 138-56.

INDEX

Highlighted People and Titles

201

ABOUT THE AUTHORS

Geoffrey Edwards is an award-winning author and stage director in both theater and opera. His production credits range from *Madama Butterfly* and *La Traviata* to *South Pacific* and *Man of La Mancha*, from *Antony and Cleopatra* and *The Cherry Orchard* to *The Misanthrope* and *The Importance of Being Earnest*. An active university educator, he has served on faculties in both the United States and Europe and is in constant demand as a speaker and lecturer. He received his PhD in Theatre and Drama from Northwestern University and has published extensively on dramatic characterization.

Ryan Edwards has received international acclaim for his vocal and dramatic interpretations of the Verdi and Puccini repertoire. As a leading baritone with the Metropolitan Opera, his numerous appearances have ranged from *Don Carlos* and *La Forza del Destino* to *La Bohème* and *Madama Butterfly*, from *Lucia di Lammermoor* and *I Pagliacci* to *Ernani* and *Werther*. His European appearances have included *Attila* and *Il Barbiere di Siviglia* at the Gran Teatro del Liceo in Barcelona, *I Puritani* at London's Royal Festival Hall, and *Caterina Cornaro* for L'Opéra de Nice and French National Radio.

Mr. Edwards has been heard on international broadcasts of over twenty operatic productions, including *Tosca*, *Aida*, and *Otello*, as well as such concert works as *Carmina Burana*. Among his television, film, and recording credits are Brahms *Requiem*, Mahler's *Symphony No. 8, The Vocal Lion*, *Caterina Cornaro*, *Maid of Orleans*, and *I Pagliacci*. As a teacher and lecturer, Mr. Edwards gives master classes throughout the United States and Europe and is a frequent judge for the Metropolitan Opera Auditions and other national competitions.

Also by the Authors:

The Verdi Baritone
Studies in the Development of Dramatic Character,
by Geoffrey Edwards and Ryan Edwards

A.K.A. Doc
The Oral History of a New Orleans Street Musician,
by Geoffrey Edwards and Ryan Edwards